T0135645

Technische Universität Braunschweig
Fachbereich für Mathematik und Informatik
Institut für Betriebssysteme und Rechnerverbund

**Internet Integration of
Vehicular Ad Hoc Networks**

Marc Bechler

Vom Fachbereich für Mathematik und Informatik
der Technischen Universität Braunschweig
genehmigte Dissertation zur Erlangung des
Grades eines Doktor-Ingenieurs (Dr.-Ing.)

Erstgutachter: Prof. Dr.-Ing. L. Wolf
Zweitgutachter: Prof. Dr.-Ing. J. Schiller

Eingereicht am 7. September 2004
Promotion am 20. Oktober 2004

Bibliografische Information Der Deutschen Bibliothek

Die Deutsche Bibliothek verzeichnet diese Publikation in der Deutschen
Nationalbibliografie; detaillierte bibliografische Daten sind im Internet über
http://dnb.ddb.de abrufbar.

ISBN 3-8325-0750-7

Logos Verlag Berlin
Comeniushof, Gubener Str. 47,
10243 Berlin
Tel.: +49 030 42 85 10 90
Fax: +49 030 42 85 10 92
INTERNET: http://www.logos-verlag.de

Always Look on the Bright Side of Life
(Monty Python)

Vorwort

„Wüsste man vor einer langen Reise über alle Schwierigkeiten bescheid, würden die meisten gar nicht angetreten." An dieses alte Sprichwort unbekannter Herkunft hat sich sicherlich der eine oder die andere während der Dissertationszeit erinnert: In gewisser Hinsicht kann die Dissertation tatsächlich als lange Reise mit vielen Höhen und Tiefen angesehen werden. Doch dabei wird gerne übersehen, dass eine solche Reise von vielen Personen begleitet wird. Diesen Personen ist es zu verdanken, dass ich eine tolle „Dissertationsreise" hatte, bei der sich Arbeit mit Freude und Vergnügen paarte. Somit erscheint mir dieses Vorwort auch die richtige Stelle des Dankes bei denjenigen zu sein, die mich in dieser Zeit in fachlicher, organisatorischer und persönlicher Hinsicht unterstützt haben.

An erster Stelle möchte ich mich ganz herzlich bei Prof. Dr. Lars Wolf bedanken, der mich während meiner Zeit am Institut für Telematik der Universität Karlsruhe (TH) und am Institut für Betriebssysteme und Rechnerverbund an der Technischen Universität Braunschweig stets gefördert und in jeder Hinsicht tatkräftig unterstützt hat. Die offene Art und Weise, die großzügigen Freiräume zur eigenen Entfaltung und zur Durchführung meiner Arbeiten, die wertvollen Diskussionen und Sachgespräche sowie die vorbildliche und unkomplizierte Betreuung haben ohne Zweifel maßgeblich zum Entstehen und zum Erfolg dieser Arbeit beigetragen. An dieser Stelle bin ich auch Prof. em. Dr. Dr. h.c. mult. Gerhard Krüger zu tiefem Dank verpflichtet, der mich nach meinem Studium in den akademischen Dienst aufgenommen hat und mich mit seinem reichhaltigen Erfahrungsschatz stets unterstützte. Durch die Förderung von Reisen auf internationale Konferenzen haben sowohl Prof. em. Dr. Dr. h.c. mult. Gerhard Krüger als auch Prof. Dr. Lars Wolf es mir ermöglicht, meine Arbeiten vorzustellen und die Kontakte zu knüpfen, die für die wissenschaftliche Weiterentwicklung unerlässlich sind.

Für die Übernahme des Korreferats bedanke ich mich ganz herzlich bei Prof. Dr. Jochen Schiller. Mit seinen fundierten Kenntnissen im Bereich der Mobilkommunikation konnte er mir bereits im Vorfeld wertvolle Hinweise für meine Arbeit geben. Er war es auch, der mich schon während des Studiums für die Mobikommunikation begeisterte und mich an die wissenschaftliche Laufbahn herangeführt hat.

Ein herzliches Dankeschön geht auch an die vielen jetzigen und ehemaligen Kollegen, die mich auf meiner „Dissertationsreise" begleitet haben. Das offene und freundschaftliche Arbeitsklima, die vorbildliche Zusammenarbeit, aber auch die zahlreichen nicht-wissenschaftlichen Aktivitäten haben stets für Spaß und Motivation bei der Arbeit gesorgt – sowohl am Institut für Telematik unter Prof. Dr. Dr. h.c. mult. Gerhard Krüger als auch am Institut für Betriebssysteme und Rechnerverbund unter Prof. Dr. Lars Wolf und Prof. Dr. Stefan Fischer. Auch haben die zahlreichen fachlichen Diskussionen und kompetenten Beiträge die Qualität der vorliegenden Arbeit verbessert. Für das Korrekturlesen danke ich besonders Ulrike Thomas, Dr. Jörg Diederich, Andreas Kleinschmidt, Oliver Storz und Oliver Wellnitz. Auch darf Ulrich Timm hier nicht unerwähnt bleiben für die hervorragende Betreuung der Rechnerlandschaft, die für Implementierung und Messungen notwendig war. Stellvertretend für das Institut für Telematik sei die traute E24-Runde genannt, bestehend aus Verena Kahmann, Daniel Kraft, Dr. Frank Pählke und Dr. Bernhard Thurm.

Wertvolle Begleiter waren auch die vielen Studenten, die im Rahmen von Studienarbeiten, Diplomarbeiten oder wissenschaftlichen Hilfstätigkeiten meine Arbeit unterstützten: Mark Arnold, Jörg Banholzer, Steffen Blödt, Stéphane Brard, Frank Dinies, André Eitner, Nikolaos Fideropoulos, Alain Gonçalvès, Dennis Gräff, Hans-Peter Gundelwein, Volker Harms, Achim Hauck, Hans-Joachim Hof, Syed M. Huq, Bernhard Hurler, Sven Jaap, Alexander Janz, Fabian Just, Florian Krako, Michael Olbrich, Tim Reinstorf, Ralf Skoda, Frank Sowinski, Oliver Storz, Paulus B. Thie, Philipp Ulrich, Harald Westphal und Mohamed Zouari. Besonders hervorheben möchte ich hierbei Sven Jaap und Oliver Storz, die durch ihren unermütlichen Einsatz einen wesentlichen Beitrag an dieser Arbeit haben.

Mein größtes Dankeschön gilt jedoch denjenigen, mit denen mich eine tiefe Liebe und Freundschaft verbindet: Meiner Lebenspartnerin Ulrike Thomas, meinen Eltern Inge und Josef, meinen Geschwistern Elke und Dirk, meinen ehemaligen Studienkollegen sowie meinem Freundeskreis, von dem ich hier stellvertretend Claudia Täubner und Helmut Jung erwähnen möchte. Sie alle haben dafür gesorgt, dass in den fröhlichen Zeiten das Leben noch strahlender ist, dass ich aber auch in den weniger schönen Momenten immer mit einem Lächeln auf den Lippen durch das Leben schreiten konnte.

Marc Bechler

Kurzfassung

Verkehrstelematik ist eine der Schlüsseltechnologien für zukünftige Entwicklungen im Automobilsektor. Von besonderem Interesse sind dabei Fahrzeugnetze, die für moderne Fahrzeuganwendungen zunehmend an Bedeutung gewinnen. Für die Fahrzeug-Fahrzeug-Kommunikation können selbstorganisierende Ad-hoc-Netze zum Einsatz kommen, die den lokalen Austausch von Daten auch über mehrere Fahrzeuge hinweg erlauben. Zusätzlich ermöglichen Zugangspunkte den Zugriff auf das Internet. Die Unterstützung von Internet-Diensten im Fahrzeug erfordert allerdings die Integration der Fahrzeugnetze in das Internet. Das Ziel ist es dabei, dass das Fahrzeugnetz als transparente Erweiterung des Internets erscheint. Die Internet-Integration ist jedoch eine große Herausforderung, da sich Kommunikation im Fahrzeugnetz und im Internet grundlegend voneinander unterscheiden. In dieser Arbeit wird mit MOCCA ein neuartiger Ansatz für die Internet-Integration von Fahrzeugnetzen vorgestellt. MOCCA verfolgt einen proxybasierten Ansatz, der die Eigenschaften des Fahrzeugnetzes verdeckt und für einen effizienten Datenaustausch zwischen Fahrzeug und Internet sorgt. Dabei kommt ein Protokoll zur Mobilitätsunterstützung der Fahrzeuge sowie ein fuzzybasiertes, skalierbares Protokoll zum Auffinden der am besten geeigneten Zugangspunkte zum Einsatz. Das Erkennen sowie das dynamische Umschalten auf besser geeigneter Kommunikationsnetze ist ebenfalls möglich. Darüber hinaus sorgt ein optimiertes Transportprotokoll für einen verbesserten Datenaustausch zwischen Fahrzeug und Proxy. Eine wichtige Eigenschaft von MOCCA ist die starke Verzahnung der Verfahren untereinander, um eine bestmögliche Effizienz zu erreichen. Für die Evaluierung werden vier fahrzeugbasierte Kommunikationsmodelle vorgestellt. Die durchgeführten Messungen mit diesen Modellen attestieren MOCCA eine bessere Leistungsfähigkeit verglichen mit gängigen Protokollen. Wie die abschließende Evaluierung zeigt, erfüllt MOCCA sämtliche Anforderungen an die Internet-Integration von Fahrzeugnetzen. Im Vergleich zu existierenden Ansätzen unterstützt MOCCA die Mobilität der Fahrzeuge, es berücksichtigt die Eigenschaften von Fahrzeugnetzen, es sorgt für einen effizienten Datendurchsatz auf der Transportschicht, und die Protokolle skalieren mit der Anzahl an Fahrzeugen. Somit ist MOCCA ein geeigneter Ansatz für die transparente Einbindung von Fahrzeugnetzen in das Internet.

Abstract

Traffic telematics is a key technology for the future development in the automotive domain. Inter-vehicle communication systems will become very important for modern vehicular applications. Such systems are based on self-organising ad hoc networks enabling autonomous communications between vehicles. This way, vehicles are able to exchange data locally even over multiple intermediate vehicles. Vehicles are also able to communicate with Internet Gateways acting as transitions points to the Internet. However, the provisioning of Internet services for the vehicles requires an integration of the vehicular network into the Internet. It has to be ensured that this network appears as a transparent extension of the Internet. The Internet integration is a very challenging task since communication in the vehicular network and in the Internet differs fundamentally. This thesis proposes MOCCA, a novel solution for the integration of vehicular ad hoc networks into the Internet. MOCCA combines a proxy-based architecture with different communication protocols to hide the characteristics of vehicular networks and to support efficient communication between vehicles and Internet hosts. It proposes a mobility management protocol for the vehicles, a scalable discovery protocol to find the most suitable Internet Gateway within the vehicular network using fuzzy logic, and it supports identification of and handover to the most suitable alternative communication system. Moreover, an optimised transport protocol enables efficient communication between proxy and vehicles. An important feature of MOCCA is that the protocols are highly integrated, i.e. they collaborate with each other in order to achieve best possible results. For the evaluation, four typical vehicular communication models are proposed to determine the performance of MOCCA. In measurements with these models, MOCCA outperforms common solutions for communication between vehicles and Internet hosts. The concluding evaluation shows that MOCCA completely fulfils the requirements for the Internet integration of vehicular ad hoc networks. Compared to related approaches, MOCCA supports the mobility of the vehicles, it considers vehicular characteristics, it enables an efficient data throughput at the transport layer, and it provides the scalability necessary for vehicular environments. The evaluation shows that MOCCA is a suitable solution for the Internet integration of vehicular ad hoc networks.

Contents

Chapter 1

Introduction

Future developments in the automobile domain are not limited to the field of automotive engineering. According to a market survey in 2003, 90 % of the innovations for automobiles are driven by electronics and software [1]. These activities also include the utilisation of communication technologies, which gain in importance for increasing vehicular safety and for improving the traffic flow on the roads. The ongoing research particularly into the field of vehicular safety shows that both active and passive safety can be significantly increased if vehicles are able to communicate with each other in order to exchange safety-relevant information [2, 3, 4]. The European Union also identified vehicular communication as an emerging technology for future intelligent transportation services [5]. A very basic vehicular application could be the warning of vehicles about dangerous situations on the road like accidents. This way, succeeding vehicles are able to slow down their speed in time or they may choose alternative routes in case of pending congestions. In such a vehicular communication scenario, low delays and moderate communication costs play an important role. Hence, direct communication via inter-vehicle communication systems presents one, probably even the most promising solution. Inter-vehicle communication systems are based on multi-hop ad hoc networks called VANETs (vehicular ad hoc networks). VANETs enable communication between two vehicles even over multiple relaying vehicles without any pre-installed network infrastructure. The vehicular communication scenario also comprises roadside installed gateways connected to the Internet. They may enable communication between two vehicles in case the communication distance between them is too large to send the data even over multiple hops.

Besides typical vehicular applications, the popularity of an ubiquitous Internet access comes along with the demand to provide Internet services in the VANET. Since the gateways are connected to the Internet, they may additionally provide temporary access to the Internet for the passing vehicles. However, communication in VANETs is fundamentally different compared to communication in the Internet. Since vehicles are highly mobile, the topology of VANETs may vary heavily and vehicles may permanently change their gateway to the Internet in different traffic scenarios on the road. The multi-hop capability of VANETs introduces additional challenges such as the mobility management of the vehicles and the discovery of the gateways even over several hops. This way, traditional Internet-based protocols cannot be used for communication between a vehicle and an Internet host. Moreover, traditional Internet protocols were not developed with respect to the unpredictable and heavily varying communication characteristics of the wireless radio transmission between vehicles, which makes them almost unsuitable for being used in vehicular communication environments.

The Internet integration, i.e. the provisioning of Internet access for VANETs, requires respective communication protocols to overcome the deficiencies and challenges of VANETs. This thesis proposes a novel communication architecture called MOCCA (mobile communication architecture) for the integration of VANETs into the Internet. MOCCA combines a proxy-based architecture with a scalable mobility management for the vehicles. The mobility management enables to discover suitable gateways from the vehicles even over multiple hops, and it hides the mobility of the vehicles. It also enables mobile devices within a vehicle to use the VANET for Internet access. Furthermore, MOCCA is able to improve communication in heterogeneous communication environments. A multiplexing mechanism is able to handover between different communication systems that are available at the same time. Thereby, a fuzzy-based protocol mechanism is able to determine the most suitable alternative communication system. At the transport layer, an optimised transport protocol improves communication efficiency while maintaining compatibility with the transport protocol TCP used in the Internet. These protocols collaborate with each other in order to improve communication between vehicles and Internet hosts. MOCCA therefore enables the deployment of IP-based applications in VANETs, which opens up the vehicular network for the Internet. This way, the VANET becomes a transparent extension of the Internet.

1.1   Contribution of this Thesis

The MOCCA architecture introduced in this thesis is a novel communication architecture for the Internet integration of vehicular ad hoc networks. MOCCA combines several highly optimised protocols with a proxy-based architecture. It therefore proposes protocols for the network layer and the transport layer of the ISO/OSI communication model. The following protocols handle the differences of communication in the VANET and the Internet and enable an efficient data exchange between vehicles and Internet hosts:

► Interoperability between the IPv6-based VANET and the IPv4-based Internet.

► Utilisation of heterogeneous communication environments using a fuzzy-based identification of and an efficient handover to the most suitable alternative communication
system if several communication systems are available simultaneously.

► Mobility of the vehicles in the VANET, including a scalable multi-hop discovery of the
most suitable gateway using fuzzy logic.

► Support of mobile devices within vehicles, which enables traditional TCP/IP-based
applications running on the passengers' mobile devices to access the Internet using
the VANET.

► A new transport protocol for efficient communication in vehicular environments.

An important feature is the integrated way MOCCA combines the communication protocols, which means that these protocols closely interact with each other. This integrated
approach is necessary for an efficient Internet access as well as for the scalability required in
vehicular environments.

This thesis also contributes communication models of four typical VANET scenarios: a
crossway in a city, a motorway at night, a motorway with a high traffic flow, and a congestion on a motorway. The models provide the communication characteristics a vehicle
experiences while travelling through the scenarios. They are used to determine the performance of MOCCA in the respective scenarios and to compare the results with alternative
common solutions for communication between a vehicle and an Internet host.

However, there are some aspects that are out of scope for the Internet integration throughout this thesis:

► *Ad Hoc Routing:* The routing protocol is vital for multi-hop ad hoc networks and it
essentially affects the communication overhead. However, it is not considered since
the routing strategy within VANETs should be transparent to the Internet.

► *Quality of Service:* Although quality of service requirements are crucial especially for
vehicular safety applications, they are of minor importance for typical IP-based applications. IP typically provides a best-effort service without any guarantees; thus,
quality of service aspects are not considered for the Internet integration.

► *Security:* Security issues are also very important for vehicular applications due to the
vulnerability of wireless links. However, they are of minor importance for the original

task of the Internet integration. This thesis discusses security considerations for several design decisions in MOCCA, but they are not considered as a requirement for the design of the architecture itself.

Furthermore, MOCCA does not address optimisations for the data link layer, although they can improve the communication efficiency further on. Such optimisations are basically out of scope for the Internet integration itself. Similarly, application-specific aspects are not considered although also they can improve the performance of applications.

1.2 Outline

The organisation of this thesis follows a modular concept. Each chapter represents a self-contained module, which basically comprises problem description and basics, related work, the proposed approach, and an evaluation. This way, basics as well as related work are thematically associated with the content of the different modules in order to improve the structural clarity. Figure 1.1 depicts the structure of this document and the corelation between the modules.

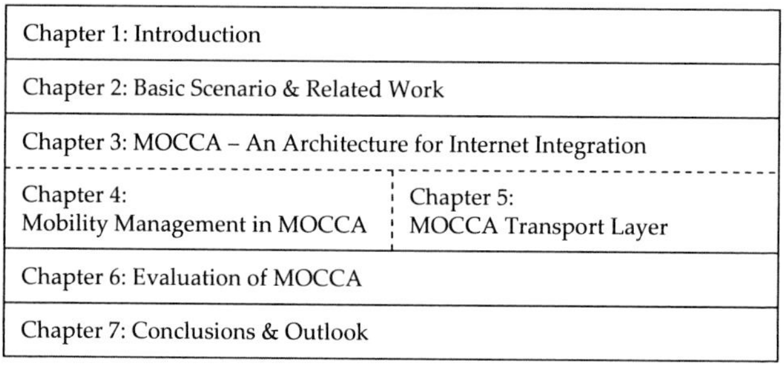

| Chapter 1: Introduction |
| Chapter 2: Basic Scenario & Related Work |
| Chapter 3: MOCCA – An Architecture for Internet Integration |
| Chapter 4: Mobility Management in MOCCA | Chapter 5: MOCCA Transport Layer |
| Chapter 6: Evaluation of MOCCA |
| Chapter 7: Conclusions & Outlook |

Figure 1.1: Outline of this Thesis

Chapter 2 addresses basics and related work on Internet integration in general: It introduces the basic communication scenario used as a reference scenario throughout this thesis and identifies the characteristics of vehicular environments. This part also derives the requirements for the Internet integration of vehicular ad hoc networks, which are used for the evaluation of Internet integration approaches. Chapter 2 also deals with related research on the Internet integration in vehicular environments. It therefore introduces important solutions and evaluates them in the context of the reference scenario.

Chapter 3 attends to MOCCA, the proposed communication architecture for the Internet integration of vehicular ad hoc networks. The first part introduces the basic concepts and principles of MOCCA. It also gives an overview on the communication protocols being used together with their close interactions. The second part is focused on communication within the vehicles and proposes the solution to integrate these appliances into the MOCCA architecture. It therefore presents a fuzzy-based solution to utilise heterogeneous communication environments in MOCCA. This chapter also discusses alternative realisation strategies and compares their strengths and weaknesses with the MOCCA approach. The following chapters 4 and 5 deal with the most important protocols in MOCCA: the mobility management and the transport protocol.

Chapter 4 is devoted to the mobility management of the vehicles at the network layer. This chapter first introduces the requirements for the mobility management of vehicular ad hoc networks and discusses Mobile IP, the protocol for mobility support in the Internet. It also evaluates related work for using Mobile IP for the mobility support of ad hoc networks. The second part introduces MMIP6, the mobility management protocol used in MOCCA. MMIP6 is extended by the DRIVE protocol, which discovers suitable gateways to the Internet from within the vehicular ad hoc network. Both protocols are finally evaluated in a qualitative and a quantitative manner.

Chapter 5 deals with the transport layer in MOCCA. This chapter first introduces TCP and its congestion control mechanisms and discusses the use of TCP for communication in vehicular ad hoc networks. Based on these observations, the requirements for a transport layer protocol in the MOCCA architecture are derived and related work on improving transport layer performance in mobile and wireless environments is observed. The second part of this chapter proposes MCTP, the transport layer protocol used in MOCCA. It therefore describes the basic functionality, the protocol state machine of MCTP, the interaction with other communication protocols, and optional optimisation strategies. Finally, MCTP is discussed and evaluated in a qualitative way in order to confirm its suitability for the Internet integration of VANETs.

Chapter 6 evaluates the MOCCA architecture in a testbed, which emulates the Internet access of a vehicle in different vehicular communication scenarios. This chapter introduces models for typical vehicular communication scenarios and compares MOCCA with an end-to-end TCP approach as well as a split TCP approach with the help of the communication models developed. Finally, MOCCA is evaluated in a qualitative way and the evaluation results are compared with the related work on the Internet integration.

Finally, chapter 7 concludes this thesis. It summarises the essential contributions of this work, their importance, and the key results of the evaluation. An outlook outlines areas for future work, which are opened up by the proposed MOCCA architecture.

Chapter 2

Basic Scenario & Related Work

According to Murphy et al. [6], an ad hoc network is "a transitory association of mobile nodes, which do not depend upon any fixed support infrastructure. [...] Connection and disconnection is controlled by the distance among nodes and by willingness to collaborate in the formation of cohesive, albeit transitory community." A VANET (vehicular ad hoc network) is such a multi-hop ad hoc network where vehicles on the move act as mobile nodes. Besides vehicle-to-vehicle communications, vehicular applications may also rely on information from the Internet, which requires an integration of the VANET into the Internet. This way, the Internet integration has to ensure efficient communication between vehicles and hosts in the Internet. Besides the Internet access for the vehicles, the Internet integration also has to provide access to services within vehicles from hosts in the Internet independent of their current locations. This way, the Internet will be opened up for the VANET, which allows the deployment of a variety of new applications in vehicular environments. However, VANETs cannot be compared neither with existing fixed networks nor with wireless networks, because they have fundamentally different communication and organisational characteristics. These differences are basic constraints for the Internet integration of VANETs.

This chapter introduces the basic scenario and discusses related work on Internet integration. It is divided into two parts. The first part attends to the VANET scenario (section 2.1), which is used as a reference scenario throughout this thesis. This part also introduces Fleet-Net, an example for an inter-vehicle communication system based on ad hoc networking. Based on this scenario, section 2.2 acquires the challenges and derives requirements for the Internet integration in the VANET scenario. These requirements are distilled in a catalogue of requirements used in the second part of this chapter for the discussion and the evaluation of related work on Internet integration in section 2.3. Finally, section 2.4 summarises this chapter.

2.1   Vehicular Networks: The Reference Scenario

Traditional road telematics applications are mainly focused on solutions for intelligent transportation systems (ITS). Examples are applications for fleet management and transportation logistics, or applications to guide a driver to the destination taking into account the current road conditions [7, 8]. These ITS applications are server-oriented, i.e. they rely on information coming from a central server. For example, vehicles travelling along a motorway request information about the current road conditions from a server in the Internet. The onboard navigation unit uses this information to determine the quickest or the shortest route to the destination and guides the driver around congested areas dynamically. Communication with the server is based on existing cellular radio access networks such as GSM [9], which provides Internet access for the vehicles on the road (cf. figure 2.1 (a)).

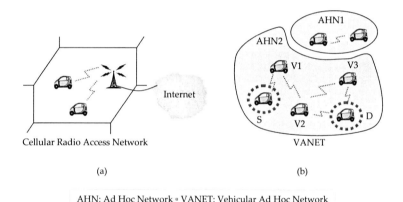

Cellular Radio Access Network   VANET

(a)   (b)

AHN: Ad Hoc Network □ VANET: Vehicular Ad Hoc Network

Figure 2.1: Comparison of Existing and Upcoming Road Telematics Applications

Besides traditional road telematics applications, the development of modern road telematics applications is focused on so-called "floating applications", which complement existing ITS services. Floating applications follow the location principle, i.e. they additionally consider the "location" of the information. This means that vehicles generate local information, distribute this information locally in the vehicular network, and consume the information generated by other vehicles. Floating applications are very interesting for vehicular environments, because they are able to improve vehicular safety and the convenience of the passengers in many situations on the road. The following examples illustrate typical applications:

► *Cooperative Driving Assistance:* These vehicle-centred applications improve the cooperation between vehicles while travelling. This allows, for instance, the development of vehicle warning systems where heavy braking vehicles notify following vehicles [10], it enables the platooning of vehicles [11], or it facilitates the ascending of vehicles on a motorway lane [12].

► *Floating Car Data:* A floating car data application collects information about a vehicle's local environment such as the current weather or road conditions and distribute this information among the other vehicles in the network. This information will be meliorated within the network when other vehicles cumulate the received information with the information generated by themselves. This way, it is possible to distribute important events locally like congestions or hazards [13, 14].

► *User Communication and Information Applications:* Example applications for improving the convenience of passengers are user chats between vehicles, the exchange of local data such as legal copies of audio files, or multi-player games [15, 16, 17].

Floating applications require a respective communication network providing the local exchange of data. For this task, cellular networks like GSM or the infrastructure mode of IEEE 802.11 are not applicable, because they require an area-wide coverage with base stations to enable communication between vehicles. In order to guarantee low delays required for the exchange of safety-related information between vehicles, modern vehicular networks are based on multi-hop ad hoc networks [18], the so-called vehicular ad hoc networks (VANETs). According to RFC 2501 [19], an ad hoc network has the following characteristics:

► It is an autonomous system of mobile nodes.

► It may operate in isolation or may have gateways to and interfaces with a fixed network.

► The mobile nodes are equipped with wireless receivers and transmitters.

This way, vehicles can transmit data to neighboured vehicles within their radio transmission range without any central infrastructure, base stations, or access points. Ad hoc networks also support multi-hop vehicle-to-vehicle communication. This requires an appropriate ad hoc routing protocol that ensures that two distant vehicles are able to communicate with each other using intermediate vehicles as relaying nodes [20, 21]. For example, in figure 2.1 (b) vehicle S is able to communicate with vehicle D using V1 and V2 as relaying nodes. Alternatively, S can communicate with D via vehicle V1, V2 and V3. Due to the mobility of the vehicles, the VANET may be partitioned into two or more autonomous ad hoc network clusters. Vehicles within a VANET cluster are able to communicate with each other, either immediately or via multi-hop communication. However, communication between the vehicles in different ad hoc networks is not possible since there is no communication link between vehicles in different ad hoc networks. For example, the VANET in figure 2.1 (b) consists of two ad hoc networks AHN1 and AHN2.

Besides (multi-hop) vehicle-to-vehicle communication, VANETs are also able to provide access to the Internet using roadside installed "Internet Gateways" (IGWs) as illustrated in figure 2.2. IGWs appear in the VANET as common (parked) vehicles providing an interconnection to the Internet. The main task of an IGW is to route data from the VANET into the Internet and vice versa. IGWs may not be mixed up with base stations (or access points) controlling the medium access of the communicating vehicles: if a base station fails, communication between vehicles will not be possible any longer. In contrast, IGWs appear as stationary nodes in the VANET. This way, communication is still possible between vehicles even if an IGW is not available.

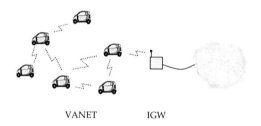

VANET   IGW

IGW: Internet Gateway ▫ VANET: Vehicular Ad Hoc Network

Figure 2.2: Internet Access for Future Vehicular Applications

An example for a VANET communication system is developed in the FleetNet project [22, 23] and its successor project NOW (Network on Wheels [24]). Besides the development and promotion of a vehicular ad hoc networking technology, FleetNet also aims at the implementation and demonstration of floating applications. The FleetNet communication system is described in the following sections in detail, because it serves as a reference implementation for an inter-vehicle communication system throughout this thesis.

2.1.1 FleetNet

Compared to communication in wired IP-based networks, the communication architecture of FleetNet differs fundamentally in many aspects. Examples are the addressing of the vehicles, the routing of data in the context of mobility, and the medium access for the wireless transmission. Figure 2.3 shows the protocol architecture of FleetNet [25, 26]. It comprises the lower three layers for inter-vehicle communications, namely FleetNet Physical Layer (FPHY), FleetNet Data Link Control Layer (FDLC), and FleetNet Network Layer (FNL). FleetNet does not specify a transport layer; instead, FleetNet applications immediately use the FNL for their communications. The FleetNet communication architecture also specifies control and management planes for both FDLC and FNL, which are not depicted in figure 2.3. The management planes control the respective layers. For example, it adapts the transmission power to the number of communicating vehicles in the VANET in order to minimise interferences.

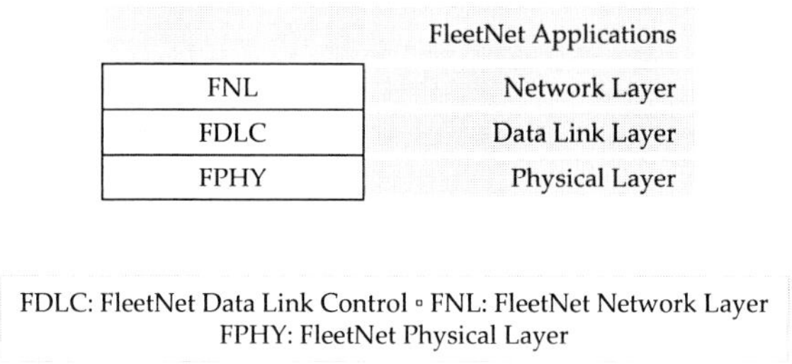

	FleetNet Applications
FNL	Network Layer
FDLC	Data Link Layer
FPHY	Physical Layer

FDLC: FleetNet Data Link Control ▫ FNL: FleetNet Network Layer
FPHY: FleetNet Physical Layer

Figure 2.3: FleetNet System Architecture

The wireless transmission of data on the lower communication layers FPHY and FDLC uses a modified UTRA TDD[1] scheme, which operates in the unlicensed UMTS band from 2.010 GHz to 2.020 GHz [27, 28, 29]. The modifications of UTRA TDD ensure a correct synchronisation between the communicating peers and define a radio resource management to support quality of service. Thereby, Code Division Multiple Access (CDMA [9]) is used to separate the communication channels of the vehicles. This capability is very important for a VANET, because it enables the deployment of time-sensitive applications. Example applications are cooperative driving assistants or applications for the platooning of cars and trucks travelling along a motorway.

---

[1]UTRA TDD: Universal Terrestrial Radio Access – Time Division Duplex

On the network layer, the FNL enables multi-hop vehicle-to-vehicle communication. The FNL therefore defines the addressing of the vehicles, the routing of data, and it supports respective quality of service mechanisms for vehicular applications. The FNL is neither based on IP technology nor compatible to IP. It is characterised by the following features:

► *Addressing:* The FNL uniquely addresses a vehicle using a "FleetNet ID" with a length of 64 bit.

► *Location Awareness:* The FNL is able to determine the geographical position of a vehicle using the Global Positioning System (GPS [30]). It therefore maps the static FleetNet ID of a remote vehicle onto its geographical position by querying a distributed location service [31]. If the location service is able to resolve the FleetNet ID, it responds to the query with the position of the FleetNet ID.

► *Location-based Routing:* The routing of data in FleetNet is based on the geographical locations instead of FleetNet IDs. If a vehicle wants to send data to a remote vehicle, the FNL first has to determine the position of the remote vehicle with the help of the location service. If this resolution is successful, the vehicle will send the data to the position of the targeted vehicle. Thereby, intermediate vehicles are responsible to forward the data towards the direction of the remote vehicle as described in [32, 33, 34, 35, 36].

The FNL provides an interface for FleetNet applications to use the FleetNet communication system. As the FNL is not based on IP technology, the interface to the FNL is different to the standardised socket interface specified for communication in the Internet. Hence, FleetNet applications are not compatible with IP-based applications. In order to support IP-based communication in FleetNet, the system architecture specifies adaptations of the FNL, which are described in the next section.

2.1.2 IP-Based Communication in FleetNet

In order to support IP-based applications, the FleetNet communication system has to bridge the functional differences between IP and the FNL. These differences are handled by an adaptation sublayer within the FNL, the FleetNet Adaptation (FNA, cf. figure 2.4). The FNA performs a bijective mapping between FNL and IP functionality. This way, the FNL additionally provides an IP interface besides the native FNL interface. A transport layer on top of the IP layer enables the end-to-end communication between IP-based applications similar to TCP and UDP in the Internet. The transport layer is not part of the FleetNet specification, because FleetNet applications immediately use the native functionality of the FNL without an intermediate transport layer.

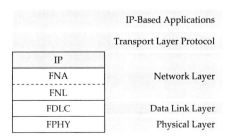

FDLC: FleetNet Data Link Control ▫ FNA: FleetNet Network Adaptation
FNL: FleetNet Network Layer ▫ FPHY: FleetNet Physical Layer

Figure 2.4: Support of IP-based Communication in FleetNet

The most important task of the FNA is the address mapping, i.e. the mapping of an IP address onto a FleetNet ID and vice versa. Besides the Internet access for the vehicles, it is important that Internet hosts can get access to vehicles for IP-based applications in FleetNet. This way, a vehicle can provide Internet services such as Web services for remote diagnostics of vehicles. This capability requires the use of a global IP addressing scheme; both private IP addresses and an arbitrary addressing scheme using address translation mechanisms similar to NAT (Network Address Translator, RFC 3022 [37]) cannot be used since they do not support the access of the vehicles. Even the combination of NAT or private addresses with Dynamic DNS (Domain Name System) does not provide vehicular access, because Dynamic DNS does not support multiple services of the same type within one local network [38]. The use of IPv4 in FleetNet is not recommended, because IPv4 does not provide enough IP addresses. In the beginning of 2004, for example, $54,082,169$ vehicles were registered in Germany [39], which is approximately 1.3% of the total IPv4 address space. Assuming a European-wide deployment and the accessibility of each controller within a vehicle, this would easily exhaust the IPv4 address space of 2^{32} addresses. Moreover, the 64 bit length of the FleetNet ID makes it impossible to map the FleetNet ID uniquely onto a 32 bit IPv4 address.

In order to avoid bottlenecks in the addressing scheme, FleetNet uses IPv6 addresses to identify the vehicles since the 128 bit address space in IPv6 provides sufficient capacity. A mapping between the FleetNet ID and the IPv6 address of the vehicle is straightforward: the FleetNet ID defines the lower 64 bits of the IPv6 address. From a conceptual point of view, the FleetNet communication system appears as a single IPv6 subnet (with a globally defined IPv6 "FleetNet prefix" assigned by IANA (Internet Assigned Numbers Authority [40]), which has to be integrated into the Internet. Within the VANET, IP-based applications communicate with each other using the FleetNet IPv6 addresses instead of the native FleetNet IDs.

2.2   Internet Integration Requirements

The Internet integration of VANETs has to enable efficient communication between a vehicle in the VANET and a host in the Internet. This task requires interoperability on the network layer, i.e. with IP. However, the characteristics of a VANET differ in many aspects from traditional IP-based networks such as LANs:

- ▶ *Wireless Links:* Communication in the VANET is based on wireless radio transmission with unpredictable and highly varying data rates, delays, and packet losses.

- ▶ *Mobility:* Typically, vehicles travel at high speeds on a motorway. This way, both the topology of the VANET and the point of attachment to the Internet change permanently. Moreover, the number of neighboured vehicles may vary since vehicles or groups of vehicles may join or leave the VANET.

- ▶ *Ad Hoc Networking:* VANETs are based on multi-hop ad hoc networks, which are subject to permanent reconfigurations. Hence, the delay between communication peers may vary heavily since it depends on the number of relaying vehicles.

- ▶ *Temporary Internet Connections:* Since an area-wide coverage with IGWs is not expected, the Internet connection will become temporarily unavailable if the vehicle cannot find an IGW.

- ▶ *Large Networks:* Vehicular ad hoc networks may become very large comprising potentially hundreds of vehicles. Hence, scalability and efficiency becomes a crucial factor for the Internet integration. Due to the potentially large number of vehicles, the vehicles must be identified by IPv6 addresses.

- ▶ *Heterogeneity:* Besides the inter-vehicle communication system, further communication networks might be available at the same time such as a GSM network or an IEEE 802.11 network at a gas station. These networks can also be used for Internet access.

Standard Internet protocols from the TCP/IP suite cannot be used for the Internet integration of a VANET: For example, IP requires a fixed network topology and does not support the discovery and handover of connections from one IGW to the next. Moreover, the

TCP performance is rather moderate in mobile environments with temporary connections and varying data transfer rates and delays [9]. This way, the integration of a VANET into the Internet has to accomplish several challenges, which basically address requirements at the network layer and the transport layer. These Internet integration requirements can be classified into four basic parts:

1. Mobility support for the vehicles.

2. Consideration of vehicular characteristics

3. Transport layer aspects.

4. Scalability issues.

These four parts are the basis for a catalogue of requirements as summarised in figure 2.5. This catalogue is used for the evaluation of related work on Internet integration in section 2.3. The four requirements are partitioned into more detailed requirements, which are explained in the following sections.

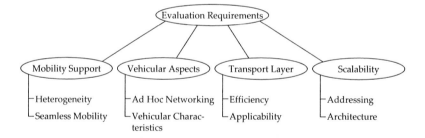

Figure 2.5: Catalogue of Requirements for the Internet Integration

2.2.1 Mobility Support

Vehicles usually travel at high speeds on a motorway. As a result, the network topology is highly dynamic and vehicles must be able to change their point of attachment to the Internet dynamically and transparently. The mobility of vehicles consists of the following two requirements: the support of heterogeneous communication environments and the provision of seamless mobility.

In the VANET scenario, vehicles typically travel in heterogeneous communication environments. The *heterogeneity* requirement reflects the ability to utilise different communication systems for the Internet access. This means that the mobility support has to be independent of the communication system. The heterogeneity requirement is very important for the adoption of further upcoming VANET communication technologies.

The *seamless mobility* support has to enable communication between vehicle and Internet host. Data to and from the Internet must be always routed to the targeted vehicle, independent of its current location and its mobility. The seamless mobility support is also known as the "Mobile IP problem" [41]. It reflects the transparency of the vehicular mobility at the network layer to the upper layer protocols in three ways:

▶ *Handover between Internet Gateways:* Seamless mobility requires protocol mechanisms to handover connections horizontally, i.e. from one IGW to another IGW within the VANET.

▶ *Handover between Communication Systems:* Besides horizontal handovers, the Internet integration has to support vertical handovers, i.e. transparent handovers between different communication systems. An example is a handover of connections from the VANET to, e.g., a wireless LAN based on IEEE 802.11.

▶ *Bi-directional Connection Establishment:* Bi-directional connection establishment means that both the vehicle and an Internet host should be able to initiate a connection setup. This is an important feature in the VANET scenario, because it enables Internet hosts to access vehicular services, e.g. for remote diagnostics.

2.2.2 Vehicular Aspects

The characteristics of a vehicular network differ from classical mobile or wireless networks with respect to the mobility and the capabilities of mobile nodes. Hence, vehicular aspects are important for the Internet integration of a VANET. In general, two evaluation parameters can be derived: The support of multi-hop ad hoc communication and the consideration of typical vehicular characteristics.

In the VANET scenario, vehicles are able to form multi-hop ad hoc networks for the local exchange of data. In order to integrate VANETs into the Internet, the *ad hoc networking* requirement has to support several features that are important for this particular type of network:

▶ *Discovery of Internet Gateways:* Vehicles should be able to identify available IGWs for Internet access. The identification must be possible even via relaying vehicles using

multi-hop communication. This problem is also known as the "service discovery problem" [42].

▶ *Selection of a suitable Internet Gateway:* In modern vehicular communication scenarios,
it might be possible that several IGWs are available simultaneously. In this case, a
vehicle should be able to select the gateway that currently fits best to the requirements
of the applications.

▶ *Interaction with the Mobility Support:* Since the mobility support (cf. section 2.2.1) inherently depends on information about available and suitable IGWs, the ad hoc networking requirement has to complement the mobility support requirement.

▶ *Independence of Ad Hoc Routing Protocols:* The Internet integration approach should be
independent of the protocols used for ad hoc networking such as the routing protocol.
This property is important, because routing in the VANET scenario will likely be different compared to routing algorithms currently discussed. Examples algorithms are
DSR (Dynamic Source Routing [43]) or AODV (Ad hoc On-Demand Distance Vector
routing, RFC 3561 [44]), which route data according to an address topology of the ad
hoc network.

The second requirement is the consideration of typical *vehicular characteristics*. Examples
are the high mobility of vehicles and the resulting temporary unavailability of Internet access, which must be taken into consideration. In contrast, classical challenges in computer-
based ad hoc networks might be of minor importance. For example, the consideration of
energy-aware protocols plays a subordinate role in the VANET scenario since power supply
in vehicles is not assumed to be as critical as with other mobile devices.

2.2.3 Transport Layer

IP-based applications use the transport layer protocols of the Internet to exchange data, i.e.
TCP and UDP. However, the communication characteristics of VANETs also have an impact
on the performance of these protocols. The transport layer issue basically addresses TCP, the
most important transport layer protocol used in the Internet. According to measurements
in 1998, 95 % of the Internet traffic was caused by TCP [45]. TCP is optimised for communication in fixed networks. However, the conservative congestion control mechanisms
implemented in TCP interfere with the characteristics of mobile environments: temporary
and error-prone connections with varying data rates, delays and error rates result in a poor
performance although a higher throughput would be possible in theory [9]. For the transport layer the following two requirements have to be addressed: communication efficiency
and applicability.

The *efficiency* addresses the performance of the transport protocol deployed in the VANET scenario in terms of data throughput and utilisation. This optimisation can be achieved either by fine-tuning standardised TCP configuration parameters, by the development of TCP extensions, or by developing a completely new transport protocol.

The second requirement is the *applicability* of the suggested transport layer solution. Since most applications in the Internet use TCP, the Internet integration has to ensure the collaboration of the transport protocol with standard TCP as well as the deployment of the transport protocol in the VANET scenario. This collaboration also considers the functionality of the transport protocol developed, which comprises the following requirements:

- ► *TCP Functionality:* Many Internet-based applications rely on different features supported by TCP such as reliability. If these applications are deployed in the VANET scenario, the transport layer of the VANET has to support a respective functionality similar to TCP.

- ► *Socket-based Application Programming Interface:* In order to alleviate the porting and deployment of existing applications in the VANET scenario, the transport protocol has to support a socket-based interface to the transport layer [46].

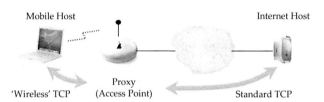

Figure 2.6: Splitting of a TCP Connection in I-TCP [47]

A subordinate aspect is the maintenance of the end-to-end semantics. TCP provides an end-to-end connection between communicating applications, which ensures that acknowledged data was received by the communication peer. In order to deploy a new transport protocol while maintaining interoperability with TCP, the transport layer connection must be split up into two parts as illustrated in figure 2.6. Thereby, communication between the proxy located on the access point and an Internet host is based on standard TCP, whereas the proxy communicates with the mobile host using an optimised 'wireless' TCP. An example protocol using the splitting technique is Indirect TCP (I-TCP [47]). However, the splitting violates the end-to-end semantics of TCP, because an acknowledgement means that the data arrived at the proxy but not at the mobile node. Hence, a failure of the proxy may result in an inconsistent view of the data transmitted.

Typically, TCP is considered to provide end-to-end semantics [48]. However, this is of less importance in practice concerning reliability [49]. The PILC (Performance Implications of Link Characteristics) working group of the Internet Engineering Task Force states that performance enhancing proxies can be used to split end-to-end connections if they offer significant advantages over an end-to-end solution [50]. Already the original TCP specification in RFC 793 [51] states that "The TCP specification describes an interface to the higher level protocols, which appears to be implementable even for the front-end case, as long as a suitable host-to-front end protocol is implemented." In case of maintained end-to-end semantics, an acknowledgement for sent data means that the data arrived at the TCP instance of the communicating peer, but not necessarily at the respective application. Even Saltzer et al. stated in [48] that "end-to-end reliability can only be implemented by applications." This way, most TCP-based applications do not rely on TCP completely. Instead, they implement the "session-like" functionality they need by themselves, or they use standardised application protocols for this task, like in the following examples:

▶ The WWW (World Wide Web) uses HTTP (Hypertext Transfer Protocol, RFC 2616 [52]);

▶ Email is based on POP3 (Post Office Protocol, RFC 1939 [53]) or IMAP-4 (Internet Message Access Protocol, RFC 3501 [54]);

However, the splitting of the end-to-end connection comes along with a loss of the end-to-end communication model, which is one of the architectural principles of the Internet [55]. This is harmful for security methods at the network layer (for example IPsec [56]) since they implicitly assume an end-to-end connection to authenticate the communication peers for secure communication. This aspect is discussed in the context of the design decisions for a communication architecture, but it is not included in the catalogue of requirements since security issues are beyond the scope of this thesis.

2.2.4 Scalability

Scalability is a crucial issue in the VANET scenario since the number of vehicles participating in the VANET potentially may be very high. The scalability requirement is necessary for the addressing of the vehicles and the communication protocols used for the Internet integration.

The *addressing* requirement has to ensure that each vehicle is identified uniquely with an IP address. As stated in section 2.1.2, both global IPv4 addresses and address translations cannot be used in the VANET scenario. Instead, vehicles have to be identified by IPv6 addresses.

Besides the addressing aspect, the solution developed for the Internet integration must be scalable, too. This way, the *architecture* requirement evaluates the scalability of communication protocols used. This requirement also considers the scalability of potential bottlenecks and single points of failure in the Internet integration solution. Therefore, it should be possible to dissolve such bottlenecks at reasonable costs.

2.2.5 Further Requirements

There are several further requirements to evaluate an Internet integration approach. The following aspects are not considered further on, because they do not have an immediate correlation with the original task of the Internet integration:

▶ *Quality of Service Issues:* Many efforts were made to support quality of service in the Internet. Examples are the Differentiated Services architecture [57] or the Integrated Services architecture [58]. There was also considerable work on improving service quality in ad hoc networks [59, 60, 61, 62, 63], which basically addresses routing and medium access control mechanisms. However, a simple adoption of the Internet quality of service concepts and guarantees to VANETs is difficult since they rely on fixed network topologies with static routing paths and reliable communication links.

▶ *Security Concerns:* Security is an important aspect for communication networks. Although the Internet community already specified a security architecture for IP (IPsec, RFC 2401 [56]), secure communication is often provided at higher protocol layers in the Internet. Examples are SSL (Secure Socket Layer [64]) and its successor TLS (Transport Layer Security [65, 66]), which both are used for securing HTTP traffic. Moreover, security also comprises protocols for authentication, authorisation and accounting of users, which are performed on the application layer [67]. The consideration of security concerns is beyond the scope of this thesis.

▶ *Support of Mobile Applications:* There was also considerable work on supporting mobile applications, e.g. by middleware-based approaches [68] or by peer-to-peer-based vehicular communication platforms [69, 70] to hide the characteristics of mobile networks. This could be very useful to improve the development of mobile applications, but it has only a minor correlation with the original task of the Internet integration.

2.3   Related Work: Internet Integration Approaches

In the last few years, communication in vehicular environments gained importance in the research community. Especially in the IST (Information Society Technologies) programs of the European Union (EU) and by the German Federal Ministry of Education and Research (BMBF) several projects were set up dealing with various aspects of communication in vehicular scenarios. The following examples give an impression on the variety of research in this area:

▶ *Chauffeur II [71] (1996 to 2002, funded by the EU):* The overall goal of Chauffeur and its successor Chauffeur II was to augment the utilisation of existing roads. Chauffeur II therefore proposed a telematics-based vehicle control system to increase the density of freight traffic in a safe manner. The project developed a radar system to link trucks electronically. This system allows a leading truck to control following trucks in a dense lane [72].

▶ *CarTALK 2000 [73] (2001 to 2004, funded by the EU):* The EU project CarTALK 2000 aims at the development of new driver assistance systems using inter-vehicle communication [10]. Inter-vehicle communication in CarTALK 2000 is based on self-organising ad hoc radio network technology [74].

▶ *MoTiV (1996 to 2000, funded by the BMBF):* One part of MoTiV was the project "Mobility in Conurbations" [75], which aimed on increasing vehicular safety and mobility by combining intermodal means of transportation. The successive research program "Mobilität und Verkehr" (mobility and transportation) deals with intelligent transportation, sustainable mobility, environmental protection, and increased safety on the road using vehicle-to-vehicle communication [76].

▶ *INVENT [77] (2001 to 2005, funded by the BMBF):* The INVENT project addresses various applications by combining traffic on the road, information, and communication technologies. Exemplary applications are driver assistance systems using inter-vehicle communication to warn vehicles about dangerous incidents or road conditions ahead [78]. Moreover, this information will be used to develop traffic management systems to dissolve – or even entirely prevent – congestions on the road [79, 80].

▶ *PATH [81] (since 1986, supported by the California Department of Transportation, USA):* PATH aims at two basic aspects: advanced transportation management and information systems, and advanced vehicle control and safety systems. In order to distribute traffic and sensor information, PATH uses Dedicated Short Range Communication

(DSRC) technology to communicate with a computer, which can be either at the road-side or within a vehicle.

These projects basically deal with vehicular applications for VANETs and the development of the VANET technology itself. However, they do not consider the integration of VANETs into the Internet. Besides these activities, there are important approaches dealing with the Internet integration of vehicular networks: DRiVE/OverDRiVE, COMCAR, IPon-Air, DriveBy InfoFueling, and CarNet. The following sections introduce these approaches[2] and evaluate their Internet integration approaches by means of the catalogue of requirements described in the previous section. Therefore, the following evaluation scale is used for the requirements:

'−−' requirement is not fulfilled

'−'   major issues of the requirement are not fulfilled

'o'   partial fulfilment of the requirement

'+'   major issues of the requirement are fulfilled

'++' requirement is fulfilled

A question mark ('?') indicates that not enough information is available to evaluate the respective requirement. Brackets denote an expected rating that was derived from the available information but could not be determined finally.

2.3.1 DRiVE/OverDRiVE

The DRiVE project (Dynamic Radio for IP Services in Vehicular Environments) [82, 83] and its successor OverDRiVE [84] were funded in the IST program of the European Union from 1998 to 2002. The objective of DRiVE was to enable spectrum-efficient high-quality wireless IP services for multimedia applications in a multi-radio vehicular network environment. In order to achieve this objective, DRiVE intends the convergence of cellular and broadcast networks. The convergence is realised by optimising the inter-working of different radio systems (GSM, GPRS, UMTS, DAB, and DVB-T) in a common dynamically allocated frequency range. The OverDRiVE project extends DRiVE by providing mechanisms for spectrum sharing between the communication systems using a dynamic allocation of the

---

[2]The FleetNet project (cf. section 2.1.1) is not discussed in this section. This is due to the fact that the FleetNet scenario is used as a reference scenario and the Internet integration in FleetNet is based on the concepts proposed in this thesis.

spectrum according to the actual load of the network. Moreover, OverDRiVE aims at the development of a vehicular router to provide multi-radio access to a moving intra-vehicular network.

Internet Integration in DRiVE/OverDRiVE

Besides spectrum efficiency, (Over)DRiVE targets on IP services in vehicular environments. DRiVE therefore implements a mobile infrastructure as illustrated in figure 2.7. This mobile infrastructure is integrated into the IPv6-based DRiVE backbone network, which interconnects the different access networks with the Internet. The access networks are connected to the DRiVE backbone network via so-called DRiVE Interface Units. Within the DRiVE backbone network, a Multi-Radio Support Node is responsible for the routing of IP packets via the "most suitable" access network to the vehicle. In order to determine the most suitable access network, DRiVE takes into account the asymmetry of communication links, the position of the vehicle, terminal decoding capacity, and user preferences in terms of delay and quality requirements [85]. The DRiVE backbone network itself is connected to the Internet via a border router.

The backbone network implements the mobile infrastructure of (Over)DRiVE. This functionality is transparent to an Internet host, i.e. modifications of hosts or routers in the Internet are not necessary. The DRiVE backbone network comprises the following functionality:

▶ *Mobility Management:* (Over)DRiVE deploys Hierarchical Mobile IPv6 (HMIPv6) [86] for the macro-mobility of the vehicles. For this purpose, the Home Agents of the vehicles are located within the DRiVE backbone network. Micro-mobility is not supported in the DRiVE network architecture since each access network is expected to handle its own micro-mobility support.

▶ *Quality of Service (QoS):* (Over)DRiVE also enables quality of service support by combining Integrated Services [58] and Differentiated Services [57].

▶ *Authentication, Authorisation and Accounting (AAA):* For the authentication, authorisation and accounting of services, DRiVE uses the Diameter protocol specified in [87].

▶ *Flow-based Host-controlled IP Forwarding:* The vehicles are able to request different types of traffic redirected via different access systems. This functionality is implemented as an extension to HMIPv6, which controls the Multi-Radio Support Node (cf. figure 2.7) to redirect the communication flow to the respective DRiVE Interface Unit [88].

▶ *Multicast Support:* OverDRiVE additionally aims at the development of efficient mobile multicast techniques for the vehicles in the DRiVE backbone network.

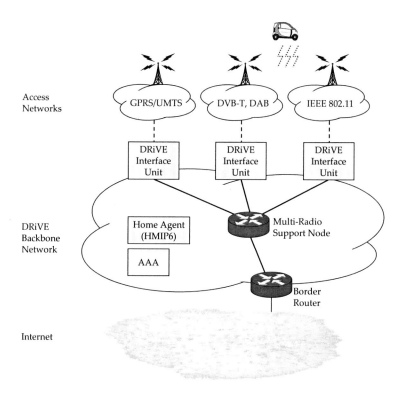

Access
Networks

DRiVE
Backbone
Network

Internet

AAA: Authentication, Authorization, Accounting ▫ HMIP6: Hierarchical Mobile IPv6

Figure 2.7: (Over)DRiVE Network Architecture [85]

Evaluation

Table 2.1 summarises the evaluation of the Internet integration in (Over)DRiVE in the context of the catalogue of requirements. Basically, (Over)DRiVE handles the mobility of vehicles sufficiently. It supports a variety of cellular communication systems, and further cellular communication systems and networks can be integrated easily by adding new DRiVE Interface Units. But, (Over)DRiVE basically uses existing cellular communication systems as access networks for the Internet. It does not provide a solution to integrate ad hoc networks, resulting in a '+' for the heterogeneity requirement. Due to the heterogeneity of the considered communication systems, (Over)DRiVE supports seamless mobility using HMIPv6 with a fixed addressing scheme. Hence, it is possible to switch between the different communication systems transparently, which fulfils the 'Seamless Mobility' requirement.

	Mobility Support		Vehicular Aspect		Transport Layer		Scalability	
Project	Hetero- geneity	Seamless Mobility	Ad Hoc Network.	Vehicular Charact.	Efficien- cy	Applica- bility	Addres- sing	Architec- ture
(Over)DRiVE	+	+ +	− −	−	−	− −	+ +	+ +

Table 2.1: Evaluation of (Over)DRiVE

(Over)DRiVE cannot be used to integrate VANETs into the Internet, because it does not provide any mechanisms for the mobility support of vehicles in ad hoc networks. Hence, the 'Ad Hoc Networking' requirement is not fulfilled. Typical vehicular characteristics play a minor role since the Internet integration approach is focused on the characteristics of available cellular communication systems and not on the vehicular environment itself. This way, the protocol mechanisms deployed in the (Over)DRiVE backbone network are basically optimised for the access networks only, resulting in a '−' for the 'Vehicular Characteristics' requirement.

(Over)DRiVE does not face any transport layer requirements. Although the impact of handovers on the performance of different TCP implementations was simulated and examined [89], (Over)DRiVE relies on standard TCP for connection-oriented communication, resulting in a '−' for the 'Efficiency' requirement. The 'Applicability' requirement is not fulfilled since TCP enhancements and optimisations require modifications in both the vehicles and all Internet hosts.

The overall scalability of (Over)DRiVE is maintained due to the IPv6-based addressing of the vehicles, resulting in a '++' for the addressing requirement. The communication architecture of (Over)DRiVE is also scalable, because potential bottlenecks in the architecture – e.g. the Home Agent, the Multi-Radio Support Node or the AAA functionality – can be designed in a scalable way within the DRiVE backbone network. Moreover, the use of Hierarchical Mobile IPv6 supports micro-mobility to reduce signalling overhead. Hence, the architecture requirement is fulfilled.

The fundamental problem of (Over)DRiVE is that it does not consider VANETs; the communication architecture cannot be used to integrate vehicular ad hoc networks into the Internet. Hence, (Over)DRiVE is not a suitable candidate for the Internet integration in the VANET scenario.

2.3.2   COMCAR

The COMCAR project (Communication and Mobility by Cellular Advanced Radio) [90, 91, 92] was part of the UMTSplus project funded by the BMBF from 1999 to 2002. The objective was the design and implementation of a mobile communication network to provide mobile, asymmetric, and interactive IP-based services in vehicles. Therefore, existing and upcoming communication systems like GSM, GPRS, HSCSD, UMTS, DVB-T, and DAB were optimised and integrated in a vehicular communication network. COMCAR basically deals with communication aspects of the lower layers such as spectrum efficiency of the supported networks. It also provides flexible mechanisms for the quality of service support in such heterogeneous communication environments. A mobile middleware supplemented this quality of service support, which allows adaptive multimedia applications to react to changes in the communication environment in a user-specific manner.

Internet Integration in COMCAR

The key idea in COMCAR is the support of vehicular applications using a communication platform (CP) located within the vehicle as depicted in figure 2.8 [93]. The CP hides the heterogeneous communication environment from the applications. This way, it controls the communication of vehicular applications with the Internet. If an application wants to establish a connection to a host in the Internet, it first has to register itself with the CP and specifies its desired quality of service. The CP then decides which available communication system is best suited to provide the requested quality of service and, if necessary, establishes a link-layer connection to use this communication system. For example, in figure 2.8 the CP decides to use GSM (marked by the arrows) and establishes a dial-up connection to the GSM provider. In case of varying resource availability, the CP reallocates resources dynamically; for example, it provides additional bandwidth using further communication systems. If the requirements of an application cannot be fulfilled, the CP notifies the respective application.

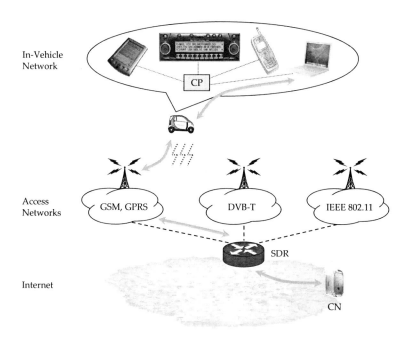

CN: Correspondent Node ▫ CP: Communication Platform ▫ SDR: Service Dependent Router

Figure 2.8: COMCAR Scenario [94]

This way, an application is able to adapt itself to the new communication characteristics reactively.

In contrast to (Over)DRiVE described in section 2.3.1, the COMCAR network architecture does not rely on an explicit backbone network infrastructure to redistribute the resources (cf. figure 2.8). Instead, a "Service Dependent Router" (SDR) is responsible to redirect the traffic flow [94]. The SDR is controlled by the CP, i.e. it receives the routing information from the CP and adapts its routing table accordingly to send data over the requested communication system. For example, if the CP currently communicates using GSM and realises the availability of an IEEE 802.11 hotspot, it will reconfigure the SDR dynamically to route the data via the IEEE 802.11 network instead of the GSM network. COMCAR uses Mobile IPv4 to handover connections seamlessly between different communication systems. The

Home Agent of a vehicle is located outside the COMCAR network in the Internet and data is always tunnelled using IP-in-IP encapsulation to the vehicle.

In case of a dynamical allocation of frequencies, the CP requires information about the available communication systems. This information is transmitted via a specific signalling channel to the vehicle, the "Common Coordination Channel" [93]. In order to support quality of service for IP, COMCAR relies on the Differentiated Services model [57]. Thereby, a number of new COMCAR-specific services [95, 96] extend the differentiated services model to support quality of service in wireless networks:

▶ A *Mobile Premium Service* providing low-loss low-latency guarantees with a statistical guarantee of handover success.

▶ A *Best-Effort Low-Delay Service* that utilises free Mobile Premium Service resources in terms of bandwidth and buffers. This service provides a low-delay service to applications, which can tolerate a certain packet loss rate [97].

Evaluation

The basic COMCAR scenario is similar to (Over)DRiVE; both rely on existing cellular communication systems used as access networks for communication with the Internet. Hence, the COMCAR approach has similar characteristics and, thus, similar evaluation results compared to (Over)DRiVE. Differences between the two approaches exist in the network topology. Whereas (Over)DRiVE implements its Internet integration functionality within a backbone network, COMCAR relies on the SDR for interconnecting the access networks with the Internet. This way, (Over)DRiVE alleviates the integration of further functionality such as IPv6 and multicast support for the vehicles, whereas COMCAR has to realise this functionality in the SDR as a part of the Internet.

Table 2.2 summarises the evaluation of the Internet integration in COMCAR. Like the (Over)DRiVE approach, COMCAR supports a variety of communication systems for the Internet access. COMCAR also considers the basic characteristics of these communication systems by implementing the Common Coordination Channel. However, it complicates the integration of a VANET since the current communication characteristics cannot be determined in advance, resulting in a '+' for the 'Heterogeneity' requirement. The use of Mobile IP enables the seamless mobility of the vehicles. However, COMCAR does not address micro-mobility aspects. The respective functionality has to be implemented within the Internet, which requires modifications of the Internet infrastructure. Hence, the seamless mobility requirement is also evaluated with '+'.

Vehicular aspects are addressed insufficiently in COMCAR. Since the underlying scenario uses existing cellular communication technologies for Internet access, it cannot deal with ad

Project	Mobility Support		Vehicular Aspect		Transport Layer		Scalability	
	Hetero-geneity	Seamless Mobility	Ad Hoc Network.	Vehicular Charact.	Efficiency	Applicability	Addressing	Architecture
COMCAR	+	+	− −	o	− −	− −	− −	−

Table 2.2: Evaluation of COMCAR

hoc networking aspects; COMCAR supports neither the mobility of ad hoc networks nor the identification of gateways to the Internet within the ad hoc networks. Similarly, typical vehicular communication characteristics are of minor importance in COMCAR. The consideration of vehicular characteristics is confined to a middleware that supports vehicular-centred applications. However, this middleware basically addresses the capabilities of cellular networks and not the vehicular environment, resulting in a 'o' for the 'Vehicular Characteristics' requirement.

COMCAR does not address transport layer requirements; it uses standard TCP for communication between the vehicle and the Internet host. Although this characteristic maintains the end-to-end semantics of TCP, the communication efficiency is expected to be poor in a real world deployment since the conservative congestion control mechanisms of TCP are confronted with the characteristics of the access networks. Hence, the 'Efficiency' requirement is not fulfilled. Like in (Over)DRiVE, the deployment of TCP enhancements or new transport layer protocols to improve communication performance would require modifications of the hosts connected to the Internet. Hence, the applicability requirement is also evaluated with '− −'.

COMCAR uses IPv4 to address the vehicles, which is not a scalable addressing solution for being deployed in large-scale vehicular environments (cf. section 2.1.2). Furthermore, the COMCAR communication architecture was not designed with respect to scalability. The introduction of the SDR can be seen as a critical component, because it is the immediate transition point between the Internet and the supported cellular communication systems. Hence, the SDR is both a single point of failure and a bottleneck, and a scalable design of this component is difficult.

Due to the similarities with (Over)DRiVE, COMCAR shares the same fundamental problem that it cannot be used to integrate VANETs into the Internet. With the unaccomplished transport layer requirements and the lack of scalability, the COMCAR approach appears as completely unsuitable for the Internet integration in the VANET scenario.

2.3.3 IPonAir

The BMBF project IPonAir started in October 2001 [98, 99] and is not finished yet. It targets on heterogeneous ad hoc networking scenarios with "typical" mobile devices like laptops, personal digital assistants (PDAs), and cellular phones. In such environments, mobile devices may support several radio technologies, which can be used for communication between the devices and to access the Internet. The goal is to integrate the different wireless and wired network technologies into an all-IP overlay network. Besides the wireless access to the Internet, IPonAir provides new services such as direct multimedia communication between mobile systems or interactive information services.

Although IPonAir is not focused on vehicular environments, it addresses many aspects of the Internet integration of ad hoc networks. This reason makes IPonAir very interesting for a further examination.

Internet Integration in IPonAir

In the IPonAir scenario, mobile devices are embedded into a highly heterogeneous communication environment. On the one hand, they can use different IP-based radio access networks (e.g., GSM, GPRS and UMTS) to access services in the Internet. On the other hand, mobile devices also are able to communicate locally with other mobile devices in an ad hoc fashion using, for example, Bluetooth or HiperLAN/2. IPonAir combines both networking scenarios to a hierarchical cellular multi-hop network [100] as exemplified in figure 2.9. In such an overlay network, a mobile node is able to access the Internet from within the multi-hop ad hoc network using mobile nodes with a connection to the Internet. In the example shown in figure 2.9, the network enables laptop L1 to access the Internet via the relaying PDAs P1 and P2 to a remote wireless LAN base station. Alternatively, L1 can connect to the Internet via multi-hop communication to a GPRS-enabled cellular phone C1.

Within the ad hoc network, mobile devices must be able to configure their IPv6 addresses dynamically. This task is handled by a novel stateless address auto-configuration protocol [102, 103]. This protocol enables a dynamic address configuration of mobile devices in large-scale ad hoc networks. Besides the addressing issues, the discovery of available services is another important topic in IPonAir. This task is achieved by a service-aware discovery protocol using an anycast communication paradigm combined with mechanisms of service information acquirement [104]. The service discovery protocol is useful, for example, to identify gateways to the Internet or to select "best-suited" servers in the ad hoc networks automatically.

The Internet integration in IPonAir integrates these heterogeneous networks into an overlay communication architecture. IPonAir therefore addresses the following issues:

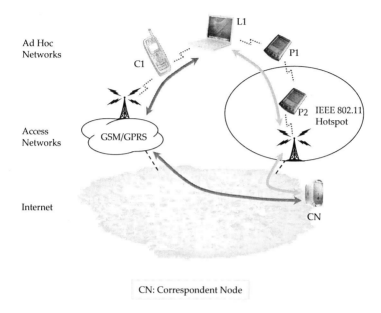

Figure 2.9: IPonAir Scenario [101]

▶ *Multi-Radio Resource Management:* Since existing radio networks operate in different frequency bands, the available resources must be managed appropriately for a high utilisation. This management allows, e.g., the deployment of advanced technologies for dynamic spectrum allocation [105].

▶ *Wireless Routing:* IPonAir also addresses routing aspects to provide efficient communication in heterogeneous environments [101]. Therefore, the quality of service support of the respective ad hoc radio technology is used to improve the efficiency of the routing protocol [106].

▶ *Hierarchical Cellular Multi-Hop Networking:* IPonAir integrates different wireless and wired networks. It addresses the interoperability between cellular and ad hoc communications [100, 101] as well as the deployment of Mobile IPv6 for the handover of connections between different communication networks [107]. The integration is enhanced by a mechanism to choose the "best" connection using a hierarchical multi-access management. This decision process considers the communication requirements in terms of quality of service, costs, availability, mobility, and user profiles.

In order to provide efficient communications within the ad hoc network, IPonAir aims at the development of a new transport protocol for ad hoc networking. This protocol should be able to balance the traffic load within the ad hoc networks in order to avoid congestion. However, details and publications about the transport protocol were not available at the time being.

Evaluation

Although IPonAir considers the concept of connecting ad hoc networks to the Internet via gateways, there are two fundamental differences to the VANET scenario:

▶ The degree of mobility is different. Since IPonAir targets on mobile devices, the mobility of the network will be rather low compared to a vehicular environment with vehicles travelling at high speeds.

▶ The characteristics of the end systems are very different. In contrast to vehicles, mobile devices have limited resources such as power supply, processing capabilities or memory.

These differences are considered in the design of communication protocols for the Internet integration in IPonAir. For example, the routing protocol developed for IPonAir has to find a balance between throughput and energy consumption, which is not necessary for vehicles with a continuous power supply.

IPonAir is an ongoing project. Hence, an evaluation of some requirements is not possible since the required information is not yet published. Table 2.3 summarises the evaluation of the Internet integration approach in IPonAir. IPonAir supports a variety of communication systems including current communication technologies for ad hoc networking. However, the resource management entails a high dependency with the supported communication systems. This aggravates the integration of a VANET technology, because additional control interfaces and adaptations are necessary. Hence, the 'Heterogeneity' requirement is not fulfilled completely and evaluated with '+'. In order to switch between the available communication networks, IPonAir uses a modified Mobile IPv6 [107] that fulfils the 'Seamless Mobility' requirement.

Ad hoc networks play an important role for communication in IPonAir. Although first publications address the wireless routing aspect in IPonAir [101, 106], they do not evaluate the integration of ad hoc networks into the Internet. Similarly, information about the context-aware service discovery of gateways is currently not available. Hence, a final evaluation of the ad hoc networking criterion is not possible at the time being, and the ad hoc networking requirement is expected to be '+'. Vehicular characteristics are not fulfilled in

Project	Mobility Support		Vehicular Aspect		Transport Layer		Scalability	
	Hetero-geneity	Seamless Mobility	Ad Hoc Network.	Vehicular Charact.	Efficien-cy	Applica-bility	Addres-sing	Architec-ture
IPonAir	+	+ +	(+)	− −	?	?	+ +	(− −)

Table 2.3: Evaluation of IPonAir

IPonAir, because the scenario focuses on mobile devices instead of vehicles. Thus, the ad hoc routing protocol in IPonAir neither utilises location information to optimise the routing nor considers the high dynamic and reconfiguration rate of VANETs.

One objective of IPonAir is to develop an optimised transport layer protocol for communication between mobile devices within the ad hoc network. However, publications about the transport layer in IPonAir are not available at present. Hence, both transport layer requirements cannot be evaluated.

In order to address mobile devices in a scalable way, IPonAir consequently builds on IPv6 technology using Mobile IPv6. Thus, the 'Addressing' requirement is fulfilled. The scalability of the communication architecture in IPonAir is difficult to evaluate. It is expected that the architecture does not scale with the number of mobile devices and gateways for the following reasons:

► The address configuration of each mobile device uses a stateless address auto configuration protocol, which scales with the number of participating mobile devices. However, this approach could be harmful in highly mobile vehicular communication environments. The IPv6 addresses of the vehicles must be reconfigured permanently in order to maintain a hierarchical address structure in the VANET.

► The anycast-based discovery protocol for finding the gateways was not evaluated yet with respect to a deployment in large-scale environments. However, both anycast and multicast show scalability problems in mobile ad hoc networks [108, 109, 110].

Hence, the 'Architecture' requirement is expected to be not fulfilled. This is also the fundamental drawback for deploying IPonAir in vehicular environments. Since IPonAir does not consider vehicular characteristics and the transport layer protocol will be optimised for mobile devices, the solution is inappropriate for the Internet integration of VANETs.

2.3.4 DriveBy InfoFueling

DriveBy InfoFueling is an ongoing research project from DaimlerChrysler Research and Technology North America [111]. The goal is to complement existing cellular communication systems, for example a CDMA-based wide area network, with high bandwidth and cost effective communication technologies for vehicular usage. DriveBy InfoFueling follows the "sometimes, somewhere" communication model. The key idea is to create an infrastructure of wireless LAN access points at strategic points along the roadside such as gas stations or convenient stores. This way, it is possible to transmit high volumes of data within the several seconds it takes for a vehicle to drive through the coverage area of an access point.

According to [112], DriveBy InfoFueling enables many new applications not feasible with today's wide area communication networks. For example, it supports access to up-to-date navigation data for the current location as well as to provide information on nearby points of interest. DriveBy InfoFueling also enables the integration of office applications and personal information managers in the vehicles, e.g. to synchronise email, calendar, and the contact database in the office with the intra-vehicle telematics platform. Another important application is the download of rich media content. This way, passengers are able to purchase a legal copy of a song currently played in the radio and to download it into the vehicle.

Internet Integration in DriveBy InfoFueling

Besides the Internet access provided by existing wide area networks, regional or metropolitan area networks, vehicles are able to communicate with the Internet using a DriveBy InfoFueling network infrastructure. This network infrastructure is based on high speed IEEE 802.11a R/A[3] technology for dedicated short-range communication (DSRC) [113]. The interconnection with the Internet is achieved by so-called "DriveBy InfoFueling stations". Figure 2.10 depicts a typical DriveBy InfoFueling scenario where a vehicle may use various network technologies for Internet access. DriveBy InfoFueling stations provide high speed data access in geographically restricted areas only. This way, it is possible to transmit multiple megabytes of data during a drive-by at vehicular speeds of 100 km/h and above. Measurements with a first prototype using common IEEE 802.11b equipment approved the usefulness of DriveBy InfoFueling in a scenario with one vehicle [114].

The DriveBy InfoFueling scenario is similar to a wireless LAN scenario, in which DriveBy InfoFueling base stations connect vehicles wirelessly to an IP-based infrastructure. Access to the Internet is, thus, straightforward, as it works in the same way like a wireless LAN. In order to improve communication efficiency, DriveBy InfoFueling supports the following features for the Internet integration:

► *Wireless Service Availability Prediction:* DriveBy InfoFueling utilises the current position of a vehicle, its navigation software, digital maps, and traffic information to predict

---

[3]IEEE 802.11a R/A (road access) is based on the IEEE 802.11a standard, which is modified to operate at the 5.850 GHz to 5.925 GHz Intelligent Transportation System band in the USA.

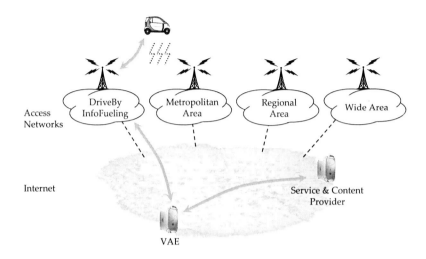

VAE: Vehicular Alter Ego

Figure 2.10: DriveBy InfoFueling Scenario [111]

when the vehicle will have access to a wireless service. This prediction comprises DriveBy InfoFueling stations as well as the coverage of the supported cellular communication systems.

▶ *Route-Dependent Communication Management:* Based on the wireless service availability prediction, DriveBy InfoFueling enables a route-dependent communication management. This means that applications can be managed to use the respective wireless technology at any time for a given route segment and for the specified application requirements. The communication management can be optimised for various goals such as minimising costs or required bandwidth.

▶ *Vehicular Alter Ego (VAE):* The VAE is an application proxy that arranges for the content retrieval in the Internet on behalf of a vehicle. This way, the VAE sustains communication with Internet hosts if vehicles are not continuously connected to DriveBy InfoFueling stations. This feature enables the implementation of mobile e-commerce applications such as financial transactions.

Although DriveBy InfoFueling supports a communication management, it does not propose a mechanism to switch between different wireless communication systems.

Evaluation

Table 2.4 summarises the overall evaluation of the Internet integration approach in DriveBy InfoFueling. The basic concept of DriveBy InfoFueling relies on the installation of a wireless LAN infrastructure for the "sometimes, somewhere" Internet access. Unfortunately, [111, 112] only give a brief overview about the project; both papers do not provide details about the Internet integration. This way, the mobility support requirements cannot be evaluated. The heterogeneity requirement is expected to be fulfilled partially (in accordance with (Over)DRiVE and COMCAR), because the DriveBy InfoFueling scenario comprises wide area networks, regional area networks, and metropolitan area networks besides the wireless LAN infrastructure. Details about the mobility support are not available. Hence, the 'Seamless Mobility' requirement cannot be evaluated since it cannot be determined whether the integration of VANETs is possible or not.

Project	Mobility Support		Vehicular Aspect		Transport Layer		Scalability	
	Hetero-geneity	Seamless Mobility	Ad Hoc Network.	Vehicular Charact.	Efficiency	Applicability	Addressing	Architecture
InfoFueling	(+)	?	– –	+ +	– –	o	(– –)	?

Table 2.4: Evaluation of DriveBy InfoFueling

The DriveBy InfoFueling concept relies on the characteristics of typical infrastructure-based networks such as the (physical) detection of base stations by link layer beacons and a link layer mobility scheme using base station handovers. DriveBy InfoFueling does not support multi-hop ad hoc communication between vehicles. This way, the ad hoc networking requirement is not fulfilled. However, DriveBy InfoFueling takes into account the characteristics and capabilities of vehicular environments. The most remarkable feature is the consideration of a vehicle's current position in combination with the navigation unit and traffic information to predict the availability of services. This is a very interesting feature to improve the communication efficiency in highly mobile environments, e.g. to minimise handover latencies. Hence, the vehicular characteristics requirement is fulfilled in DriveBy InfoFueling.

Another important feature is the VAE that introduces a session management for communication with the vehicle. A vehicle immediately communicates with the VAE, which itself acts in the Internet on behalf of the vehicle. DriveBy InfoFueling relies on standard TCP and does not address any optimisations. Hence, the 'Efficiency' requirement is not fulfilled.

Although not addressed in the DriveBy InfoFueling project, the VAE can be used to incorporate optimisations on the transport layer: A vehicle uses the VAE as a proxy and, thus, as a communication endpoint, which alleviates the deployment of TCP optimisations between the VAE and the vehicles. However, the VAE is only used as a proxy for the applications it supports. Hence, each new vehicular application requires an enhancement of the VAE functionality resulting in an average rating of the 'Applicability' requirement.

DriveBy InfoFueling uses IPv4 to address the vehicles, which is not suitable for vehicular environments. With the available information, it was not possible to determine whether an integration of IPv6 into the DriveBy InfoFueling architecture is possible or not. Hence, the addressing requirement is not expected to be fulfilled. The scalability of the architecture itself cannot be determined. In general, the architecture is expected to scale with the number of communicating vehicles if it is possible to set up a scalable IEEE 802.11-based DriveBy InfoFueling network infrastructure. As information about the mobility support and the route-dependent communication management is not available yet, the protocols being deployed cannot be evaluated with respect to scalability.

The Internet integration approach in DriveBy InfoFueling cannot be used for the integration of VANETs. It neither supports multi-hop ad hoc networks nor does it provide the requested scalability. Hence, DriveBy InfoFueling is not a suitable approach for the Internet integration in the VANET scenario.

2.3.5 CarNet

CarNet is a testbed for the evaluation of communication protocols for ad hoc networks [115]. It supports IP connectivity as well as vehicular applications such as cooperative highway congestion monitoring, fleet tracking, discovery of nearby points of interest, location-directed multicast, over-the-horizon radar detection, and inter-vehicle chat. The objective of CarNet is to deploy a large-scale ad hoc network. Hence, an important design issue was the scalability without requiring a fixed network infrastructure to route messages between vehicles. The key idea of CarNet is to locate radio nodes in vehicles that communicate with each other using a geographic forwarding algorithm called "Grid". Grid is based on a scalable distributed location service to route packets to the targeted vehicle without flooding the network. This geographic forwarding works as follows: If a Grid node wants to send IP packets to another Grid node, it queries a location service for the position of the destination instead of using the Address Resolution Protocol (ARP, RFC 1042 [116]). The location service is distributed over all the vehicles in order to ensure its availability and robustness [117]. After receiving the position of the destination, the IP packets are forwarded to this geographical position using the Greedy Perimeter Stateless Routing (GPSR) protocol [118].

Internet Integration in CarNet

The underlying communication scenario in CarNet is very similar to the VANET scenario described in section 2.1. Hence, CarNet has to face similar challenges for the Internet integration. The vehicles on the road form one IPv4 subnet. This subnet is interconnected with the Internet using fixed Grid-to-Internet gateways. Figure 2.11 exemplifies this scenario. Similar to the configuration of an Internet host, each vehicle has an IP address from within the subnet, a subnet mask (equal for all vehicles), and a default gateway. A basic feature of CarNet is that all Grid-to-Internet gateways participate in the Grid protocol using the same (unicast) IPv4 address. As a result, the default gateway configured for each vehicle is this pre-specified IPv4 address.

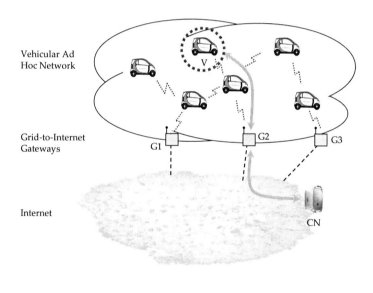

CN: Correspondent Node

Figure 2.11: Exemplary CarNet Scenario

The Internet access from the vehicles is similar to communication with the Internet in a local area network. If vehicle V in figure 2.11 transmits an IP packet to the Internet host CN, the IP packet is delivered to the pre-defined default gateway. Instead of using ARP, Grid queries the location service for the position of the default gateway. The location query will find the Grid-to-Internet gateway nearest to the vehicle, which is gateway G2 in figure 2.11. Finally, the IP packet is routed to the position of this Grid-to-Internet gateway, which itself forwards the IP packet to the correspondent node CN in the Internet.

Vice versa, the IP packets from the CN to the vehicle are routed to the IP address of the pre-defined default gateway. Traditional Internet routing protocols such as BGP (Border Gateway Protocol, RFC 1771 [119]) or OSPF (Open Shortest Path First, RFC 2328 [120]) typically route the IP packets to the Grid-to-Internet gateway that is closest to the Internet host. This gateway then has to forward the IP packets to the Grid-to-Internet gateway that is currently closest to the vehicle. CarNet therefore deploys a protocol similar to the inter-mobile support station forwarding in the Columbia Mobile*IP system [121]. Columbia Mobile*IP relies on a centralised instance to manage the current positions of all vehicles and their closest Grid-to-Internet gateway.

Evaluation

The evaluation of the Internet integration in CarNet is summarised in table 2.5. The communication infrastructure of CarNet is of very elementary nature: The vehicles communicate with each other using the ad hoc mode of IEEE 802.11. Hence, CarNet does not fulfil the 'Heterogeneity' requirement, because the concept does not incorporate further communication technologies. For the same reason, the seamless mobility requirement is not fulfilled, which implicitly presumes such a heterogeneous environment. However, the Columbia Mobile*IP used in CarNet could be extended accordingly to provide seamless mobility if the scenario supports heterogeneity. Hence, the 'Seamless Mobility' requirement is expected to have an average rating.

Project	Mobility Support		Vehicular Aspect		Transport Layer		Scalability	
---------	Hetero-geneity	Seamless Mobility	Ad Hoc Network.	Vehicular Charact.	Efficiency cy	Application bility	Addressing sing	Architecture ture
CarNet	– –	(o)	+ +	+ +	– –	– –	– –	–

Table 2.5: Evaluation of DriveBy CarNet

Vehicular aspects are very important in CarNet. The Grid routing protocols uses the current positions of the vehicles to forward the data towards the destination. Moreover, Grid inherently forwards data to the closest Grid-to-Internet gateway, which is very efficient in vehicular environments [31]. Hence, CarNet fulfils both vehicular requirements, the ad hoc networking and the vehicular characteristics.

CarNet does not address any transport layer issues. The end-to-end communication is based on standard TCP without any modifications, i.e. it does not improve the communication efficiency of TCP. Hence, the 'Efficiency' requirement is not fulfilled. Also, the deployment of TCP extensions to improve efficiency is practically impossible in CarNet, because it requires modifications on both the communication platforms in the vehicles and on the hosts connected to the Internet. This way, the 'Applicability' requirement is not fulfilled, too.

Finally, CarNet is not scalable in both concerns, the addressing scheme deployed and the architecture itself. The IP-based addressing does not scale, because the number of participating vehicles is restricted to one IPv4 subnet. Only minor issues of the architecture requirement are fulfilled: Although the Grid routing protocol is highly scalable and efficient, the Columbia Mobile*IP also could be a bottleneck in a large-scale environment due to its centralised management of the current vehicular positions. Moreover, CarNet requires a close cooperation of the involved Grid-to-Internet gateway operators, which is hard to achieve in a commercial deployment scenario. Hence, the architecture requirement is evaluated with a '–'.

Although CarNet is focused on ad hoc communication in vehicular environments, its Internet integration approach neither provides the required scalability nor fulfils the transport layer requirements. Hence, the CarNet approach is unsuitable for the VANET scenario.

2.4 Summary

The communication characteristics in VANETs are fundamentally different compared to typical mobile computing scenarios. VANETs are based on multi-hop ad hoc networks established between the communicating vehicles on the road. Due to the mobility of the vehicles, these ad hoc networks are highly dynamic, i.e. their topology changes permanently. These characteristics are reflected in the FleetNet communication system, which serves as a reference for the VANET used in this thesis. The Internet integration of such a VANET is more complex than just interconnecting the vehicular network via a gateway with the Internet. Besides the handling of the vehicles' mobility, the Internet integration has to deal with wireless transmission characteristics, temporary Internet connections, scalability, and heterogeneous communication environments. Hence, the Internet integration requires a communication architecture in order to provide efficient communications between vehicles and the Internet. This communication architecture has to comprehend several protocol aspects on both the network layer and the transport layer.

Project	Mobility Support		Vehicular Aspect		Transport Layer		Scalability	
	Hetero-geneity	Seamless Mobility	Ad Hoc Network.	Vehicular Charact.	Efficien-cy	Applica-bility	Addres-sing	Architec-ture
(Over)DRiVE	+	+ +	− −	−	−	− −	+ +	+ +
COMCAR	+	+	− −	o	− −	− −	− −	−
IPonAir	+	+ +	(+)	− −	?	?	+ +	(− −)
InfoFueling	(+)	?	− −	+ +	− −	o	− −	?
CarNet	− −	(o)	+ +	+ +	− −	− −	− −	−

Table 2.6: Summary Evaluation for Internet Integration

There are a number of projects dealing with communication in vehicular environments. Table 2.6 summarises these projects and the evaluation of their Internet integration approach. The evaluation is based on a catalogue of requirements reflecting the challenges of the Internet integration: mobility support for the vehicles, consideration of vehicular characteristics, transport layer requirements, and scalability issues. A general result is that none of the existing approaches fulfils the requirements sufficiently. Most of these projects, namely DRiVE/OverDRiVE, COMCAR, and DriveBy InfoFueling, are focused on the radio technology of cellular access networks and their usage for vehicle-to-Internet communication. Only two projects, IPonAir and CarNet, deal with the integration of ad hoc networks into the Internet. However, the protocols used in IPonAir are not designed for vehicular environments, and CarNet does not provide the required scalability for being deployed in large-scale. Another interesting observation is that – apart from IPonAir – none of these approaches address transport layer requirements.

The basic weakness of all projects is that they do not provide a flexible solution for the Internet integration of a VANET. Such a solution requires a respective communication architecture in order to address mobility, vehicular characteristics, transport layer efficiency, and scalability. The following chapters introduce such an Internet integration communication architecture providing a solution for these requirements.

Chapter 3

MOCCA – An Architecture for Internet Integration

A fundamental characteristic of the VANET scenario is that the vehicles are organised in multi-hop ad hoc networks to exchange data locally. In this scenario, Internet Gateways couple the VANET with the Internet. The basic task of the Internet integration is to provide communication protocols to "inter-connect" the VANET seamlessly with the Internet, i.e. that the VANET becomes a transparent extension of the Internet. The previous section showed that existing related work does not fulfil the Internet integration requirements and motivated the need for a communication architecture. This chapter introduces MOCCA, a MObile CommuniCation Architecture for the Internet integration of VANETs. MOCCA is a novel integrated approach based on a specific performance enhancing proxy concept. In general, MOCCA is not restricted to vehicular environments; the communication architecture can be used to integrate various types of ad hoc networks into the Internet. However, the protocols used in MOCCA are designed and developed with respect to the typical characteristics of vehicular networks, i.e. they deal with mobility support, vehicular aspects, transport layer issues and scalability.

This chapter gives a general overview of MOCCA. Section 3.1 proposes the basic MOCCA communication architecture. The communication protocols deployed in MOCCA are introduced in section 3.2 covering interoperability, mobility support, and the transport layer. Section 3.3 describes the communication within the vehicles, which comprises the interworking with communication systems that might be available in heterogeneous environments and the support of mobile devices within the vehicles. A possible alternative approach of such a communication architecture is discussed in section 3.4. Finally, section 3.5 concludes this chapter with a summary.

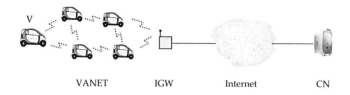

CN: Correspondent Node ▫ IGW: Internet Gateway ▫ VANET: Vehicular Ad Hoc Network

Figure 3.1: Basic VANET Scenario

3.1 MOCCA Communication Architecture

The basic VANET scenario is illustrated in figure 3.1. If a vehicle V sends data to a correspondent node (CN) in the Internet, intermediate vehicles in the VANET forward the data to an appropriate Internet Gateway (IGW). From the IGW, the data is routed through the Internet to the targeted CN, as described in section 2.1. In this scenario, the Internet integration has to meet the following four requirements (cf. section 2.2):

1. Mobility support for the vehicles.

2. Consideration of vehicular aspects such as ad hoc networking.

3. Transport layer efficiency.

4. Scalability.

MOCCA is a mobile communication architecture for the Internet integration of VANETs. This communication architecture combines various protocols in an integrated way: On the one hand, the protocols are optimised for being deployed in a vehicular environment. On the other hand, they closely interact with each other and their functionality is highly geared for being syntonised to the VANET scenario.

3.1.1 Basic Principles of MOCCA

The key principle of MOCCA is the combination of a proxy-based communication architecture with a mobility management in order to meet the challenges of the Internet integration. Figure 3.2 illustrates the basic concept of MOCCA from a topological point of view. A central element in this architecture is the *MoccaProxy*, which is located in the Internet, e.g. in the domain of an Internet Service Provider (ISP). Its basic task is to handle the differences of the protocols in the vehicular environment and the Internet. This way, the MoccaProxy brings together the higher communication layers of the VANET and the Internet, i.e. the network layer and the transport layer in the ISO/OSI communication model [122]. This property implies that the communication flow between vehicular network and Internet always has to pass the MoccaProxy as illustrated in figure 3.2. From the Internet point of view, the MoccaProxy can be seen as a transition point to the vehicular network that opens up the VANET for the Internet.

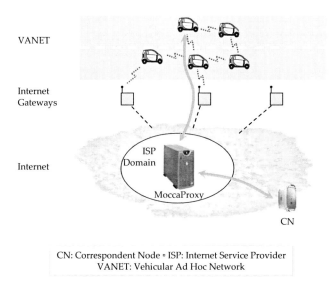

CN: Correspondent Node ▫ ISP: Internet Service Provider
VANET: Vehicular Ad Hoc Network

Figure 3.2: MOCCA's Proxy-Based Communication Architecture

The proxy functionality of the MoccaProxy also includes a transparent termination of TCP connections between vehicles and CNs. This way, the MoccaProxy acts as a representative for both the Internet and the VANET: For the vehicles, the MoccaProxy represents the CN in the Internet, and vice versa the MoccaProxy represents the vehicles for the CNs. Therefore, the MoccaProxy splits up the end-to-end transport layer connection into two segments as illustrated in figure 3.3:

1. Communication in the Internet, i.e. between Internet host and MoccaProxy.

2. Communication in the VANET cloud, i.e. between vehicles and MoccaProxy.

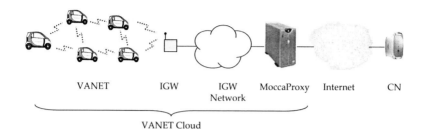

CN: Correspondent Node ∘ IGW: Internet Gateway ∘ VANET: Vehicular Ad Hoc Network

Figure 3.3: Logical View on MOCCA

The VANET cloud comprises the segment between a vehicle and the MoccaProxy, i.e. it comprises the VANET and the IGW network. The IGW network represents a "virtual" network that connects the IGWs to the Internet. It may represent a dedicated ATM (Asynchronous Transfer Mode) network, the IGWs could be connected to an ISP via xDSL technology, or the IGW network may represent the Internet. Thereby, the ISP that hosts the IGW network (and, thus, the IGWs itself) need not necessarily be the same ISP that hosts the MoccaProxy.

According to RFC 3135 [50], the MoccaProxy is a 'Split Connection PEP' (Performance Enhancing Proxy) providing transport layer transparency. The splitting of the transport layer connection comes along with the loss of the end-to-end semantics (see section 2.2.3 for a detailed discussion). This property is still in accordance with RFC 3135 because Split Connection PEPs can be used if they offer significant advantages over an end-to-end solution. A significant advantage in MOCCA is that the splitting allows the deployment of a highly optimised transport protocol in the VANET cloud which is detailed in section 3.2.3. Due to the different communication characteristics in VANETs and the Internet, Split Connection PEPs even promise an additional performance enhancement compared to common transport layer PEPs like Mobile TCP (M-TCP [123]), which maintain the end-to-end semantics. A very basic difference between MOCCA and existing Split Connection PEPs is the location of the PEP: Existing approaches like Indirect TCP (I-TCP [47]) and Mobile TCP locate the proxy functionality very close to the mobile node, which would be the IGWs in the VANET scenario. In contrast, MOCCA deploys the proxy functionality at a fixed point in the Internet, i.e. within the domain of an ISP. This feature has several advantages in the VANET scenario as shown in section 3.4.

The MoccaProxy always should be seen as a virtual entity. In order to avoid bottlenecks and single points of failure, the MoccaProxy may represent a cluster of MoccaProxies. Moreover, there can be several MoccaProxies acting as transition points between the VANET cloud and the Internet. They may be hosted, e.g., by the ISPs of different car vendors or OEM suppliers. This way, the use of several MoccaProxies and proxy clusters maintains the scalability of the architecture and avoids bottlenecks. The further description of MOCCA assumes one such "virtual" MoccaProxy for a better clarification of the concepts. Without the loss of generality, it can be always substituted by a proxy cluster or several MoccaProxies.

3.1.2 Addressing of Vehicles

In order to scale with the number of communicating vehicles, MOCCA supports an IPv6-based addressing scheme in the VANET (cf. section 2.1.2). Every vehicle has a global IPv6 address from a reserved address space, i.e. each IPv6 address of this space uniquely identifies a vehicle. The IPv6 address will be assigned statically to each vehicle, e.g. by a pre-configuration of the communication hardware shipped with the vehicles. Hence, all vehicles share one common IPv6 prefix and, thus, represent one large IPv6 subnet. Like in typical ad hoc networking scenarios, there is no hierarchical relationship between the IPv6 addresses of the vehicles within the VANET although each vehicle acts as both an end system and a router. This characteristic results from the following properties:

▶ Due to the mobility of the vehicles, the topology of the ad hoc network changes permanently. Since the global IPv6 address of a vehicle is static, the address structure within the VANET is subject of a permanent reconfiguration and address hierarchies cannot be established.

▶ VANETs rely on a location-based forwarding algorithm to route data between vehicles, i.e. the forwarding is based on geographical coordinates instead of IPv6 addresses (cf. section 2.1.1). Hence, the routing protocol itself does not consider any address hierarchies in order to deliver the data to the targeted vehicle or IGW.

As a result, the VANET cloud appears as one common IPv6 subnet (with a global IPv6 address prefix) with one logical access router, the MoccaProxy. If there is more than one MoccaProxy, each vehicle is represented in the Internet by exactly one MoccaProxy. Each MoccaProxy has the same global IPv6 prefix, so the VANET cloud still appears as one IPv6 subnet. However, each MoccaProxy forms its own logical IPv6 subnet within the VANET cloud. Figure 3.4 gives an example with two MoccaProxies. In this example, the VANET cloud is identified by the global IPv6 prefix 001A:BBBB:CC::/40. This subnet is logically partitioned into two subnets:

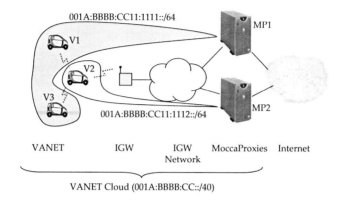

VANET Cloud (001A:BBBB:CC::/40)

IGW: Internet Gateway ∘ VANET: Vehicular Ad Hoc Network

Figure 3.4: Address with Multiple MoccaProxies

1. MoccaProxy MP1 with the IPv6 prefix 001A:BBBB:CC11:1111::/64 comprising vehicles V1 and V3,

2. MoccaProxy MP2 with the IPv6 prefix 001A:BBBB:CC11:1112::/64 comprising vehicle V2.

This logical hierarchy ensures that IP packets from the Internet are always routed to the correct MoccaProxy representing the respective vehicle. Within the VANET, this logical partitioning is not relevant. The vehicular ad hoc routing protocol considers the global IPv6 prefix of the VANET cloud to determine whether an IPv6 packet is delivered locally or whether it addresses a correspondent node in the Internet.

3.2   MOCCA Protocol Functionality

In order to bridge the protocol differences between the VANET and the Internet, the MoccaProxy is responsible for the adaptation of the different protocols. Protocol translations occur on both the network layer and the transport layer. Figure 3.5 summarises the protocol functionality for coupling the protocols from the Internet and the VANET.

The network layer addresses two important tasks: (i) the interoperability between the IPv4-based Internet and the IPv6-based VANET and (ii) the management of the vehicular

| Efficient Communication | Transport Layer |
| IPv4/IPv6 Interoperability
Mobility Management
Intra-Vehicle Communication | Network Layer |

Figure 3.5: Protocol Functionality in MOCCA

mobility. Furthermore, the network layer in MOCCA has to deal with intra-vehicle communication aspects in order to integrate the mobile devices of the passengers into the VANET. On the transport layer, the protocol for data exchange between the applications must be very efficient in order to handle the unpredictable characteristics of the VANET. Interoperability, mobility management and transport layer issues are carried out by the MoccaProxy and are discussed in the following sections. Section 3.3 attends to the intra-vehicle communication aspects in MOCCA, which is handled in the vehicle only.

3.2.1 Interoperability

On the network layer, interoperability is an essential condition in order to enable communication between a vehicle and the Internet. The VANET is based on IPv6 whereas nowadays the Internet mainly uses IPv4 technology. Since IPv6 is not backward compatible to IPv4, the MoccaProxy has to ensure IPv4/IPv6 interoperability between the Internet and the VANET cloud until the Internet is migrated to IPv6 technology.

Several solutions are possible to provide interoperability between IPv4-based and IPv6-based communication networks. They can be categorised into the following classes:

▶ *IPv4/IPv6 Dual Stack:* A router implements IPv4 and IPv6 stacks in parallel. RFC 2893 specifies such a dual stack scheme [124].

▶ *IPv4/IPv6 Tunnelling:* Tunnelling approaches "bridge" two networks of the same type over a different network via tunnels. This way, two separated IPv6 network domains can communicate with each other using a tunnel through an IPv4-based network. Examples implementing tunnelling mechanisms are 6over4 (RFC 2529 [125]), Configured IP-in-IP Tunnelling (RFC 3053 [126]), and 6to4 Automatic Tunnelling (RFC 3056, [127]).

▶ *Translator Approaches:* Translator approaches convert IPv4 and ICMPv4 packets into IPv6 and ICMPv6 packets and vice versa. Currently, several translation protocols are available such as BIS (RFC 2767 [128]), NAT-PT (RFC 2766 [129]), SIIT (RFC 2765 [130]), SOCKS64 (RFC 3089 [131]), and TRT (RFC 3142 [132]).

Only translation mechanisms can be used to enable communication between an IPv4-based host and an IPv6-based vehicle. Both dual stack and tunnelling enable the interconnection of two networks of the same type; yet this is not the case in the targeted VANET scenario. From the translator approaches, only two protocols provide a translation between IPv4 and IPv6 in both directions: NAT-PT and SOCKS64. The other protocols translate in one direction only, i.e. either IPv4-to-IPv6 or IPv6-to-IPv4 but not both. NAT-PT is more flexible and requires modification in the routers only, whereas SOCKS64 additionally requires modifications in the end systems [133, 134]. For this reason, MOCCA deploys NAT-PT for the interoperability between the Internet and the VANET.

The key concept behind NAT-PT (Network Address Translation – Protocol Translation) is that IPv6-based vehicles specify their destinations using IPv4 addresses that are embedded into a specific IPv6 address class, the 'IPv4-compatible IPv6 addresses' [135]. The NAT-PT protocol running on the MoccaProxy extracts this IPv4 address and uses it to communicate with the destination. The source IPv6 address of the vehicle is mapped dynamically onto a global IPv4 addresses located with the MoccaProxy. Therefore, NAT-PT requires a certain amount of (global) IPv4 addresses. An optional feature of NAT-PT is to utilise transport layer identifiers for the address translation in order to attenuate the address space restrictions of IPv4. This way, TCP and UDP port numbers can be used in addition to an IPv4 address, which allows the mapping of several IPv6 addresses onto one IPv4 address.

The interoperability aspect unavoidably re-introduces the scalability problems coming along with the use of IPv4. In general, two configurations of NAT-PT are possible:

▶ *Dynamic Mapping:* If a vehicle wants to communicate with an Internet host, NAT-PT maps the IPv6 address of a vehicle arbitrarily to one of its available IPv4 addresses. This configuration does not allow the access of the vehicles from an Internet host, because Internet hosts do not know the currently mapped IPv4 address of the vehicle. But, the dynamic mapping weakens the scalability problems since TCP and UDP port numbers can be used in addition to the IPv4 address.

▶ *Static Mapping:* Access to services in vehicles from Internet hosts requires a static mapping between IPv4 and IPv6 addresses, which can be compared with the representative IPv4 address of a vehicle in the Internet known by all Internet hosts. However, this configuration limits the number of vehicles having Internet access to the number of IPv4 addresses assigned to the MoccaProxy, because the additional use of port numbers is not possible.

These unavoidable restrictions occur for IPv4-based communication with the Internet only; they are not of relevance for IPv6-based hosts and applications. This way, the restrictions must be accepted as long as the Internet does not support IPv6 natively. Since the Internet still evolves towards IPv6, the interoperability should be kept in mind as a necessary migration step towards an IPv6-based Internet. Hence, the further description supposes an IPv6-based Internet and does not attend to the interoperability further on in order to improve the clarifications of the basic concepts and protocol mechanisms.

3.2.2 Mobility Management

The second important task of the network layer is the mobility management of the vehicles within the VANET cloud. Vehicles travelling on a motorway typically drive at high speeds. Hence, they change their point of attachment to the Internet permanently. The basic requirements of the mobility management are threefold:

▶ *Vehicle-to-Internet Communication:* If a vehicle wants to send data to an Internet host, it has to find a suitable IGW in the VANET.

▶ *Internet-to-Vehicle Communication:* Conversely, the mobility management must be able to route the data flow from the Internet to the vehicle via the respective IGW. If a handover to another IGW occurs, the data flow from the Internet must be rerouted dynamically to the new IGW.

▶ *Accessing the Vehicles:* Since vehicles might also provide Internet-based services, it must be possible to initiate a connection from an Internet host to a vehicle independent of the current location of the vehicle.

A challenging aspect of the mobility management is the multi-hop capability of VANETs, where a vehicle is able to communicate with an IGW over several hops. This capability requires protocol support in order to identify IGWs even if they are not located in the radio transmission range of a vehicle. Such a solution must be highly scalable since the VANET might become very large. In order to handle the mobility of the vehicles, MOCCA provides two interacting protocols that are detailed in chapter 4:

▶ *MMIP6 (MOCCA Mobile IPv6)*: MMIP6 is the core protocol of MOCCA for the mobility management of vehicles.

▶ *DRIVE (Discovery of Internet Gateways from Vehicles)*: MMIP6 is closely related with DRIVE, a protocol to discover suitable Internet Gateways within the VANET.

3.2.3 Transport Layer in MOCCA

The original idea of TCP is to provide a reliable and connection-oriented data transfer between communicating peers. In general, TCP works well in networks with a static topology with reliable communication links such as the Internet, a LAN, or even a wireless LAN. However, the conservative congestion control in TCP prevents an efficient communication in mobile ad hoc networks like VANETs [9, 42, 136, 137]. The deployment of a non-standard transport protocol is practically not possible since it would require modifications in all hosts attached to the Internet. Hence, the MoccaProxy acts as a PEP splitting up the transport layer connection into two parts as illustrated in figure 3.6: One connection in the VANET cloud between a vehicle and the MoccaProxy and another connection in the Internet between the MoccaProxy and a correspondent node CN[1].

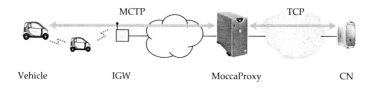

CN: Correspondent Node ▫ IGW: Internet Gateway ▫ MCTP: MOCCA Transport Protocol

Figure 3.6: Transport Layer in MOCCA

The splitting of the end-to-end connection increases communication efficiency, because it decouples different network segments with different characteristics. This way, the MoccaProxy prevents the propagation of the VANET characteristics into the Internet. Moreover, it is possible to deploy optimised transport protocols within the VANET cloud without modifications of the end systems connected to the Internet. Hence, the MoccaProxy communicates with the vehicles using the optimised transport protocol whereas communication between the CN and the MoccaProxy still relies on standard TCP. The optimised transport protocol developed for MOCCA is called *MCTP*, the MOCCA Transport Protocol (cf. figure 3.6). Thereby, the MoccaProxy translates between TCP and MCTP and vice versa. MCTP is detailed in chapter 5.

---

[1]The PEP functionality is only of relevance for connection-oriented services. The connectionless and unreliable User Datagram Protocol UDP [138] is not considered further on in this work. UDP traffic will not be affected by the MoccaProxy.

3.2.4   Security Considerations

A general problem of PEP-based architectures is that security protocols operating on the network layer cannot be used. Solutions like IPsec [56] are based on end-to-end connections since they typically authenticate and/or encrypt the complete transport layer segment including its header. This way, the PEP is not able to "read" the content of an IP packet. A similar problem for IPsec occurs when a host uses a private IP address that is translated onto a global routable IP addresses using NAT [139]. Regarding this problem, the IPSec working group of the Internet Engineering Task Force is currently working on a solution called NAT-Traversal for IPsec [140].

Security protocols on the upper layers should be interoperable with MOCCA despite some minor restrictions caused by their implementation. For example, SSL/TLS [65, 66] can be used in the MOCCA architecture since it encrypts the content of the TCP packets and not their headers. Problems may only occur in case SSL/TLS tries to validate the domain name of the peer with the corresponding entries given in the certificate exchanged. Therefore, it depends on the way the implementation handles such potential inconsistencies.

In order to overcome the problems of securing IP traffic between a vehicle and an Internet host, the following three solutions are conceivable:

1. *Alternative Security Means:* An obvious solution is to use other available security methods that are interoperable with MOCCA in order to secure communication between vehicle and Internet. This solution requires that the peer in the Internet supports the respective protocol, but it could be a suitable approach for, e.g., access to a virtual private network (VPN).

2. *Supporting End-to-End Connections:* Another approach could be the use of end-to-end connections for security-based connections. Therefore, the MoccaProxy does not split the TCP connection if the peers want to communicate securely. However, this solution comes along with a loss of efficiency since it uses standard TCP for communication between vehicle and Internet host. Thus, the potential of MCTP cannot be utilised.

3. *Trust Models:* A promising option is to consider the MoccaProxy as a trusted entity, which acts on behalf of the vehicle. Thereby, the vehicles communicate securely with the MoccaProxy, which appears as a representative for the vehicle (and maintains its cryptographic keys) that itself communicates securely with the Internet host. A security solution for such a scenario is described in [141]. However, this solution requires an appropriate trust model between the service provider of the MoccaProxy and the vehicle since the service provider needs to preserve the privacy of confidential user data.

The most suitable solution ultimately depends on the deployment scenario, e.g. whether it is possible to use alternative protocols to secure communication or whether the service provider of the MoccaProxy is able to ensure a respective trust model.

3.2.5   Protocol Summary and Example

Figure 3.7 summarises the mechanisms and communication protocols deployed in the network layer and the transport layer of MOCCA. The IPv6-based network layer of MOCCA consists of MMIP6 for the mobility management of the vehicles. MMIP6 is deployed in all participating components, i.e. MoccaProxy, IGW, and vehicle. Within the IGW and the vehicle, DRIVE supplements MMIP6 for the discovery of the Internet Gateways from within the VANET. In order to ensure IPv4-IPv6 interworking, the MoccaProxy implements NAT-PT. Handovers in heterogeneous communication environments are handled by the Mocca-Muxer (cf. section 3.3.2) located in the vehicle and the MoccaProxy. The transport layer of MOCCA consists of MCTP, which ensures an efficient data exchange between vehicle and the MoccaProxy. Thereby, the MoccaProxy has to translate between MCTP and TCP.

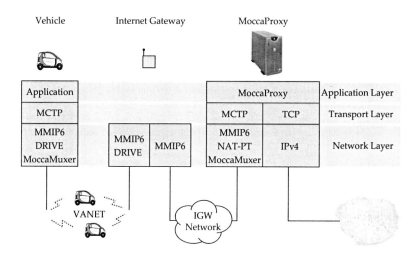

DRIVE: Discovery of Internet Gateways from Vehicles ▫ IGW: Internet Gateway
NAT-PT: Network Address Translation – Protocol Translation ▫ MIP6: MOCCA Mobile IPv6
MCTP: MOCCA Transport Protocol ▫ VANET: Vehicular Ad Hoc Network

Figure 3.7: Communication Protocol Overview in MOCCA

The communication example in figure 3.8 demonstrates the benefits of the proposed proxy-based approach in MOCCA. On the left side, vehicle V1 is able to access the Internet through IGW1. If V1 requests a web page from the correspondent node CN, an MCTP connection c1 is established via IGW1 to the MoccaProxy, which itself establishes a second connection c2 using standard TCP to the CN. While receiving the data, V1 moves out of the radio transmission range of IGW1 and cannot access further IGWs via other relaying vehicles. Hence, V1 temporarily gets disconnected from the Internet, i.e. c1 is turned into an "idle" mode where no data exchange occurs, whereas the data exchange using c2 is still possible. This way, the buffers of the MoccaProxy are filled with data from the CN.

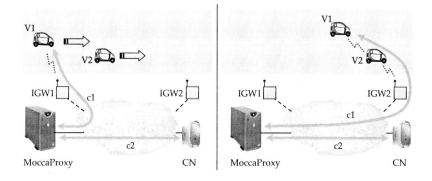

CN: Correspondent Node ▫ IGW: Internet Gateway

Figure 3.8: Communication Example

If vehicle V2 moves into the radio transmission range of IGW2 (right-hand side in figure 3.8), the DRIVE protocol enables V1 to identify IGW2 although it is not yet in the immediate transmission range of V1. Hence, MMIP6 registers V1 with IGW2 as its new point of attachment to the Internet. The VANET supports multi-hop communication between V1 and IGW2 using V2 as a relaying vehicle. Afterwards, the buffered data in the MoccaProxy can be transmitted to V1 through connection c1 very efficiently using MCTP. This example demonstrates the benefits of MOCCA:

▶ DRIVE and MMIP6 enable the Internet access for vehicles within the VANET even over several relaying vehicles, i.e. they integrate VANETs into the Internet.

▶ MMIP6 provides a transparent mobility support for upper layer protocols. This way, the communicating peers MoccaProxy and V1 are not affected since the handover does not require a context transfer to another peer. This is due to the fact that IGWs do not keep any state of upper layers.

▶ The MoccaProxy decouples the characteristics of the VANET from the Internet without requiring modifications of the Internet hosts. In the example given above, MCTP is able to transmit the outstanding data to V1 after the vehicle reconnects to IGW2 in an efficiently manner.

3.3 Intra-Vehicle Communication

Using the communication protocols described in the previous section, data can be transmitted to the vehicle efficiently. However, it is not possible to support existing TCP/IP-based applications and services for mobile devices within the vehicle. These applications are considered in the MOCCA concept, too, as described in section 3.3.1. Moreover, a vehicle's communication platform, which implements the MOCCA functionality, may support a variety of further communication systems to communicate with an Internet host. In this case, it is preferable to utilise this heterogeneity by using the communication system that currently fits best to the requirements of the applications and the user. Section 3.3.2 deals with this heterogeneity support.

3.3.1 Support of Legacy Applications

Within MOCCA-enabled vehicles, passengers likely want to use their mobile equipment to access the Internet using the VANET. This way, passengers are able to synchronise their personal applications running on a laptop or PDA, or they can download legal copies of audio files. These "legacy" Internet-based applications running on the mobile devices typically use standard TCP/IP or UDP/IP for their communications. The mobile devices can be connected to the communication platform of the vehicle using intra-vehicle networks such as a MOST bus (Media Oriented Systems Transport [142]), a CAN bus (Controller Area Network [143]), Ethernet, IEEE 1394 ("Firewire"), Bluetooth or an IEEE 802.11 network. However, the mobile devices cannot use the VANET for the following reasons:

▶ If mobile devices are connected to an intra-vehicle network, they require protocol drivers for using the MOCCA functionality, i.e. for the mobility management and the transport protocol.

► Every mobile device needs a unique address identifier, i.e. it requires a predefined and static IPv6 address from within the VANET cloud. Moreover, the mobile devices need a static VANET-compliant identification for the routing purposes. For example, in FleetNet every device would require its own FleetNet ID (cf. section 2.1.1).

In order to ensure interoperability of legacy applications with the VANET, MOCCA deploys a second proxy located within the vehicle, the *VehicleProxy*. This way, the communication platform in the vehicle acts as a proxy for legacy applications running on mobile devices within the vehicle. This proxy translates (back) the MOCCA communication protocols into standard Internet protocols. Figure 3.9 illustrates this concept when legacy applications on a laptop communicate with the Internet using the VANET. The VehicleProxy again separates the end-to-end connection. Hence, the overall end-to-end connection between the mobile device within the vehicle and an Internet host is partitioned into three segments:

1. Communication between Internet host and MoccaProxy.

2. Communication between the MoccaProxy and the VehicleProxy.

3. Communication between the VehicleProxy and the mobile device.

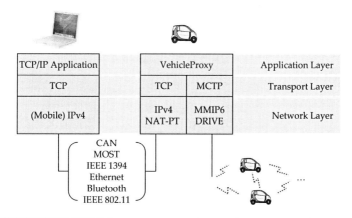

CAN: Controller Area Network ▫ DRIVE: Discovery of Internet Gateways from Vehicles
MCTP: MOCCA Transport Protocol ▫ MOST: Media Oriented Systems Transport
MMIP6: MOCCA Mobile IPv6 ▫ NAT-PT: Network Address Translation – Protocol Translation

Figure 3.9: Integration of Mobile Devices in MOCCA

Figure 3.9 also depicts the communication protocols deployed for supporting legacy applications. The VehicleProxy communicates in the VANET cloud using MCTP, the optimised MOCCA transport protocol. Within the vehicle, TCP (and UDP) is used for communication with the mobile device. The VehicleProxy thereby translates between MCTP and TCP. On the network layer, NAT-PT (again) performs the transparent translation between IPv4-based intra-vehicle addresses and the IPv6 addresses used in the VANET (see section 3.2.1). This solution is more efficient than a tunnelling of IPv4 packets through the VANET for two reasons:

▶ It avoids additional overhead caused by the encapsulation of IP packets within the VANET.

▶ This solution enables the communication of legacy applications using TCP/IP while directly utilising the optimised MOCCA communication protocols simultaneously.

The VehicleProxy only supports the mobility of the vehicles, not the mobility of the mobile devices inside the vehicles. This means that MOCCA always delivers the data to the VehicleProxy if the vehicle is able to communicate with an IGW. In the scenario illustrated in figure 3.9, a mobile device will usually obtain a private IPv4 address (e.g., from the Dynamic Host Configuration Protocol DHCP [144]) which is valid within the vehicle only. Hence, the VehicleProxy hides the mobile devices inside the vehicles so they cannot be accessed from hosts in the Internet; it is only possible that mobile devices access services in the Internet.

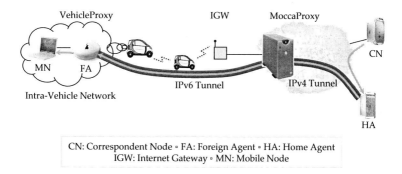

CN: Correspondent Node ▫ FA: Foreign Agent ▫ HA: Home Agent
IGW: Internet Gateway ▫ MN: Mobile Node

Figure 3.10: Mobility Support for Legacy Devices

In order to ensure an overall mobility for the mobile devices within the vehicles, these devices have to support Mobile IPv4 (according to RFC 3344 [145]) as illustrated in figure 3.10. In this configuration, the following functionality is necessary:

▶ The Mobile Node (MN) is located within the vehicle.

▶ The Home Agent (HA) of the MN is located in the home network of the MN in the Internet.

▶ The Foreign Agent (FA) is located on the communication platform within the vehicle, which implements the MOCCA functionality and the VehicleProxy.

IP packets from the CN to the MN flow as follows: First, the packets are routed to the home network of the MN. As specified for Mobile IP (see section 4.2), the HA in this network accepts the IP packets on behalf of the MN and forwards them through an IPv4 tunnel to the FA the MN is currently registered with. Since the IPv4 address of the FA is located within the VANET, the MoccaProxy acts on behalf of the FA, i.e. the IP packets are sent to the MoccaProxy. The MoccaProxy itself translates the IPv4 address of the FA to the respective IPv6 address of the vehicle where the FA is located. Hence, the MoccaProxy translates the IPv4 tunnel into an IPv6 tunnel, and the original IP packets are tunnelled through the IGW and the VANET to the vehicle in which the MN is located. Within the vehicle, the VehicleProxy translates back the IPv6 tunnel to the IPv4 tunnel with the FA as the tunnel endpoint since the CoA is not co-located with the MN. This way, the tunnelled IP packets arrive at the FA that finally unpacks the original packets and forwards them to the MN.

3.3.2 Utilising Heterogeneity

Vehicles typically move in highly heterogeneous communication environments. Besides the inter-vehicle communication system, several other (cellular and ad hoc) networks and communication systems might be available simultaneously in an overlaid fashion. Figure 3.11 depicts an example of such an overlay network. This heterogeneity can be used to improve both connectivity and quality of service (QoS) support as illustrated by the following examples:

▶ A vehicle can use either the VANET or alternatively a GSM, GPRS, or UMTS network to access the Internet.

▶ If an IGW is currently not available in the VANET, the vehicle can handover its connections to another available communication network.

▶ If the vehicle passes a gas station, it may have a temporary high-speed Internet access via the IEEE 802.11 network of the gas station. In this case, it can handover its connections temporarily to the IEEE 802.11 network.

However, the handover to another communication network requires respective management mechanisms. This section introduces the approach used in MOCCA to utilise the heterogeneity in such a communication environment. The utilisation of heterogeneity is an important feature but not a necessary requirement for the Internet integration of a VANET. Hence, this section is focused on the general approach in MOCCA and leaves a detailed discussion of related work and the evaluation to references on published work [146, 147, 148, 149].

Objectives and Existing Approaches

The overall objective is to utilise heterogeneity in order to improve the QoS for communications in the VANET scenario. However, the available networks typically have different characteristics: Whereas an IEEE 802.11 network may provide gross data rates of up to 54 Mbit/s in a restricted geographical area, cellular communication systems like GPRS provide area-wide data rates of up to 384 kbit/s. The QoS support also depends on the requirements of the IP-based applications running on the communication platform (CP) located in the vehicle. In order to bring together these different QoS issues, protocol mechanisms are needed which fulfil the following basic requirements [68, 150, 151]:

▶ It must be possible to handover connections seamlessly between the different communication systems, which is also called a vertical handover.

▶ It must be possible to determine the most suitable communication system.

A noticeable amount of work exists to providing seamless handovers in mobile and wireless networks. Examples are the BARWAN project [152, 153], MosquitoNet [154], a handover scheme for mobile networks proposed by Pahlavan et al. [155], the Smart Decision Model proposed by Chen et al. [156], and approaches using a dynamic network reconfiguration of mobile devices [157]. A detailed description and discussion of this research with respect to the requirements for utilising heterogeneity can be found in [158, 159]. In summary, these approaches share two basic drawbacks: First, they provide vertical handovers in overlay networks with only a few communication systems. Second, these approaches do not define mechanisms to decide which network fits best to the QoS requirements of the running applications.

MoccaMuxer

MOCCA implements a management entity called *MoccaMuxer* located in both the CP inside the vehicle and the MoccaProxy as illustrated in figure 3.11. The MoccaMuxer hands over

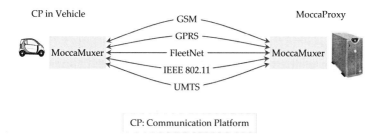

Figure 3.11: MoccaMuxer in the VANET Scenario

connections dynamically between different network interfaces. The following example illustrates the basic principle of the MoccaMuxer. If a vehicle wants to communicate with an Internet host, it establishes a transport layer connection through the VANET, an IGW, and the MoccaProxy as described in section 3.2.5. Thereby, the MoccaProxy splits up this transport layer connection. If the vehicle moves out of the service area of an IGW and an alternative IGW cannot be found in the VANET, further communication with the Internet will not be possible. In this case, the MoccaMuxer realises that the MoccaProxy becomes unreachable in the VANET and hands over the connections to an alternative communication system like GPRS. This way, the communication flow is routed via GPRS to the MoccaProxy instead of the inter-vehicle communication system. If the vehicle gets back access to another IGW, the ongoing connections can be handed over back to the VANET.

Figure 3.12 illustrates the integration of the MoccaMuxer in the MOCCA architecture. The central element is a *DeviceMultiplexer* that is responsible for switching between the different network interfaces dynamically. If the receiver becomes unreachable in the network actually used, the DeviceMultiplexer queries a *Management Information Base* (MIB) providing information about alternative networks to communicate with the peer. Then, the DeviceMultiplexer determines the most suitable alternative (see next section), establishes an IP tunnel to the alternative IP address of the MoccaProxy, and forwards the IP packets through this tunnel. This tunnelling mechanism, which is the main principle of Mobile IP [145], is performed by a redirector in the DeviceMultiplexer that calls the IP stack a second time and, thus, redirects every IP packet to another network device. When an encapsulated packet arrives at the MoccaProxy, the MoccaMuxer within the MoccaProxy first establishes a tunnel back to the sender. Hence, the communication path from the MoccaProxy to the vehicle is also tunnelled through the alternative communication system. This way, "half-directional" communication is avoided since common wireless communication systems provide duplex communication paths. Afterwards, the DeviceMultiplexer unpacks the original IP packet

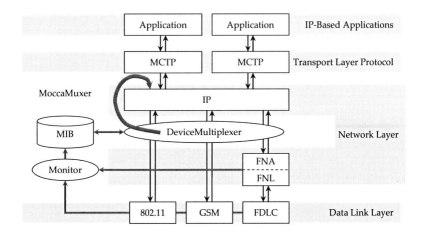

FDLC: FleetNet Data Link Control ▫ FNA: FleetNet Network Adaptation
FNL: FleetNet Network Layer ▫ MCTP: MOCCA Transport Protocol
MIB: Management Information Base

Figure 3.12: MoccaMuxer

and forwards it to the upper layer protocols. Further details about the DeviceMultiplexer and its implementation can be found in [146].

The MIB contains information about the available communication systems and alternative IP addresses of the corresponding peer. A *Monitor* within the network layer is responsible for updating the MIB entries. Therefore, it collects relevant information from both the network layer and the link layer, which can be used to determine the current state of a network interface. Another important information is the tunnel endpoint, which is needed in case of a handover. This tunnel endpoint is the MoccaProxy, i.e. its address can be configured statically in the MIB. Detailed information about the Monitor can be found in [148].

Finding the Most Suitable Alternative

In order to determine the most suitable communication system, the DeviceMultiplexer considers basic information of a network device provided by the MIB (cf. figure 3.12). This basic information is classified in the following way:

▶ *Static Information* such as pay scales for the transmission costs or the maximum data rate of a network (e.g., in case of GSM the price per minute and 9.6 kbit/s as maximum gross bandwidth).

▶ *Dynamic Information* like the currently available bandwidth or the current error rate of a network device. This information is derived from the kernel of the operating system [148].

This basic information is the input for a fuzzy controller used in the MoccaMuxer. The use of fuzzy controllers is a suitable method for the decision process, because they describe a system intuitively using linguistic variables [160, 161]. The fuzzy controller in the MoccaMuxer implements a two-tier decision process as illustrated in figure 3.13. For each network device, an *Abstraction Controller* processes the basic information and generates a set of generic parameters. These parameters are the input for the second tier, the *Decision Controller*. The Decision Controller finally determines the "rating" of a communication system represented by a numerical value. Such a decision is performed for each available communication system. Finally, the MoccaMuxer finds the most suitable network device by comparing the ratings. If a more suitable communication system is available, the DeviceMultiplexer performs a handover to this communication system as described in the previous section.

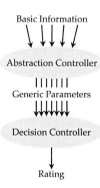

Figure 3.13: Fuzzy Controller for the Decision Process

A prototype of the MoccaMuxer was implemented to demonstrate the usefulness and to prove the concepts introduced. The prototype comprises a basic set of parameters, which is described in appendix A. Further parameters like quality of service requirements for the applications can be integrated by creating new fuzzy rules. However, their consideration requires a detailed analysis of the application requirements, which is out of the scope for the original task of the Internet integration of VANETs.

MoccaMuxer: Evaluation Summary

The MoccaMuxer enables a seamless handover between different communication systems in order to utilise heterogeneity for an improved QoS support. Thereby, communication between vehicle and MoccaProxy can be switched over to alternative communication systems if the MoccaProxy becomes unreachable in the network currently used or in case a better suited communication system is found. An important concept of the MoccaMuxer is the consideration of the communication characteristics for the alternative networks. This static and dynamic information is used for finding the most suitable alternative network to continue communication. The MoccaMuxer therefore implements a fuzzy controller system, which can be extended to take into account the QoS requirements of the applications running in the vehicle.

An evaluation of the MoccaMuxer showed that the delay caused by the DeviceMultiplexer handover is very short and does not affect the performance of TCP significantly [147]. However, the transport protocol MCTP should be able to adapt to the new network characteristics after a handover very quickly since the performance of the communication systems may be very different.

3.4   Alternative Proxy Concepts

An alternative Internet integration concept for VANETs would be an infrastructure based on mobile agents [162, 163]. In such an infrastructure, an agent can be regarded as object code that fulfils a "task" elsewhere on a remote system. An example is a "search agent" to find a specified document in libraries. Once instructed by the user, the search agent wanders through the Internet to the databases of different libraries where its search code is executed. The search agent collects the information about the specified document and finally returns back to the user with the respective result or with the document itself. An agent-based infrastructure for mobility support uses mobile agents as "personal" proxies for the mobile devices, i.e. the mobile agents act in the Internet on behalf of the mobile devices. Thereby, the agents are located very close to the mobile devices [164].

Referred to the VANET scenario, a suitable location for the mobile agents would be the Internet Gateway. Since a vehicle always communicates with its mobile agent, the agent has to "travel" with the vehicle as illustrated in figure 3.14: If a vehicle hands over its connections from the lower IGW to the upper IGW, the complete context of the mobile agent

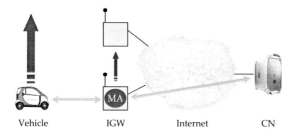

CN: Correspondent Node ∘ IGW: Internet Gateway ∘ MA: Mobile Agent

Figure 3.14: Mobile Agents Concept

must be transferred to the new IGW. In contrast to MMIP6 used in MOCCA, a completely new and heavy-weighted signalling protocol would be necessary to realise the movement of mobile agents. Since the delays for sending IP packets between MoccaProxy and IGW are expected to be low compared to the delays in the vehicular ad hoc network, mobile agents on the IGWs promise no further benefits. In contrast to the mobile-agent-based approach, MOCCA provides a better flexibility and less complexity for several reasons:

▶ *Complexity:* Since mobile agents in IGWs "travel" with the vehicles, complex protocol mechanisms and more hardware resources are required for the IGWs to maintain the agents and their signalling protocol.

▶ *Connection Management:* TCP connections to the mobile agent must be migrated in case of a handover to another IGW. This migration is not necessary in MOCCA, because the vehicles always communicate with the stationary MoccaProxy in the Internet – independent of the IGW currently used.

▶ *Security:* Since personal proxies (and, thus, mobile agents) act as a communication peer, data will be always accessible in the hardware the proxy runs. However, it is easier for attackers to infiltrate mobile agents on IGWs than the MoccaProxy located in the network of a service provider. This network can be secured by powerful firewalls, packet filters, or intrusion detection systems, whereas passing vehicles can attack the IGWs easily using the wireless link.

▶ *Scalability and Management:* Since the MoccaProxy is located in the fixed Internet, it is easier to design a scalable system using powerful proxy clusters with proper load balancing and replication strategies. In contrast, the restricted resources of outdoor IGWs aggravate the realisation of a scalable system. Moreover, locating the MoccaProxy in the network of a service provider alleviates its management and administration.

▶ *Costs:* Using mobile agents, IGWs become more expensive and more vulnerable to hardware failures, because mobile agents require more computation capabilities and memory resources. MOCCA shifts this functionality into the MoccaProxy in the Internet. This allows the development of cheap and lightweight IGWs.

Another benefit of the proxy-based approach in MOCCA is the possibility to deploy highly customised (provider-specific) services easily. Examples are the use of application-specific proxies, e.g. for WWW traffic [165]. Such a proxy may also perform a transcoding of content in order to adapt the content to the hardware capabilities within the vehicles [153, 166, 167, 168]. These provider-specific services can improve the efficiency of vehicular Internet-based applications further on. They are not discussed further on since application-specific enhancements are not of relevance for the original task of the Internet integration.

3.5 Summary

The integration of VANETs into the Internet is a very challenging task. This section proposes MOCCA, a communication architecture for the Internet integration of vehicular ad hoc networks. MOCCA combines a proxy-based communication architecture with a mobility management scheme for vehicles. Thereby, a MoccaProxy acts as a connection split performance enhancing proxy separating the vehicular ad hoc network (and the network that interconnects the Internet Gateways) from the Internet. This separation additionally allows for the deployment of a highly optimised transport protocol for communication with the vehicles to improve communication efficiency. In contrast to existing approaches using mobile agents, MOCCA provides less complexity, an easier management, better scalability, and less monetary costs for its maintenance.

In order to fulfil the requirements of the VANET scenario, MOCCA comprises several communication protocols. In order to ensure interoperability with the IPv4-based Internet, the MoccaProxy implements NAT-PT for the translation between IPv6 and IPv4. A VehicleProxy located within the vehicle integrates IP-based applications running on mobile devices inside the vehicles into the MOCCA concept. This way, passengers can use the VANET with their mobile equipment. Furthermore, a MoccaMuxer located within the vehicles is able to switch seamlessly between the available communication systems in the vehicular overlay network. The MoccaMuxer implements a fuzzy controller system to determine the most suitable communication system for Internet access, which enables an efficient utilisation of heterogeneous communication environments.

MOCCA		
MMIP6 (Mobility Management)	DRIVE (Gateway Discovery)	MCTP (Transport Layer)
Section 4.4	Section 4.4.2	Chapter 5

Figure 3.15: Communication Protocols in MOCCA

Besides these protocols, the core functionality of MOCCA for the Internet integration is the mobility management of the vehicles. This task is handled by two different protocols as summarised in figure 3.15. MMIP6 realises the basic functionality of the mobility support, i.e. it ensures that IP packets are always routed to the vehicle via the correct Internet Gateway. MMIP6 is supplemented by DRIVE, a service discovery protocol for the discovery of Internet Gateways in vehicular multi-hop ad hoc networks. On the transport layer, MCTP allows the efficient exchange of data between the MoccaProxy and the vehicles instead of TCP. MMIP6, DRIVE, and MCTP are detailed in the following two chapters.

Chapter 4

MMIP6 – Mobility Management in MOCCA

The mobility management of the vehicles plays an important role for the Internet integration. Communication in the Internet requires a fixed network topology with a hierarchical IP addressing scheme. In contrast, vehicles are highly mobile and may travel at high speeds. Hence, the topology of the VANET is subject to a permanent reconfiguration and vehicles permanently change their point of attachment to the Internet. This way, Internet Gateways temporarily appear like common mobile nodes within the VANET and can be used for Internet access in this certain period of time. In such a dynamic environment, vehicles must be able to find suitable Internet Gateways even over several relaying vehicles in order to communicate with the Internet. Reversely, data from the Internet must always be routed appropriately to reach the targeted vehicle; i.e. through the Internet Gateway the targeted vehicle currently passes.

The mobility support in MOCCA has to ensure that the VANET becomes a transparent extension of the Internet. This section proposes MMIP6 (MOCCA Mobile IPv6), the mobility management protocol used in MOCCA. This protocol handles the mobility of the vehicles and enables the Internet access for the vehicles as well as the access of services within the vehicle from Internet hosts. MMIP6 deploys a novel service discovery protocol called DRIVE to identify Internet Gateways within the vehicular ad hoc network in a scalable and efficient way. DRIVE also provides a fuzzy-based solution to determine the suitable Internet Gateway if several gateways are available simultaneously. MMIP6 is highly correlated with the MOCCA architecture, i.e. it is tightly geared with communication protocols used in MOCCA. In general, MMIP6 can be used for the mobility support of arbitrary multi-hop ad hoc networks. However, its basic protocol mechanisms are designed with respect to the specific characteristics of VANETs.

This chapter is organised as follows: Section 4.1 specifies the requirements for supporting mobility in VANETs followed by the fundamental techniques for supporting mobility in
the Internet using Mobile IP in section 4.2. Section 4.3 discusses and evaluates the related
work for the mobility support of ad hoc networks. Section 4.4 is focused on the mobility
management protocol MMIP6 and proposes the core protocol functionality, the discovery
of Internet Gateways using DRIVE, and the handover procedure. Furthermore, this section describes optimisations in MMIP6 to improve communication efficiency in the VANET
scenario. MMIP6 is evaluated in both a quantitative and a qualitative way in section 4.5.
Finally, a brief summary in section 4.6 concludes this chapter.

4.1 Requirements for Mobility Management

Communication in the Internet is based on hierarchical IP addresses with a static (address)
topology to route IP packets appropriately. In contrast, VANETs are highly mobile: The
VANET topology changes dynamically and vehicles permanently change their gateway to
the Internet while travelling at high speeds. Hence, the Internet integration of VANETs requires a transparent mobility management for the vehicles, which means that the VANET
should appear as a (static) part of the Internet. In the MOCCA architecture, the MoccaProxy
brings together the Internet and the VANET cloud. Hence, the MoccaProxy is responsible
for the mobility management of the vehicles, i.e. it has to combine the proxy-based communication architecture with a respective mobility management as illustrated in figure 4.1.

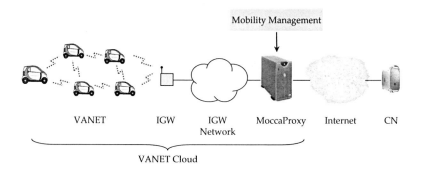

CN: Correspondent Node ▫ IGW: Internet Gateway ▫ VANET: Vehicular Ad Hoc Network

Figure 4.1: Mobility Management in MOCCA

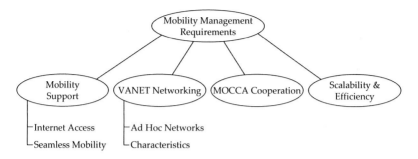

Figure 4.2: Requirements for the Mobility Management

The mobility management in the VANET scenario has to satisfy several requirements summarised in figure 4.2. The most important requirement is the *mobility support* of the vehicles in the VANET cloud [41, 151]. The mobility support comprises the following two sub-requirements:

▶ *Internet Access:* Vehicles should be able to access resources in the Internet, independent of the IGW they currently use. This requirement has to ensure a correct IP packet flow between a vehicle and an Internet host in both directions. IP packets from the vehicle have to be routed through an appropriate IGW to the Internet host. Vice versa, IP packets from an Internet host must be delivered through an appropriate IGW to the vehicle. A transparent Internet access also requires support for handovers between IGWs. If a vehicle discovers a more suitable IGW, it should be possible to handover its connections to the new IGW in a transparent manner.

▶ *Seamless Mobility:* Besides the Internet access, IP services within the vehicles should be also accessible from Internet hosts. Therefore, an Internet host should be able to establish a connection with a vehicle, independent of the IGW the vehicle currently uses. In order to hide the mobility of the vehicles, seamless mobility requires global and location-independent IP identifiers for the vehicles.

The mobility management additionally has to consider the *VANET networking* environment, i.e. the two sub-requirements (i) ad hoc networks and (ii) characteristics have to be taken into account. The *ad hoc networks* requirement claims that the protocol mechanisms for the mobility management have to be compatible to the multi-hop capability of the VANET. Therefore, vehicles must be able to identify the most suitable IGW within the VANET even if they are several hops away. Furthermore, the mobility management has to consider the *characteristics* of the VANET. This requirement comprises, e.g., the use of IPv6 for identifying the vehicles and the specific capabilities of the VANETs as described in section 2.2.

The mobility management also must be compatible to the MOCCA architecture. The *MOCCA cooperation* requirement reflects that the mobility support should not affect communication in the Internet, i.e. the mobility support has to avoid the need for modifications of Internet routers and hosts connected to the Internet. As a result, it must be possible to integrate the mobility support seamlessly into the VANET cloud that has to hide the mobility of the vehicles for the Internet. Due to the proxy-based design of MOCCA, the 'MOCCA Cooperation' requirement ensures that the IP packets are always routed through the MoccaProxy.

Finally, the mobility management must be *scalable and efficient* in the following ways:

► The protocols used for mobility support have to scale with both the number of vehicles and their degree of mobility.

► The protocol mechanisms must be efficient in terms of the overhead caused in the VANET. The efficiency also comprises the overhead that may occur if an IGW is currently not available.

4.2   Mobile IPv4

Mobile IPv4 [145] is the standardised communication protocol to manage host mobility in the Internet. It provides protocol enhancements for a transparent routing of IP packets to mobile nodes (MNs) in the Internet. Each MN is always identified by its home address regardless of its current point of attachment to the Internet. From the topological point of view, the home address is located in the home network of the MN. While situated away from its home network, an MN is also associated with a care-of address (CoA) providing information about the MN's current point of attachment to the Internet. Therefore, Mobile IPv4 deploys an agent-based system comprising of a *Home Agent* (HA) and a *Foreign Agent* (FA) as illustrated in figure 4.3. If a correspondent node (CN) in the Internet sends an IP packet to the home address of the MN, the packets will be routed to the home network of the MN. In case the MN is currently located in a foreign network, the HA of the MN in the home network accepts the IP packets on behalf of the MN. The HA then encapsulates the IP packet and tunnels it to the current CoA of the MN. In the example depicted in figure 4.3, the CoA of the MN is located with the FA of the foreign network. The tunnelling is realised by putting a new header in front of the original IP header with the CoA as the new destination address and the HA as the source address. Hence, the packet is forwarded through the Internet to the FA, which unpacks the IP packet and forwards it to the MN. Vice

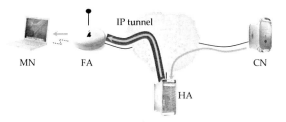

CN: Correspondent Node ▫ FA: Foreign Agent ▫ HA: Home Agent ▫ MN: Mobile Node

Figure 4.3: Mobile IPv4

versa, IP packets from the MN to the CN are transmitted either directly to the CN or they are first tunnelled back to the HA ("reverse tunnelling" according to RFC 3024 [169]), which unpacks the IP packets and forwards them through the Internet to the CN.

Mobile IPv4 basically requires that an MN is able to discover an FA when it enters a foreign network. Therefore, an FA advertises its presence (and its CoA) periodically using *agent advertisements*. Agent advertisements are special ICMP messages broadcasted periodically in the local network of the FA. The transmission of agent advertisements can be additionally triggered by the MN. For this it sends an *agent solicitation* message that will be responded by the FA with an agent advertisement. If the MN receives the agent advertisements of a new FA, it has to register itself with both the FA and the HA in order to notify both agents about its new location. Therefore, the MN sends a *registration request* message to the FA. The FA then adds the MN to its registry and forwards the registration request to the HA. Finally, the HA updates the (new) CoA of the MN and responds to the request with a *registration reply* message to the MN. A detailed description of the protocol processing and the message formats can be found in [145].

An alternative variant of Mobile IP is based on co-located CoAs (CCoAs). In this case, the FA functionality is integrated into the mobile nodes since the CoA is co-located with the MN. If an MN enters a foreign network, it receives a temporary CCoA from within the foreign network. This CCoA can be configured either statically by the user or dynamically using, e.g., the Dynamic Host Configuration Protocol (DHCP [144]). The MN then registers the CCoA with its HA. Thus, the MN has a topologically correct IP address being used for further communication. IP packets sent by a CN are routed to the home network of the MN. The HA in this network accepts the IP packets on behalf of the MN and tunnels them to the CCoA of the MN. On the MN, the additional tunnel IP header is stripped off and the original packet is delivered to the upper protocol layers. Alternatively, the MN can notify

its CNs directly about its CCoA with a *binding update* message. In this case, the CN can send
the IP packets directly to the MN since it knows the current CCoA of the MN.

Mobile IP is also specified for IPv6, which makes it an interesting solution for the VANET
scenario.

4.2.1   Mobile IPv6

Mobile IPv6 [170] adds mobility support for IPv6-based nodes. MNs are thus able to move
between wireless IPv6 networks. For this purpose, Mobile IPv6 is based on an agent-based
system similar to Mobile IPv4 using co-located CoAs. An important difference to Mobile
IPv4 is that Mobile IPv6 does not use any Foreign Agents. If an MN moves to a new point
of attachment in another subnet, it has to acquire a new valid IPv6 address from within this
foreign network, the CoA. As with Mobile IPv4, the HA of the MN in the home network acts
as a representative while the MN is located in a foreign network. In contrast to Mobile IPv4,
the MN in Mobile IPv6 has to register its current CoA not only with its HA but also with the
CNs it currently communicates with. The association made between the home address and
the current CoA of an MN is also called a *mobility binding*.

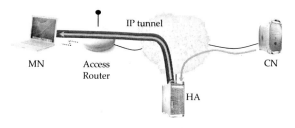

CN: Correspondent Node ▫ HA: Home Agent ▫ MN: Mobile Node

Figure 4.4: Mobile IPv6

An MN detects its movement into a new subnet by analysing router advertisements
broadcasted periodically by the access routers of the foreign network. An MN can also
request an access router of a foreign network with a router solicitation message [171] to
transmit a router advertisement. The information contained in the router advertisements
allows the MN to create its new care-of address autonomously. Therefore, the MN performs
following three steps [172]:

1. The MN performs a duplicate address detection algorithm on its assigned link-local IPv6 address to verify the uniqueness of the link-local address [171].

2. Afterwards, the MN generates a topologically correct IPv6 CoA using either stateless [173] or stateful [174] address configuration.

3. The generated CoA is verified for its uniqueness using duplicate address detection [171].

Once the CoA construction is finished, the MN updates the mobility bindings in the HA and its current CNs by sending a *mobility binding update* message with the new CoA.

In order to communicate with an MN, a CN first queries the stored mobility bindings for the IP address of the MN. If it finds an (updated) mobility binding, it will communicate with the MN directly using the current CoA. Otherwise, the CN sends the IPv6 packets to the home address of the MN. The HA then receives the IPv6 packets and tunnels them to the current CoA of the MN using IPv6 encapsulation [175] as illustrated in figure 4.4. The other direction from the MN to the CN follows the same way, i.e. IPv6 packets from the MN are tunnelled back to the HA, which unpacks the original IPv6 packets and forwards them to the CN.

Mobile IPv6 requires various modifications of the original IPv6 protocol to realise its protocol functionality. The following protocol mechanisms of IPv6 must be adapted [170]:

▶ *IPv6 Protocol Extensions:* Mobile IPv6 introduces a new mobility header and a protocol extension necessary to handle the mobility bindings of an MN.

▶ *New IPv6 Destination Option:* When an MN in a foreign network sends an IPv6 packet to a CN, the Home Address Destination Option informs the CN about the home address of the MN.

▶ *New ICMPv6 Messages:* Mobile IPv6 requires new ICMPv6 messages for the dynamic discovery of Home Agents and for the mobile prefix discovery in a foreign network.

▶ *Modified IPv6 Neighbour Discovery:* The format of the router advertisement message and the prefix information must be modified for the discovery of both the mobile prefix in the foreign network and the Home Agent in the home network.

▶ *New Routing Header:* Mobile IPv6 defines a new routing header variant for routing IPv6 packets directly from a CN to the CoA of the MN.

Mobile IPv6 additionally provides enhancements for the handover procedure such as the simultaneous support of several access routers and a forwarding mechanism for former access routers. Moreover, several extensions were proposed to improve handovers, for example Fast Handovers [176, 177]. Further mechanisms address the micro-mobility support of Mobile IP to reduce the handover latency. Examples are Hierarchical Mobile IPv6 [86] (including optimisations like S-MIP [178]), Cellular IP [179, 180, 181], and HAWAII (Handoff-Aware Wireless Access Internet Infrastructure [182, 183, 184]). A detailed discussion and comparison of these extensions can be found in [185].

In addition to the mobility support of single nodes, the NEMO (Network Mobility) working group of the Internet Engineering Task Force develops enhancements for Mobile IPv6 to manage mobility of an entire network, which changes its point of attachment to the Internet [186, 187]. Examples of mobile networks include, for instance, personal area networks, sensor networks, access networks, and ad hoc networks. In these networks, one or more mobile routers connected to the Internet provide connectivity and reachability for the nodes inside this subnetwork. For the mobility support, a bi-directional tunnel is maintained between the mobile router and its HA. This way, IPv6 packets from a CN to the MN inside the subnet of the mobile router are routed to the home network of the mobile router. The HA of the mobile router accepts these packets and tunnels them to the CoA of the mobile router. Finally, the mobile router decapsulates the IPv6 packets and forwards them to the MN. Vice versa, IPv6 packets from the MN are tunnelled back via the mobile router to the HA, which unpacks the original IPv6 packets and forwards them the targeted CN.

4.2.2   Evaluation: Mobile IPv6 in the VANET Scenario

Mobile IPv6 was designed for the mobility support of MNs moving between wireless IPv6 networks. Applied to the VANET scenario, the vehicles act as MNs, the access routers are the IGWs, and the HAs are maintained by the MoccaProxy. However, Mobile IPv6 cannot be used to integrate multi-hop ad hoc networks into the Internet. The most fundamental problem is that most protocol mechanisms in Mobile IPv6 require link-local multicast support. For example, router solicitations and router advertisements for identifying the access routers (see previous section) are sent to a link-local multicast address. This feature is harmful in the VANET scenario in several ways:

► The use of link-local addresses implies that router advertisements are only transmitted to the vehicles within the direct transmission range of an IGW. This is in contrast to the multi-hop property of VANETs.

► In VANETs, a vehicle typically acts as both a router and an end system. This way, a vehicle will permanently receive router advertisements from its adjacent vehicles. This implies that all neighbouring vehicles are access routers to the Internet, too, which is not true in the VANET scenario.

▶ Since each vehicle acts as a router, the use of CoAs co-located with the vehicles impress a hierarchical address structure for the VANET that can be hardly established and maintained due to the mobility of the vehicles. This address hierarchy also contradicts to the notions of ad hoc networking which generally do not suppose any hierarchical relation between the mobile nodes.

▶ The support of multicast is hard to achieve in large VANETs with a high degree of mobility [108, 109, 110]. It is also very difficult to map the multicast support onto the geographical address scheme used for communication within the VANET.

The evaluation of Mobile IPv6 for the VANET scenario is summarised in table 4.1. In general, Mobile IPv6 enables the mobility support for the vehicles. Once a vehicle detects an access router to the Internet, it can communicate with hosts in the Internet using its CoA. Mobile IPv6 also supports handovers between IGWs. In this case, the CoA must be reconfigured each time a vehicle changes its IGW to access the Internet. Hence, the 'Internet Access' requirement is evaluated with a '+'. Mobile IPv6 completely fulfils the 'Seamless Mobility' requirement, because an Internet host can communicate with an MN using the home address of an MN. Hence, an Internet host can establish a connection to an MN independent of the current location of the MN.

Approach	Mobility Support		VANET Networking		MOCCA Coopera- tion	Scalability & Efficiency
	Internet Access	Seamless Mobility	Ad Hoc Networks	Charac- teristics		
Mobile IPv6	+	++	− −	− −	o	− −

Table 4.1: Evaluation of Mobile IPv6

Mobile IPv6 enables the mobility support of MNs moving between wireless IPv6 networks. However, it was not designed for the mobility support of VANETs. The use of link-local IPv6 addresses prevents the discovery of Internet Gateways in multi-hop environments. Mobile IPv6 will, thus, only find IGWs situated in the immediate transmission range of a vehicle. The NEMO enhancements for Mobile IPv6 are also not suitable since they provide the mobility of the network itself but not of the nodes within this network. Hence, the 'Ad Hoc Networks' requirement is not fulfilled. Similarly, Mobile IPv6 does not consider the characteristics of VANETs: Since it is based on IPv6, it requires an IPv6 address hierarchy within the VANET and a respective multicast support. This way, the 'Characteristics' requirement is not fulfilled.

In general, Mobile IPv6 can be integrated into the IPv6-based MOCCA architecture. However, the mobility binding updates to the CNs may prevent that IP packets are always routed through the same MoccaProxy. Hence, the 'MOCCA Cooperation' requirement is evaluated with 'o'. The protocol mechanisms of Mobile IPv6 are neither scalable nor efficient for communication in the VANET scenario. Due to the mobility, the neighbourship between vehicles changes permanently. Hence, the vehicles permanently have to update their link-local IPv6 addresses to maintain the address consistency of the network. In order to identify new or better suited IGWs, vehicles permanently have to transmit router solicitations in the VANET. This causes overhead even when IGWs are not available. If a vehicle finds a more suitable IGW, the automatic address configuration of IPv6 consumes additional resources [188]. Furthermore, the tunnelling of the IPv6 packets directly to the MN causes additional overhead within the ad hoc network.

As a result, Mobile IPv6 cannot be used for the mobility management in the VANET scenario. The most fundamental problem is that the protocol mechanisms in Mobile IPv6 are not suitable for the mobility support of multi-hop ad hoc networks. Since both the router solicitations and the router advertisements are sent using the link-local multicast addresses, the IGWs cannot be identified over multiple hops. Moreover, the automatic address configuration in Mobile IPv6 and the discovery of routers using solicitations are not scalable for large vehicular ad hoc networks. This way, solutions for the mobility management of VANETs explicitly have to extend Mobile IPv6 to support multi-hop ad hoc networking. The following section discusses available solutions developed for the mobility support of ad hoc networks.

4.3   Related Work

Numerous research projects have already investigated solutions for supporting mobility in multi-hop ad hoc networks. Existing related work is not only concerned with handling mobility at the lower communication layers, i.e. physical layer, data link layer, and network layer. A considerable amount of work proposes solutions for the mobility support on the upper communication layers. Examples are the following:

▶ *Application Layer:* Several approaches handle mobility at the application layer. A particular example is the intentional naming system proposed by Adjie-Winoto et al. [189], which identifies an MN by its domain name and maps this name onto the current IP address of the MN.

▶ *Session Layer:* Another possibility is to support host mobility at the session layer [190]. Thereby, applications specify their notion of a session by joining related transport layer connections. Session layer approaches also handle disconnections and reconnections in a consistent fashion. An example is SLM, a framework for session layer mobility management proposed by Landfeldt et al. [191].

▶ *Transport Layer:* Various approaches were developed to handle host mobility at the transport layer by supporting interfaces-independent transport layer connections. Examples are mobile sockets [192, 193] or multi-homing protocols like the mobile Stream Control Transmission Protocol (mSCTP [194, 195]), Multi-homed TCP [196], and Multi-Homing Translation Protocol (MHTP [197]).

These approaches rely on a topological correct IP addressing scheme in the multi-hop ad hoc network. However, this is not given in the VANET scenario. Moreover, new transport layer protocols and session layer protocols typically introduce new programming interfaces, which require fundamental modifications of existing IP-based applications to adapt them to the new protocols. Hence, such approaches do not solve the Internet integration of VANETs sufficiently. For this reason, the further investigation of the related work is focused on network layer approaches for the mobility management of multi-hop ad hoc networks. Several approaches were proposed for Mobile IP to support mobility in ad hoc networks. This related work can be classified into three categories:

1. Ad hoc routing extensions.

2. Multicast extensions for Mobile IP.

3. Application-specific enhancements.

The following sections propose and evaluate the three categories using a representative approach to exemplify the fundamental characteristics of each category. Although other approaches of the same category might use different protocol mechanisms, they show the same fundamental strengths and weaknesses. The examination also considers IPv4-based approaches since they provide interesting protocol mechanisms for the Internet integration of ad hoc networks.

4.3.1   Ad Hoc Routing Extensions

One possibility for the mobility management in ad hoc networks is to extend the ad hoc routing protocol to support Mobile IP protocol mechanisms. Ad hoc routing extensions were developed for Mobile IPv4 only. A basic principle of these approaches is to use IP broadcasts for the Foreign Agent detection instead of using link-local broadcasts specified in Mobile IP. Hence, the ad hoc network is flooded with agent advertisements as well as agent solicitations. The routing protocol has to be modified accordingly to support the respective IP broadcast functionality. It also must be able to determine whether a host is located inside or outside the ad hoc network. Several approaches were developed for different ad hoc routing protocols:

► Broch et al. [198] extend the Dynamic Source Routing (DSR [43]).

► Randhawa et al. [199] proposed an extension for the Optimised Link State Routing (OLSR [200]).

► Lei et al. [201] describe a general solution for using Mobile IP on top of a proactive routing protocol.

► MIPMANET [202] is a routing extension for using Mobile IP together with the Ad Hoc On-Demand Distance Vector (AODV [44]) routing protocol.

Other approaches developed a completely new ad hoc routing protocol to integrate Mobile IP and ad hoc networks. An example is the Flow-Oriented Routing Protocol (FORP [203]). In the following, MIPMANET will be used as an example for ad hoc routing extensions, because it addresses issues similar to the VANET scenario like the presence of several available IGWs (cf. section 2.1).

MIPMANET

MIPMANET is based on Mobile IPv4, i.e. it uses Foreign Agents located on the gateways to the Internet as illustrated in figure 4.5. A layered tunnelling approach is used for Internet traffic to separate the Mobile IPv4 functionality from the ad hoc routing protocol. This makes it possible for MIPMANET to provide Internet access with the ability for nodes to select a suitable FA and to perform handovers between FAs. The discovery of FAs and the registration procedure are similar to those of Mobile IPv4: The FAs flood the ad hoc network periodically with agent advertisement messages using IP broadcasts. If an MN misses three consecutive agent advertisements, it floods the ad hoc network with an agent solicitation to request the FAs for an agent advertisement. After receiving the agent advertisement, the MN registers itself with the FA and its HA as specified for Mobile IPv4 (see section 4.2). Figure 4.5 also depicts the communication flow in MIPMANET. Communication from MN1 to a CN in the Internet is based on tunnelling. If MN1 wants to send an IP packet to the Internet, it tunnels the packet through the ad hoc network to the FA. The FA unpacks the IP packet and tunnels the original IP packet to the HA using reverse tunnelling. Finally, the HA unpacks the tunnelled IP packet and forwards the original packet through the Internet to the targeted CN.

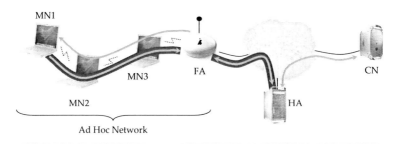

CN: Correspondent Node ▫ FA: Foreign Agent ▫ HA: Home Agent ▫ MN: Mobile Node

Figure 4.5: Communication in MIPMANET

IP packets from a CN in the Internet to the MN are treated like in Mobile IPv4 (cf. figure 4.5). The IP packets are first routed to the HA of the MN, which tunnels them to the FA by common Mobile IP mechanisms. After unpacking the IP packets, the FA delivers them to the MN in the ad hoc network. MNs that do not require Internet access will use the ad hoc network in the common way, because they consider the ad hoc network as a stand-alone network. As a result, the ad hoc network becomes transparent to Mobile IPv4.

MIPMANET was developed for on-demand routing protocols like AODV or DSR. It requires modifications of the routing protocol to forward IP packets to the FA if the destination host is not found in the ad hoc network. Moreover, several configuration parameters in AODV were modified to ensure proper functionality of MIPMANET. The basic protocol mechanisms of Mobile IPv4 are also implemented in MIPMANET. However, the following settings of Mobile IPv4 must be adapted to cooperate with MIPMANET:

▶ Since multi-hop ad hoc networks do not provide link layer connectivity between all mobile nodes, the protocols in Mobile IPv4 have to use IP addresses instead of link layer addresses.

▶ In order to reduce the overhead within ad hoc networks, MIPMANET increases the agent advertisement periodicity in Mobile IPv4 from 1 s to 5 s. If an MN does not receive any agent advertisements, it broadcasts an FA solicitation to retrieve available FAs.

An interesting feature of MIPMANET is the introduction of a movement detection mechanism that is used if several FAs are available within the ad hoc network. MIPMANET therefore uses the hop counter as a metric to decide whether an MN should perform a handover or not: An MN should register itself with another FA if it is at least two hops closer to

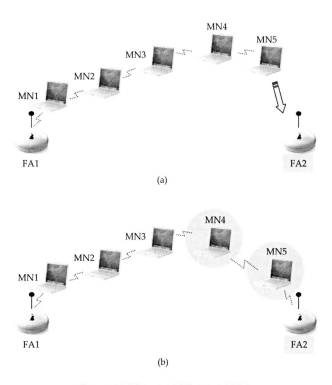

(a)

(b)

FA: Foreign Agent ▫ MN: Mobile Node

Figure 4.6: Movement Detection in MIPMANET

this FA for two consecutive agent advertisements than to its current FA. The example given in figure 4.6 illustrates this movement detection mechanism. In figure 4.6 (a), all five MNs are registered with FA1. If MN5 gets in contact with FA2 and receives two consecutive agent advertisements from FA2, the nodes MN4 and MN5 will decide to handover to FA2 (figure 4.6 (b)) since both nodes are at least two hops closer to FA2 than to FA1. The other three MNs remain registered with FA1.

Evaluation

Table 4.2 summarises the evaluation of MIPMANET – and, thus, of ad hoc routing extensions in general – in the context of the requirements defined in section 4.1. MIPMANET
supports the mobility of nodes within the ad hoc network using Mobile IPv4. In contrast
to Mobile IPv6, MIPMANET identifies each MN by its global home address only. This way,
MIPMANET fulfils the two mobility support requirements 'Internet Access' and 'Seamless
Mobility'.

Approach	Mobility Support		VANET Networking		MOCCA Coopera-tion	Scalability & Efficiency
	Internet Access	Seamless Mobility	Ad Hoc Networks	Charac-teristics		
Ad Hoc Routing Extensions	+ +	+ +	+ +	– –	–	– –

Table 4.2: Evaluation of Ad Hoc Routing Extensions

With the tunnelling of Internet traffic from the MN to the FA, the ad hoc network becomes
transparent to Mobile IPv4 in MIPMANET. Together with the use of IP broadcasts for agent
advertisements and agent solicitations, the mobility support is possible for multi-hop ad
hoc networks, which fulfils the 'Ad Hoc Networks' requirement. However, ad hoc routing
extensions are not compatible to the VANET characteristics for several reasons:

► The approaches are based on Mobile IPv4 only and an adaptation of the basic protocol
  mechanisms to IPv6 is not possible without a complete modification of Mobile IPv6.

► Due to the high degree of mobility experienced in VANETs, the decreased frequency
  of the agent advertisements may cause a long idle time before the FA is identified.
  Moreover, the movement detection mechanism requires additional 10 s (i.e. the period
  for two advertisements) before a handover to a newly detected FA is performed.

► Ad hoc routing extensions are highly correlated to the routing protocol used in the
  ad hoc network. Hence, a mapping of these extensions to the location-based ad hoc
  routing protocol of the VANET might be difficult or even impossible.

► The movement detection mechanism is not suitable if several IGWs are available. Since
  it relies on the number of hops to the FA only, it is too inflexible to find the most suitable gateway. Moreover, the number of hops for IP packets in a VANET cannot be
  determined, because the location-based routing protocol forwards IP packets transparently and, thus, each vehicle is exactly one IP hop away from the IGWs.

In general, ad hoc routing extensions can be integrated in the MOCCA architecture to manage the mobility of the vehicles since they can be configured to route IP packets through the MoccaProxy. However, these approaches were developed for Mobile IPv4 only; they do not solve the basic problems of providing mobility support in IPv6-based ad hoc networks. The 'MOCCA Cooperation' requirement is thus evaluated with '−'.

Due to the use of Mobile IPv4, ad hoc routing extensions are not scalable. The address space of IPv4 is not scalable and the overhead caused by agent solicitations to find FAs increases with the number of vehicles. In case of MIPMANET, the tunnelling of Internet traffic from the MN to the FA additionally increases the overhead within the VANETs. As a result, the 'Scalability & Efficiency' requirement is not fulfilled.

In summary, ad hoc routing protocol extensions are not a suitable solution for the mobility management of ad hoc networks. They highly depend on the routing protocol deployed in the ad hoc network and they are available for Mobile IPv4 only. These characteristics together with the limited scalability make it almost impossible to deploy such ad hoc routing protocol extensions in the VANET scenario.

4.3.2 Multicast Extensions for Mobile IP

IP multicast [135, 204, 205, 206] provides a location-independent addressing and IP packet delivery to a set of hosts that belong to a multicast group. It also provides mechanisms for hosts to join and leave multicast groups. This way, IP multicast can be combined with Mobile IP to integrate ad hoc networks into the Internet[1]. The general idea is to use Mobile IP for the mobility support of the mobile nodes, whereas the discovery of gateways within the ad hoc networks is based on IP multicast. Several protocols were developed using multicast:

▶ The Internet Engineering Task Force introduced a multicast-based discovery of gateways for IPv6-based networks, which extends IPv6, ICMPv6 and Mobile IPv6 to support global connectivity for mobile nodes [210]. However, this activity was not continued.

▶ MMP (Multicast for Mobility Protocol) published by Mihailovic et al. [211] uses multicast operation to find FAs in Mobile IPv4.

▶ The multicast mobility solution proposed by Tseng et al. [212] additionally takes the characteristics of ad hoc networks into account. This solution is proposed in the following section as a representative for multicast extensions.

---

[1]Approaches which identify a mobile node by an IP multicast group [207, 208, 209] are not discussed further on, because it is not possible to use TCP over IP multicast in the Internet. Hence, most IP-based applications cannot be deployed since they rely on TCP.

A Multicast Mobility Solution

The communication scenario used in [212] is similar to MIPMANET (see section 4.3.1). It is also based on IPv4 and each gateway between an ad hoc network and the Internet additionally serves as a Foreign Agent. In this scenario, Mobile IP handles the mobility of the mobile nodes. The discovery of an FA works in the following way: The FAs periodically broadcast agent advertisements in the local ad hoc network to advertise their service. Each FA is associated with a parameter n that defines the service range (in hops) of the FA. The service range specifies the area in which the FA can be discovered. The limitation of the number of hops is achieved by setting the time-to-live field in the IP packet to n. This way, any mobile host within a range of n wireless hops receives the agent advertisements of the FA and, thus, can register itself with the FA. In the example depicted in figure 4.7, n was set to two hops and, thus, node MN1 cannot detect the FA.

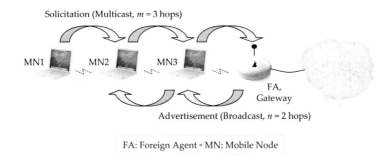

Figure 4.7: FA Discovery using Multicast

If an MN does not receive an agent advertisement for a certain period of time, it sends a multicast agent solicitation with a time-to-live equal to m hops. This value is gradually increased in order to avoid broadcast storms within the ad hoc network caused by flooding [213]. The destination address of the solicitation message is the "all routers" IP multicast address 224.0.0.2. If $n < m$ and the gateway is less than or equal to m hops away from the MN, the FA will receive the solicitation and can increase its service range to m hops. For example, if the solicitation of MN1 in figure 4.7 has a time-to-live of $m = 3$ hops and FA uses $n = 2$ hops, the FA will receive the solicitation and may decide to increase its n to three hops. In this case, MN1 will also receive the agent advertisements of the FA and will be able to register itself with the FA and its HA using the Mobile IP registration procedure.

An alternative deployment of IP multicast to discover FAs completely avoids broadcasts in the ad hoc network [214]. In this approach, the FAs do not broadcast the ad hoc network with agent advertisements. If a mobile node joins an ad hoc network, it sends an agent solicitation to a pre-defined multicast group, which identifies all FAs within an ad hoc network. This way, the agent solicitation will be routed to the FAs that joined this multicast group. Each FA receiving the solicitation responds to the mobile node with an agent advertisement message using unicast.

Evaluation

Table 4.3 summarises the evaluation of multicast extensions for Mobile IP for being deployed in the VANET scenario. Multicast extensions for Mobile IP were developed with respect to the mobility support of mobile nodes. The gateway discovery mechanism enables the deployment of Mobile IP for ad hoc networks; MNs can access the Internet and Internet hosts can access the mobile nodes using standard Mobile IP. Hence, both mobility support requirements are fulfilled.

| Approach | Mobility Support | | VANET Networking | | MOCCA Cooperation | Scalability & Efficiency |
	Internet Access	Seamless Mobility	Ad Hoc Networks	Charac- teristics		
Multicast Extensions	+ +	+ +	+	– –	o	– –

Table 4.3: Evaluation of Multicast-Based Approaches

The gateway discovery of multicast extensions enables the deployment of Mobile IP in multi-hop ad hoc networks. However, multicast extensions for Mobile IP always require an ad hoc routing protocol that supports multicast. Hence, the 'Ad Hoc Networks' requirement is fulfilled with limitations only. In contrast, the 'Characteristics' requirement is not fulfilled for two reasons:

▶ Current location-based ad hoc routing algorithms for (vehicular) ad hoc networks do not support multicast.

▶ Although multicast-based approaches can be used to discover gateways in ad hoc networks, they do not provide a solution to find the most suitable gateway if several gateways are available simultaneously.

Although multicast extensions were originally developed for Mobile IPv4 for the purpose of identifying FAs in ad hoc networks, they can be also used in IPv6-based networks since multicast is specified for both IPv4 and IPv6. Approaches like [214] even propose a multicast extension for using Mobile IPv6 in ad hoc networks, so they can be easily integrated into the MOCCA architecture. However, such approaches do not ensure that IP packets always pass the MoccaProxy, which is a general drawback of Mobile IPv6 (see section 4.2.1). Thus, the 'MOCCA Cooperation' requirement is evaluated with 'o'.

Multicast support in ad hoc networks is neither scalable nor efficient [108, 109, 110]. Moreover, all approaches basically rely on solicitations to find gateways or FAs if mobile nodes do not receive any advertisements from them. Sending these solicitations causes overhead within the ad hoc network even if a gateway is not available at the moment. Hence, the 'Scalability & Efficiency' requirement is not fulfilled.

The most fundamental drawback of multicast extensions for Mobile IP is that they require the ad hoc routing protocol to support multicast. Since VANETs may become very dense comprising potentially hundreds of vehicles within the service area of an IGW, multicast-based routing as well as a flooding of multicast messages does not provide the scalability and efficiency necessary for the VANET scenario. Hence, a solution based on multicast is unsuitable for the mobility management in the VANET scenario.

4.3.3 Application-Specific Enhancements

A completely different approach is the deployment of application-specific enhancements for Mobile IP. Whereas both routing protocol extensions and multicast-based approaches are implemented at the network layer, the approaches discussed in this section implement application-specific enhancements to use Mobile IP in ad hoc networks. Two different types of application-specific enhancements are possible: *Application Layer Mobile IP* and *Service Discovery Enhancements*.

Application Layer Mobile IP

The basic idea of Application Layer Mobile IP is to implement application-specific enhancements to provide Mobile IP functionality in ad hoc networks. These enhancements are independent of the underlying ad hoc routing protocol. An Application Layer Mobile IP solution was proposed by Striegel et al. for Mobile IPv4 [215], which is discussed in this section.

Striegel et al. proposed a gateway model that provides a uniform set of services for mobile nodes. This model is independent of the underlying ad hoc routing protocol, i.e. it works together with existing ad hoc routing protocols as well as with Mobile IPv4 to provide seamless Internet access for mobile nodes. Figure 4.8 depicts such a scenario. The basic

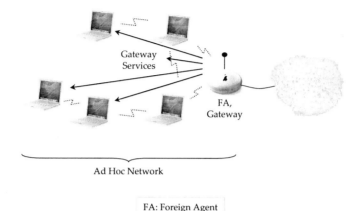

Ad Hoc Network

FA: Foreign Agent

Figure 4.8: Mobile IP with Application-Specific Enhancements

idea is that the gateways announce their service of providing Internet access for the ad hoc network. In contrast to agent advertisements, the announcements are generated at the application layer. The gateway model consists of two modules, an application module and a node support module. The *application module* is responsible to route packets between the ad hoc network and the Internet in the following way:

► For packets from the Internet, the application module responds to ARP requests and promiscuously monitors and forwards the IP packets to the ad hoc network.

► For IP packets from the ad hoc network, the application module has to monitor messages defined by the gateway services described below.

The *node support module* of the gateway model is responsible for connecting an MN to the gateway application module using the gateway services. Hence, each MN that wants to access the Internet must run the node support module.

In order to implement Mobile IPv4 in ad hoc networks, gateways act as Foreign Agents for the nodes in the ad hoc network as illustrated in figure 4.8. The FA component of a gateway may be independent of the gateway application module itself; gateway discovery and registration procedure are entirely independent from the mechanisms used in Mobile IPv4. In order to deploy Mobile IPv4 in the ad hoc network, the gateway model can replace the FA discovery and the FA registration in Mobile IPv4. Alternatively, it can control these protocol mechanisms in Mobile IPv4. Both implementation strategies make the ad hoc network transparent to Mobile IPv4. Therefore, the application module provides the following four services similar to Mobile IPv4:

1. *Advertisement:* A gateway announces its presence within the ad hoc network by sending an advertisement message to the "all nodes" multicast address 224.0.0.1. Similar to Mobile IP, an MN additionally sends a solicitation message to the "all routers" multicast address 224.0.0.2 if it does not receive any advertisements for a longer period of time. The gateways then respond to this solicitation with an advertisement either by broadcast or by addressing the MN directly.

2. *Registration:* In order to use the services of the gateway, an MN has to register itself with the gateway to reserve the necessary resources. Therefore, the MN sends a registration request to the gateway (based on the information received in the advertisement received), and receives a registration response from the gateway. The registration process has to cooperate with the registration procedure used in Mobile IP, either by replacing or by triggering the registration procedure of Mobile IP.

3. *Node Location:* Since a node may be found outside the ad hoc network, an MN should be able to query the gateway to determine if the correspondent node can be found externally or internally.

4. *Data:* In order to send IP packets to a node found externally in the Internet, the packets must be appropriately routed to the gateway. Therefore, the IP packets are tunnelled from the mobile node to the gateway.

With these services, MNs can discover gateways and register themselves with the FAs on the gateways from within the ad hoc network. Communication in the Internet between FA, HA, and CN is handled by standard Mobile IP.

Service Discovery Enhancements

In large-scale networks, the configuration and usage of mobile devices could be very difficult. A new user may have to configure her or his mobile device manually if the device is not registered with the DHCP server of the new network to obtain a valid IPv4 address automatically. The use of services within the network, e.g. printing a document on the nearest printer, requires configuration efforts, too, and is at least annoying to the user. Service discovery protocols address these problems. They enable users, mobile devices, and applications to discover services in a network with a minimum of knowledge.

The problem of finding IGWs in VANETs is similar to the discovery of services in ad hoc networks. Although several papers suggest service discovery protocols for finding gateways to the Internet within ad hoc networks [216, 217, 218, 219], none of them proposes a solution to combine the service discovery protocol with Mobile IP. Currently, various service discovery protocols are available such as the Service Location Protocol (SLP [220, 221]), Universal Plug and Play (UPnP [222]), Jini [223], the Bluetooth Service Discovery Protocol (SDP [224]), and Salutation [225]. These protocols were developed for different application scenarios. Hence, their functionality and their requirements are very different [226]. UPnP, Salutation and the Bluetooth SDP are not relevant for the VANET scenario, because they were developed for small ad hoc networks and they highly depend on the operating system (UPnP and Salutation are currently available on Microsoft Windows platforms only) and the underlying radio technology (Bluetooth SDP). Jini is also not a suitable candidate, because it requires a central instance that manages the available services within the network. In the following, SLP will be used to describe the basic service protocol mechanisms; in contrast to Salutation, SLP originated from the Internet community and, thus, is based on TCP and UDP natively.

In 1999, the SRVLOC Working Group of the Internet Engineering Task Force standardised SLP (version 2) in RFC 2608 [220]. SLP for IPv6 followed in RFC 3111 [221]. The very basic components in SLP are so-called agents, which appear in three types:

1. *Service Agent (SA):* Service Agents act on behalf of service providers. Their task is to propagate addresses and characteristics of the provided services.

2. *Directory Agent (DA):* Directory Agents optionally implement a service directory that manages the available services within a network. Service Agents therefore have to register their services with the Directory Agent.

3. *User Agent (UA):* User Agents are consulted by applications to find specified services in a network. User Agents therefore communicate with Service Agents and Directory Agents.

SLP specifies two interaction modes to discover services in ad hoc networks. The first mode operates without DAs as depicted in figure 4.9. Each SA has to join a predefined multicast group. If a mobile device requests for a service in the network, the UA running on the mobile node queries the available SAs directly. It does so by sending a Service Request (SrvRqst) message to the predefined multicast address. If an SA receives a SrvRqst message, it will respond to the query with a Service Reply (SrvRply) message directly to the UA using unicast. The SrvRply message contains information about the service provided by the SA in the form of a Service URL (Uniform Resource Locator). The Service URL specifies the type

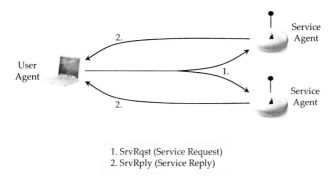

1. SrvRqst (Service Request)
2. SrvRply (Service Reply)

Figure 4.9: Protocol Interaction of SLP without Directory Agents

and location of a service according to RFC 2609 [227]. This way, the UA receives information about available services in the ad hoc network from all SAs that received the service request. A very interesting feature in SLP is the use of attributes describing a service. UAs can specify attributes in the SrvRqsts to find appropriate services. If an SA receives such a SrvRqst, it will respond only if its service matches to the specifications in the attributes. For example, an attribute for a printer may define the room where the printer is installed. If a mobile user wants to print a document, the User Agent specifies the room number attribute and receives SrvRplys from all printers in the respective room. This way, the UA is able to send the document to one of the printers in this room.

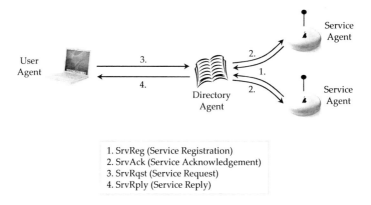

1. SrvReg (Service Registration)
2. SrvAck (Service Acknowledgement)
3. SrvRqst (Service Request)
4. SrvRply (Service Reply)

Figure 4.10: Protocol Interaction of SLP using Directory Agents

The second interaction mode, shown in figure 4.10, deploys one ore more Directory Agents managing the available services in the network. In this case, each SA within the network has to register its service(s) with the DA using a Service Registration (SrvReg) message (step 1). The DA acknowledges the registrations with a Service Acknowledgement message SrvAck in step 2. UAs request services immediately from the DAs. They send a SrvRqst to the DA (step 3), which replies with the registered services using a SrvRply (step 4). In this interaction mode, the DAs need to be discovered as described in the first interaction mode. Alternatively, the IP address of a DA can be configured manually.

The use of Directory Agents is optional in SLP. However, they are recommended to improve the scalability of the available services particularly in large-scale ad hoc networks.

Evaluation

The evaluation of application-specific enhancements for Mobile IP is outlined in table 4.4 for both Application Layer Mobile IP and Service Discovery Enhancements. In general, application-specific enhancements for Mobile IP support the mobility of devices. Both approaches enable the Internet access independent of a node's current location. Since they are based on Mobile IP for the mobility support, application-specific enhancements also fulfil the 'Seamless Mobility' requirement.

Approach	Mobility Support		VANET Networking		MOCCA Coopera-tion	Scalability & Efficiency
	Internet Access	Seamless Mobility	Ad Hoc Networks	Charac-teristics		
Application-Layer Mobile IP	+ +	+ +	+ +	– –	– –	– –
Service Discovery Enhancements	+ +	+ +	+ +	–	o	– –

Table 4.4: Evaluation of Application-Specific Enhancements

Application Layer Mobile IP and Service Discovery Enhancements were both developed with respect to the mobility support of devices located within ad hoc networks resulting in a '++' for the 'Ad Hoc Networks' requirement. A very basic characteristic of application-specific enhancements is that they are independent of the underlying ad hoc routing protocol. However, several drawbacks make application-specific enhancements an unsuitable solution for being deployed in VANETs:

▶ Both solutions rely on multicast support to find Internet Gateways using solicitations.

▶ They do not handle the problem of finding the most suitable gateway among a number of available gateways.

▶ Application Layer Mobile IP was specified for Mobile IPv4 only and requires a complicated mechanism to decide whether or not a node is located within the ad hoc network. These mechanisms are not necessary in the VANET scenario where the vehicles form one logical IPv6 subnet

Hence, Application Layer Mobile IP is evaluated with a '$--$' for the 'Characteristics' requirement. Since some service discovery protocols are also specified for IPv6, they can be deployed in VANETs more easily. Hence, the 'Characteristics' requirement is rated with '$-$'.

Approaches for Application Layer Mobile IP were specified for Mobile IPv4 only; Striegel et. al. pointed out that their approach alleviates the transition to IPv6 since the nodes within the ad hoc network do not necessarily need to support IPv6. However, these approaches cannot be implemented in the IPv6-based MOCCA architecture: Their mechanisms cannot be applied for IPv6-based networks and approaches for extending Mobile IPv6 with application-specific enhancements are not yet available. Hence, the 'MOCCA Cooperation' requirement is not fulfilled for Application Layer Mobile IP. Since service discovery protocols like SLP are also specified for IPv6-based networks, they can be used in MOCCA to enhance Mobile IPv6 for ad hoc networks. However, the mobility binding updates of Mobile IPv6 may prevent that the IP packets between vehicles and Internet always pass the MoccaProxy. Hence, the 'MOCCA Cooperation' requirement is evaluated with 'o' for Service Discovery Enhancements.

Application-specific enhancements are neither scalable nor efficient: Besides the limited address space of IPv4 for Application Layer Mobile IP, the proposed approaches rely on solicitations if a mobile node cannot find a gateway. Hence, overhead even occurs if an Internet Gateway is not available. The tunnelling of IP packets from the MNs to the gateway is in contrast to an efficient communication within the ad hoc network, resulting in a '$--$' for the 'Scalability & Efficiency' requirement for both types of application-specific enhancements.

In general, application-specific enhancements are an interesting approach for mobility support of VANETs. They support the mobility of nodes organised in ad hoc networks and they are independent of the ad hoc routing protocol being deployed. However, such approaches cannot be used in the MOCCA architecture. Application Layer Mobile IP does not exist for IPv6-based networks and Service Discovery Enhancements do not solve the problems of integrating Mobile IPv6 into MOCCA for the mobility management. Moreover, a proposal for using service discovery enhancements together with Mobile IP is currently not available. Since both types of application-specific enhancements are neither scalable nor efficient, they are not suitable for the management of mobility in the VANET scenario.

4.3.4   Discussion of Related Work

Each category of related work comprises several approaches having different advantages and drawbacks. However, the approaches in each category have the same fundamental characteristics that can be used for a general evaluation using a representative solution of each category. Table 4.5 summarises the comparison of the different categories. The evaluation comprises the following basic requirements for the mobility management in the VANET scenario: mobility support of the nodes, consideration of VANET networking characteristics, cooperation with MOCCA, scalability and efficiency.

Approach	Mobility Support		VANET Networking		MOCCA Coopera-tion	Scalability & Efficiency
	Internet Access	Seamless Mobility	Ad Hoc Networks	Charac-acteristics		
Mobile IPv6	+	++	– –	– –	o	– –
Ad Hoc Routing Extensions	++	++	++	– –	–	– –
Multicast Extensions	++	++	+	– –	o	– –
Application-Layer Mobile IP	++	++	++	– –	– –	– –
Service Discovery Enhancements	++	++	++	–	o	– –

Table 4.5: Summary Evaluation for Mobility Management

A general observation is that the proposed categories can be used for the mobility support of nodes organised in multi-hop ad hoc networks; mobile nodes can access the Internet using multi-hop communication with an Internet Gateway, and IP packets from the Internet are dynamically routed to the mobile nodes independent of their current position. However, a basic problem of all approaches is the lack of scalability and efficiency for the following reasons:

▶ *IP Addressing:* Most approaches were developed for IPv4-based networks and, thus, are not able to address all vehicles uniquely. In contrast, IPv6-based approaches require local IPv6 auto configuration mechanisms, which are hard to implement in ad hoc networks and which are not considered as scalable (cf. section 4.2.2).

▶ *Network Structure:* The approaches discussed do not consider the ad hoc network as one logical subnet of the Internet. This does not reflect the structure of networks in the context of VANETs. Hence, these approaches have to provide complex and scalable mechanisms to determine if a mobile node is located within the ad hoc network or elsewhere in the Internet.

▶ *Multicast:* Despite some few routing extension approaches like, e.g., MIPMANET, most approaches require a multicast support within the ad hoc networks, which cannot be designed in a scalable and efficient way for VANETs [108, 109, 110].

▶ *Solicitations:* All approaches rely on solicitations initiated by mobile nodes to find gateways or FAs and are therefore not scalable in the context of large-scale ad hoc networks. As a result, overhead even occurs if IGWs are currently not available.

Another interesting observation is that none of the solutions for the mobility management of vehicles can be properly integrated with the MOCCA communication architecture. Most approaches were developed for the mobility support of IPv4-based multi-hop ad hoc networks. Hence, these approaches cannot be integrated into the IPv6-based MOCCA architecture. There are also approaches in each category based on IPv6. However, these solutions have the problem that Mobile IPv6 in general does not ensure that the communication flow between VANET and Internet always passes the same proxy.

Finally, the related work does not consider the VANET networking characteristics sufficiently. Especially routing extensions and multicast-based approaches are highly correlated with the ad hoc routing protocol deployed in the VANET. This correlation aggravates their deployment in the VANET scenario using a location-based routing protocol. Furthermore, the selection of the most suitable IGW plays a minor role in the related work. Only a few approaches like MIPMANET introduce algorithms to select an appropriate gateway if several gateways are available simultaneously. These algorithms only consider the number of hops to the gateway. However, in the VANET scenario several parameters are more important for selecting the most suitable gateway. Examples are the current number of users and the utilisation of the gateway, the position of the gateway, user preferences, or the distance to the gateway. These parameters cannot be considered by existing approaches, since these approaches cannot be extended accordingly.

The examination of related approaches showed that they are not suitable to manage the mobility of vehicles organised in VANETs; a novel solution is necessary to fulfil all requirements. The following section presents such a solution.

4.4 MMIP6

MOCCA deploys a mobility management protocol called MMIP6 (MOCCA Mobile IPv6), which handles the mobility of vehicles in the VANET. MMIP6 is based on the principles of Mobile IPv4, but was designed to support IPv6-based mobile nodes organised in ad hoc networks. In contrast to related work on mobility support for ad hoc networks, MMIP6 was specifically developed with respect to the VANET scenario, i.e. the protocol mechanisms take into account the characteristics of VANETs described in section 2.2. This section introduces MMIP6 and its protocol mechanisms. The formats of the protocol data units in MMIP6 are specified in appendix B.

4.4.1 Protocol Overview

In MOCCA, all vehicles in the VANET form one single IPv6 subnet connected to the Internet via Internet Gateways. From a logical point of view, the MoccaProxy provides access to this vehicular network, which is called the VANET cloud (cf. section 3). In this scenario, each vehicle is identified by a globally unique and permanent IPv6 address. A very important feature of MMIP6 is that it relies on this global IPv6 address only, i.e. the vehicle always uses this IPv6 address for its communications. MMIP6 consequently avoids link-local and site-local IPv6 addresses. This way, it does not require stateful or stateless automatic address configuration used in IPv6, which conserves bandwidth resources in the ad hoc network.

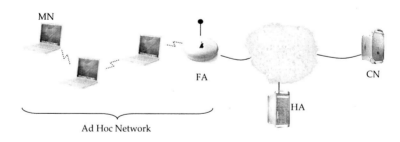

CN: Correspondent Node ▫ FA: Foreign Agent ▫ HA: Home Agent ▫ MN: Mobile Node

Figure 4.11: Agent-Based System of MMIP6

In order to manage the mobility of vehicles, MMIP6 deploys an agent-based system similar to Mobile IP. Thereby, a Home Agent represents each MN in the Internet, as illustrated in figure 4.11. In contrast to Mobile IPv6, MMIP6 reintroduces the functionality of Foreign

Agents representing MNs in the foreign ad hoc network using care-of addresses (CoAs). This agent-based architecture is combined with the proxy-based architecture of MOCCA: From a topological point of view, the IPv6 addresses of the vehicles are located at the MoccaProxy, i.e. the MoccaProxy maintains the HAs of the vehicles (cf. figure 4.12). This way, the MoccaProxy acts as a representative for the vehicles in the Internet and is therefore able to manage the mobility of vehicles. The FA functionality is located at the IGW, i.e. each IGW maintains an FA and, thus, represents a vehicle in the VANET by associating the vehicle with its CoA.

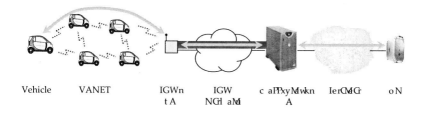

Vehicle	VANET	IGWn	IGW	c aPxyMwkn	IerCMG	o N
		t A	NGl aM		A	

t Adt aMSpe :ApCer:ᵖ HA: Home Agent ▫ IGW: Internet Gateway
VANET: Vehicular Ad Hoc Network

Figure 4.12: Communication Flow in MMIP6

If a vehicle discovers a new FA as described in section 4.4.2, it first has to register itself with both the new FA and its HA in order to communicate with Internet hosts (see section 4.4.3). This way, the MoccaProxy always knows the current CoA of the vehicle and, thus, the IGW that can be used to communicate with the vehicle. Figure 4.12 illustrates the routing of IPv6 packets in this scenario between a vehicle and a CN in the Internet[2]:

1. If a CN wants to send IPv6 packets to a vehicle, it always uses the global IPv6 address of the vehicle. Hence, the IPv6 packets are routed through the Internet to the HA of the vehicle maintained by the MoccaProxy.

2. The HA in the MoccaProxy receives the IPv6 packets on behalf of the vehicle and tunnels them to the CoA the vehicle is currently registered with. This way, the packets are

---

[2]For a better clarification, this scenario assumes IPv6-based communication between correspondent node in the Internet and vehicle. Using IPv4 for the CN with respective translation mechanisms in the MoccaProxy is described in section 3.2.1.

routed to the IGW currently used by the vehicle. For the tunnelling, MMIP6 uses either IPv6-in-IPv4 tunnelling [125, 126, 127] or IPv6-in-IPv6 tunnelling [175] depending on the technology supported by the IGW network.

3. The FA on the IGW unpacks the encapsulated IPv6 packets and forwards them to the vehicle using the location-based ad hoc routing protocol of the VANET.

Conversely, a vehicle that wants to send IPv6 packets to a CN first has to decide whether the packets should be delivered to another vehicle in the VANET or to a CN in the Internet. This can be easily done by comparing the IPv6 prefix of the destination address with the prefix specified for the VANET, because all hosts in the VANET cloud share one common IPv6 prefix. If a vehicle wants to send IPv6 packets to a CN in the Internet, the packets will be delivered to the IGW that maintains the FA the vehicle is currently registered with. This mechanism is similar to communication in IPv6-based LANs where IP packets to the Internet are sent to a "default gateway". At the IGW, the outgoing IPv6 packets are accepted by the FA that tunnels the IPv6 packets back to the HA using reverse tunnelling [169]. Finally, the HA unpacks the tunnelled IPv6 packets and forwards them to the CN addressed in the original IPv6 packet. Therefore, all IP packets are implicitly routed via the MoccaProxy.

Although the use of Foreign Agents in MMIP6 seems to be a step backwards towards Mobile IPv4, it is an indispensable feature of MMIP6 to manage the mobility of vehicles in the VANET. FAs avoid the use of link-local addresses as well as co-located CoAs for the vehicles and shift potential tunnelling overhead from the VANET into the IGW network. Additionally, the FAs enable the deployment of IPv4 tunnels in the IGW network. This way, even the IPv4-based Internet can be used for communication between HA and FA. The use of reverse tunnelling from an FA to its HA is necessary to ensure that all IPv6 packets from a vehicle to a CN in the Internet pass the MoccaProxy. This is a mandatory feature for splitting up the transport layer connection as is described in chapter 5.

4.4.2 DRIVE – Discovery of Internet Gateways

An important challenge in MMIP6 is the discovery of IGWs in the VANET, which maintain the Foreign Agents for the vehicles. The existing approaches discussed in section 4.3 are basically reactive, i.e. a mobile device looking for a gateway to the Internet has to "initiate" the discovery process[3]. Applied to the VANET scenario, vehicles permanently have to discover new IGWs to achieve a consistent view on the varying topology of the VANET. Depending on the routing algorithm, the multi-hop capability of the VANET may multiply this effect.

---

[3]Although many approaches deploy advertisements to announce their services, they always require solicitations from the mobile nodes.

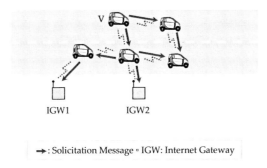

IGW1   IGW2

→ : Solicitation Message ▫ IGW: Internet Gateway

Figure 4.13: Reactive IGW Discovery in the VANET Scenario

For example, if the position of an IGW cannot be determined, the location service of the routing algorithm needs to flood the VANET locally to resolve the IPv6 address of the IGW onto its location [117]. This worst-case scenario is illustrated in figure 4.13 where a vehicle V initiates the discovery of an IGW. The solicitation of V will be reproduced in the multi-hop ad hoc network along the arrows until it finally reaches at the available gateways IGW1 and IGW2. These solicitations will be sent out periodically by each vehicle, even if IGWs are not present in the VANET.

MMIP6 uses a novel IGW discovery protocol called DRIVE (Discovery of Internet Gateways from Vehicles). DRIVE was developed to find the most suitable Internet Gateway in large-scale multi-hop ad hoc networks. It is based on service discovery protocol concepts for ad hoc networks. According to the categories derived in section 4.3, DRIVE can be classified in the following way:

▶ *Application-Specific Enhancements:* MMIP6 combines the mobility management with DRIVE running on the application layer. Since DRIVE implements service discovery concepts, it belongs to the subcategory 'Service Discovery Enhancements'.

▶ *"Inverse" Ad Hoc Routing Protocol Extensions:* Instead of modifying the routing protocol, DRIVE adapts its provided services to the ad hoc routing protocol.

The service discovery process in DRIVE comprises two functional tasks proposed in the following sections: the discovery of available IGWs and the selection of the most suitable gateway. A detailed description of message formats and the prototype implementation is given in appendix C.

Finding Available Internet Gateways

The key concept of DRIVE is that it completely avoids the reactive approach used in traditional service discovery protocols. Thereby, the behaviour of users (vehicles) and service
providers (Internet Gateways) are exchanged: IGWs do not wait for requests from the vehicles. Instead, IGWs themselves announce their service of providing gateway and Foreign
Agent functionality proactively. Vehicles looking for an IGW are passive, i.e. they do not
discover the IGWs actively. This kind of discovery process will be called "passive discovery"
further on.

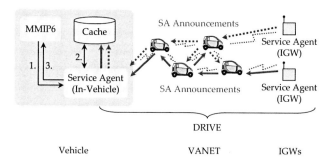

·➤ ➔ : SA Announcements ▫ DRIVE: Discovery of Internet Gateways from Vehicles
IGW: Internet Gateway ▫ VANET: Vehicular Ad Hoc Network ▫ MMIP6: MOCCA Mobile IPv6

Figure 4.14: DRIVE Discovery Process

In DRIVE, a *Service Agent* (SA) represents the FA functionality of an IGW and therefore
the service of providing Internet access. In order to enable passive discovery, DRIVE splits
up the SA functionality into two distributed functional units as illustrated in figure 4.14.
The first unit is located at the IGWs, and the second unit resides within the vehicles. The
IGW unit of the SA periodically announces the IGW service of providing gateway and FA
functionality in a locally restricted area around the IGW. It therefore transmits *Service Agent
Announcements* (SA Announcements) into the VANET that are distributed among the vehicles in this restricted area by the VANET routing protocol. The local restriction is achieved
by specifying the geographical region where the location-based routing protocol has to distribute the SA Announcements. Alternatively, the distribution of SA Announcements can
be restricted by limiting the number of hops SA Announcements are propagated.

The in-vehicle unit of the SA represents the IGW functionality within a vehicle. It therefore receives the SA Announcements from available IGWs, extracts the information contained in them and caches the information locally. Due to the periodicity of the SA Announcements, a vehicle is able to infer whether an IGW is available or not: if the SA Announcements of an IGW fail to appear after the specified announcement period, the service will be either unavailable, or a relaying vehicle discarded the SA Announcements, e.g. because of irreparable transmission errors. In DRIVE, this value was set to two times of the transmission frequency of the SA Announcements. In this case, the orphaned cache entry of the IGW will be removed from the in-vehicle SA. Hence, the cache contains information about the IGWs currently available in the VANET.

From the MMIP6 point of view, the discovery of an FA is reduced to a search in the local cache as shown in figure 4.14. Therefore, MMIP6 periodically polls the cache to detect modifications[4]. If so, the following three steps are performed:

1. In the first step, MMIP6 queries the in-vehicle SA for a new IGW (and, thus, its FA).

2. The in-vehicle SA searches the local cache. If the search is successful, the Service Agent will respond with the respective IGW. Otherwise, DRIVE assumes that an IGW is currently not available.

3. Finally, the result is returned to MMIP6 in step 3.

In contrast to existing approaches, DRIVE prevents copious transmissions of service requests from the vehicles. Figure 4.15 visualises the differences between reactive approaches used in traditional service discovery protocols and the passive discovery approach deployed in DRIVE. Whereas the number of messages transmitted for traditional service discovery approaches in figure 4.15 (a) depends on the number of vehicles, the transmitted messages in DRIVE are proportional to the number of IGWs (figure 4.15 (b)). This figure also shows that the overhead caused by both methods is determined by the rate of the SA Announcements and the Service Requests as well as the routing protocol used in the VANET. This aspect is discussed in section 4.5.1. Another important benefit is that multicast traffic is not generated in the VANET since the SA Announcements in DRIVE use geocast (or hop-limited broadcast) transmission only [228]. The overhead for the discovery of IGWs in DRIVE is correlated with the location of the services. This way, overhead occurs only in the service area of an IGW: In traditional service discovery protocols, vehicles permanently have to scan

---

[4]An alternative implementation strategy may be a notification of MMIP6 if the cache was modified. This may reduce the in-vehicle processing overhead, but requires fundamental modifications and additional interfaces in the MMIP6 implementation. However, it does not affect the communication performance and signalling overhead in the VANET.

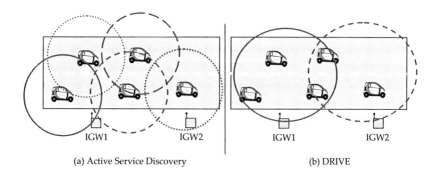

(a) Active Service Discovery   (b) DRIVE

DRIVE: Discovery of Internet Gateways from Vehicles ▫ IGW: Internet Gateway

Figure 4.15: DRIVE Discovery Process

their environment for (newly) available IGWs in order to find better-suited alternative IGWs
– even if IGWs are not available. In DRIVE, the proactive SA Announcements generate network load, too. However, this overhead occurs in a locally restricted area only since the SA
Announcements only attain to the vehicles within the service area of an IGW.

Selection Process

In the VANET scenario, the cache of the in-vehicle SA possibly contains entries of several
available IGWs. Some of them might be within the immediate transmission range of the
vehicle, or they might be accessible through several vehicles driving in front of or behind
one particular vehicle. In this situation, DRIVE has to select the "most suitable" IGW to be
used. The outcome of this selection process significantly influences the quality of service
experienced by the applications while using the selected gateway for Internet access. For
example, selecting an IGW that resides within the direct radio transmission range of a vehicle will help to keep the communication delay between vehicle and IGW low. However, it is
very likely that a new IGW must be discovered after driving out of the transmission range
of the current IGW, leaving the vehicle with a potential period of disconnection.

In order to be able to make an optimised selection, the decision process has to consider
the quality of service expectations of the applications. Therefore, DRIVE uses a flexible and
extensible classification scheme to estimate these expectations. For example, the classification scheme of the DRIVE prototype implementation comprises the properties interactivity,
streaming and real-time as described in appendix C.2. In the following, n specifies the num-

ber of different classifications for the application properties. Besides the requirements of applications, the selection mechanism in DRIVE also takes into account various sources for state information. For example, vehicles are able to determine the current traffic density based on information from other vehicles in their vicinity. IGWs provide additional state information related to the Internet access service. SA Announcements therefore carry additional information by means of attributes describing the provided service. Examples are:

▶ The current number of vehicles registered with the FA on an IGW.

▶ The utilisation of an IGW's available bandwidth.

▶ The geographical position of an IGW.

▶ Additional location-based services provided by the IGW.

The geographical position of the IGW is a very interesting information, which is used to estimate the duration of a connection as well as the communication delay between vehicle and IGW. Further parameters might also be relevant for the selection process depending on the nature of future applications deployed in the VANET scenario. These parameters can be easily integrated in DRIVE as described in appendix C.

The selection of the most suitable IGW cannot be performed with traditional mathematical methods. It is almost impossible to formalise typical traffic scenarios since the movements of vehicles depend – among other factors – on the behaviour of their human drivers. Without a detailed model of the scenario, predictions are only possible at a very high level of abstraction. Hence, DRIVE uses a fuzzy-logic-based approach [161, 160] to carry out the selection process. Fuzzy-logic-based approaches allow the formulation of coherences on very high levels of abstraction. This makes them suitable candidates for the process of selecting the most suitable IGW. A detailed discussion about the suitability of fuzzy logic for this decision process in DRIVE can be found in [229, 230, 231]. The fuzzy logic system in DRIVE implements three steps as illustrated in figure 4.16. In the first phase, a number of fuzzy engines process the available state information received from all available sources in order to predict the expected quality of service for each individual IGW. The expected quality of service is represented by expected values for communication-based parameters. Examples include the expected bandwidth, the expected number of users, or the expected packet loss rate. These predictions are very important for the decision process, because applications are more interested in the expected communication behaviour than in the current communication performance.

The second phase of the DRIVE decision process implements further fuzzy engines to evaluate the predicted quality of service by means of the application requirements. Assum-

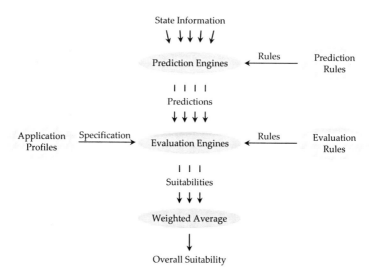

Figure 4.16: DRIVE's two-step Selection Process

ing n application classes, the fuzzy engine calculates the suitability of an IGW for each application class i $(1 \leq i \leq n)$. The defuzzification using the centroid method [160] maps the suitability for each application class onto a numerical result $s_i \in [0, 1]$. Thereby, 1 represents perfect suitability whereas a value of 0 indicates that an IGW is unsuitable for that particular application class. Finally, the third step calculates the overall suitability s for each IGW by computing a weighted average of the s_i. Thereby, weight $w_i (1 \leq i \leq n$ and $\sum_i w_i = 1)$ for an application property i expresses the preferences of the user for this application class. Hence, the overall suitability s is determined as follows:

$$s = \frac{1}{n} \cdot \sum_{i=1}^{n} w_i s_i \tag{4.1}$$

The result of this process is a list of available IGWs ordered by the overall suitability of the individual IGWs. DRIVE then returns information about the IGW with the highest overall suitability back to MMIP6. If this IGW is different from the one currently used, MMIP6 will perform a handover to the more suitable IGW as described in the following section. A high IGW density may introduce handover oscillations since the decision process is performed individually by each vehicle. This way, additional filters may be necessary to minimise such oscillations. This aspect is not considered further on since suitable filters are basically determined by the characteristics experienced in a real-world deployment of a VANET.

4.4.3   Handover Procedure

After the discovery of a more suitable IGW, the vehicle will handover its connections to the new IGW by initiating a registration procedure. Therefore, the vehicle has to register itself with both the new FA and its HA as illustrated in figure 4.17. The registration procedure is based on two messages, a *registration request* and a *registration reply*, and comprises the following four steps:

1. The vehicle sends a registration request to the FA on the prospective IGW to initiate the registration.

2. The FA processes the registration request and updates its internal list of visitors. Afterwards, it relays the registration request to the HA.

3. The HA processes the registration request by updating its mobility bindings and responds with a registration reply message to the FA to grant or to deny the request.

4. Finally, the FA processes the registration reply message and relays it to the vehicle to inform it of the disposition of its request.

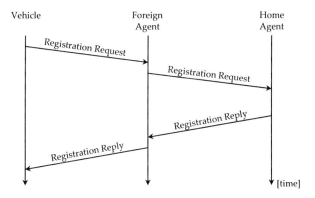

Figure 4.17: Registration Procedure in MMIP6

The specification of the message formats is given in appendix B. After the registration process has been finished successfully, the handover to the new FA is complete and communication between vehicle and Internet can be continued.

Due to the mobility of the vehicles, registrations with an IGW may become orphaned. For example, if a vehicle performs a handover to a new IGW, the former IGW still holds the vehicle in its list of visitors. The implementation of a deregistration mechanism with an IGW is not a suitable solution, because a vehicle may loose the contact to an IGW at any time and is therefore not able to explicitly deregister itself with the IGW. In order to avoid orphaned registrations, MMIP6 deploys a soft state approach similar to the design in Mobile IPv4. Thereby, the IGWs hold a soft state for the lifetime of a registration. If the lifetime of a registration expires, the IGW will delete the respective registration entry in its visitor list. The vehicle also has to hold this soft state for its registration. Before the lifetime of the state expires, the vehicle has to renew the registration with its current Foreign Agent. The lifetime is specified in the registration request message (see appendix B). In standard Mobile IPv4, the default value for the lifetime is set to 1800 s. MMIP6 does not use static values for the lifetime. Instead, MMIP6 dynamically determines the lifetime by calculating the estimated time the vehicle travels through the service area of an IGW. The lifetime can be approximated by dividing the diameter of the service area of the IGW through the current speed of the vehicle. This dynamic calculation reduces the number of renewals for the registration; in the best case, exactly one registration is necessary while travelling through the service area of an IGW.

In order to avoid vulnerabilities by non-authorised vehicles or devices, both registration request and registration reply messages can be authenticated. The authentication scheme is similar to the concept specified for Mobile IPv4 but uses the global IPv6 addresses of the vehicles instead of IPv4. Thereby, each vehicle, Foreign Agent, and Home Agent are able to support a mobility security association for mobile entities. Further details on the authentication scheme can be found in [145].

4.4.4 Optimisations

The basic protocol mechanisms of MMIP6 have been further optimised for the VANET scenario. The optimisations described in this section improve the connectivity between vehicles and reduce both the signalling overhead of MMIP6 and the overhead for communication between vehicle and IGW.

Home Address Forwarding

An important optimisation is the "Home Address Forwarding" resulting from the cooperation between the global IPv6-based address scheme and the location-based routing protocol. Figure 4.18 depicts this situation. If an IP-based application of vehicle V1 wants to communicate with another vehicle V2, the location-based routing protocol will try to find out the

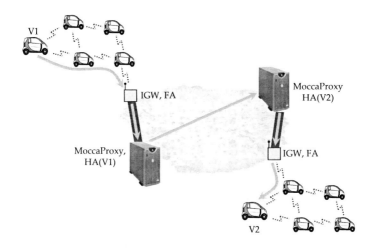

FA: Foreign Agent □ HA: Home Agent □ IGW: Internet Gateway

Figure 4.18: Home Address Forwarding

geographic position of V2 (see section 2.1.1). If multi-hop communication is not possible
between V1 and V2, e.g. due to a broken link in the route between V1 and V2, the routing
protocol will not be able to provide the position of V2. In this case, the Home Address Forwarding in MMIP6 forwards the IPv6 packets from V1 to the IGW that maintains the current
FA of V1. Therefore, it temporarily modifies the location table in order to route the IP packets for the unreachable vehicle to the FA. The FA then accepts the IP packets and tunnels
them to the HA of V1 (denoted as HA(V1)), which unpacks the IPv6 packets and forwards
them to the targeted destination address, i.e. to the IPv6 address of V2. The IPv6 packets are
then routed to the Home Agent of V2 since the IPv6 address of a vehicle always represents
the vehicle in its home network[5]. The HA of V2 treats the IPv6 packets like packets from
the Internet, i.e. they are tunnelled from HA(V2) to the current FA of V2, which unpacks the
IPv6 packet and forwards them to V2.

This way, the Home Address Forwarding enables the communication between two distant vehicles connected to the Internet via different IGWs.

---

[5]This example assumes that HA(V1) and HA(V2) are located at different MoccaProxies (cf. section 3.1.1).
Obviously, they can also be located at the same MoccaProxy.

Hierarchical Mobility Management

A second optimisation is the deployment of a hierarchical IPv6-based micro-mobility management similar to Hierarchical Mobile IPv4 [232]. This mechanism relieves the MoccaProxy from the flood of registration requests and improves the handover latency. Typically, the MoccaProxy maintains the Home Agents for several vehicles, e.g. for all vehicles from one car manufacturer. This way, the MoccaProxy has to process the incoming registration requests of all these vehicles. Moreover, the distance between the Internet Gateways and the MoccaProxy might become large. For example, if a vehicle performs handovers in a foreign country, the registration request must be processed in its Home Agent far away resulting in a handover latency of possibly several seconds.

In order to relieve the MoccaProxy and to improve the handover latency, MMIP6 allows the deployment of a hierarchy of Foreign Agents in the IGW network as exemplified in figure 4.19. Each FA implements parts of the Home Agent functionality and stores local mobility bindings for the vehicles. The FAs on the lowest layer, i.e. the FAs located on the IGWs, are called LFAs (Lowest Foreign Agents), the FAs following immediately after the HA are the HFAs (Highest Foreign Agents). Foreign Agents between HFAs and LFAs in this hierarchy are called IFAs (Intermediate Foreign Agents). If a vehicle registers itself the first time with an LFA, the registration request passes up the hierarchy until it reaches the HA. Thereby, each FA along that path to the HA establishes a mobility binding for the IPv6 address of the vehicle with the previous FA.

For example, the vehicle in figure 4.19 is first registered with LFA1 and, thus, with IFA1, HFA1, and the HA. If the vehicle performs a handover to LFA2 and initiates a registration procedure, each FA on the path along the hierarchy to the HA first checks if it has a mobility binding for the IPv6 address of the vehicle. The first FA with such a mobility binding responds with a registration reply message and updates its mobility bindings accordingly, i.e. IFA1 in figure 4.19. This way, the registration request of the vehicle is processed in LFA2 and IFA1 only. Mobility binding updates for the upper-layered HFA1 and the HA in the hierarchy are not necessary. This way, the latency of a handover can be reduced if a vehicle hands over its connections between two LFAs connected to the same IFA or HFA. Further details about the hierarchical micro mobility management of MMIP6 and its implementation can be found in [233].

Efficient IGW Address Resolution

MMIP6 additionally improves communication efficiency by minimising the routing protocol overhead. In the VANET scenario, the ad hoc routing protocol forwards data based on the location of vehicles. Before a vehicle is able to send data to a corresponding node in the

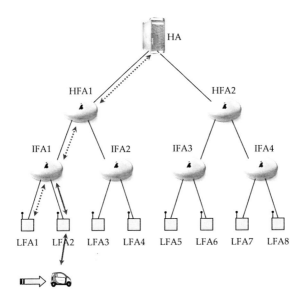

HA: Home Agent □ HFA: Highest Foreign Agent
IFA: Intermediate Foreign Agent □ LFA: Lowest Foreign Agent

Figure 4.19: Hierarchical Micro Mobility in MMIP6

Internet, the routing protocol first has to determine the geographical position of the IGW in order to be able to route the data properly (see section 2.1). For example, the location-based ad hoc routing algorithm in FleetNet has to query the location service for the position of the respective IGW. Hence, a "start-up phase" may occur before the transmission of data from the vehicle to the IGW.

However, the SA Announcements of the DRIVE protocol already contain information about the geographical position of IGWs in order to determine the distance between vehicle and IGW. Since IGWs are static and do not change their position, the vehicles can use this information to improve the latency caused by the location-based routing protocol. If MMIP6 decides to handover to a more suitable IGW, the handover procedure is extended in the following way:

1. The vehicle initiates the registration procedure.

2. After receiving a positive registration reply message from its HA, the vehicle updates

its location table with the location of the new IGW. The location table contains mappings between the IPv6 addresses of vehicles and IGWs in the VANET and their current positions.

3. Finally, MMIP6 updates its internal default gateway to the Internet with the IPv6 address of the new IGW, which completes the handover procedure.

If the vehicle sends IP packets to an Internet host through the new IGW for the first time, the location-based routing protocol will forward the data immediately since it will find an updated position for the IGW in its location table. Hence, the ad hoc routing protocol does not require a location update and, thus, avoids potential start-up phases before sending data to the Internet.

Further Optimisations

Both the handover performance and the selection of the most suitable IGW can be improved further on. Vehicles may be equipped with a navigation system providing a road map. Together with the destination, the navigation system dynamically calculates the optimal route and guides the driver to the desired destination. The navigation system may also comprise a dynamically updated map of installed Internet Gateways. This way, a vehicle has additional situation awareness and can provide predictions about its future movements, which can be utilised by MMIP6 in the following ways:

▶ The selection process of DRIVE can consider the IGW map in order to determine the most suitable IGW more accurately.

▶ The handover procedure itself can be improved, for example by using pre-registrations with a new IGW via the old IGW if the vehicle predicts both a temporary disconnection and potential IGWs in advance.

There is noticeable work on improving handovers with location-awareness [203, 234, 235, 236]. However, this aspect is not described in any more detail since it first assumes the availability of a navigation unit and a road map in the vehicle and second it is not vital for the Internet integration of VANETs.

MMIP6 also notifies the MOCCA transport layer in case of specific events such as a pending handover. This information is processed by the MOCCA transport protocol in order to react appropriately to potential short-term packet losses due to the handover. This aspect is seized in chapter 5.

4.5   Evaluation

This section evaluates MMIP6 in a quantitative and a qualitative way in order to determine the efficiency and suitability of MMIP6 in the VANET scenario. In the quantitative evaluation, the performance of DRIVE and MMIP6 is derived mathematically and compared with the performance characteristics of related work. The results are also an important input parameter for the overall evaluation of the MOCCA architecture described in chapter 6. Finally, a qualitative evaluation determines the suitability of MMIP6 for being deployed in the VANET scenario.

4.5.1   Quantitative Evaluation of DRIVE

DRIVE was designed to discover IGWs in VANETs in a scalable and efficient way. Hence, the quantitative evaluation in this section has two major goals:

1. Determine the bandwidth requirements for the IGW discovery.

2. Comparison with traditional discovery methods.

Related approaches implement different mechanisms for the discovery of IGWs and, thus, have different strengths and weaknesses. However, a fundamental principle of these approaches is the active discovery of the IGWs where vehicles actively have to discover their environment for available IGWs. The active discovery basically results in similar performance characteristics for these approaches. In order to compare DRIVE with active discovery approaches, the Service Location Protocol SLP (see section 4.3.3) is used as a representative. The SLP extension for Mobile IP belongs to the category of application-specific enhancements, which was proved to be the most suitable solution of all competing protocols with respect to the discovery of IGWs (see section 4.3.4).

The evaluation considers bandwidth requirements for the discovery of IGWs only; it does not take into account CPU and memory requirements. These requirements basically depend on the target platform and the software used for the implementation. Although they are not yet specified and standardised for automotive environments, the hardware is expected to be powerful since requirements regarding both power supply and physical space for the hardware are fulfilled in vehicles. Moreover, the evaluation only considers application-specific characteristics; the overhead caused by lower communication layers was not considered since it varies from the protocols being deployed on the lower layers.

Initial Considerations

Being radio-based, the VANET represents a physical broadcast medium. If a vehicle sends a data packet, the other vehicles in the radio transmission range will receive this packet. Vice versa, a vehicle receives every packet transmitted in its radio transmission range. This way, the average required bandwidth Bw in bits per second is determined by

$$Bw = R \cdot P \tag{4.2}$$

where R is the number of packets a vehicle receives and P is the packet size. A basic problem is to determine R appropriately since it depends on the way a packet is forwarded and distributed in the VANET. Thereby, the ad hoc routing protocol plays a fundamental role. This evaluation assumes two routing approaches reflecting the best-case scenario and the worst-case scenario as illustrated in figure 4.20:

▶ *Optimal Routing:* An optimal routing protocol minimises the number of transmissions necessary to forward a packet to its destination. In the example given in figure 4.20 (a), only the neighbouring vehicle V2 forwards the data packet towards the IGW. This way, a vehicle receives a message up to two times: from the previous forwarder of the packet, and from the next forwarder of the packet[6].

▶ *Flooding with Duplicate Detection:* Flooding means that every vehicle forwards the packets it receives. Data packets are distinguished from each other by a sequence number. If an incoming packet has the same sequence number as an already forwarded packet, the packet will be dropped in order to avoid circulating packets [237]. Hence, a data packet from vehicle V1 to the IGW in figure 4.20 (b) is forwarded by every vehicle.

Both routing protocols assume that vehicles and IGW use the same radio transmission range. The best-case scenario and the worst-case scenario considered for the evaluation represent an upper and lower boundary for the performance of an ad hoc routing protocol being deployed in a real-world VANET scenario. In contrast to the routing protocol, the IGW discovery protocol determines the number of transmitted messages. In case of traditional approaches like SLP, every vehicle transmits service request messages periodically. The number of transmitted messages in a geographical area is, thus, proportional to the number of vehicles within this area. The latter parameter is determined by the traffic density ρ. The following considerations assume a motorway or a rural area, in which ρ represents the number of vehicles per km and lane[7]. On a street segment of l km length with

---

[6]Exceptions are the vehicles at the border of the service area: they only receive data packets once.

[7]This definition is useful for the consideration of "longer" street segments. In other scenarios like a city, a more suitable definition of ρ would be the number of vehicles per km^2.

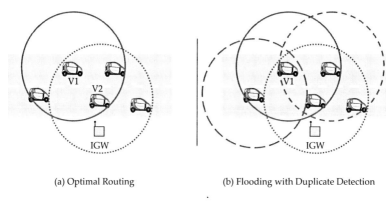

(a) Optimal Routing   (b) Flooding with Duplicate Detection

Figure 4.20: Best-Case Routing vs. Worst-Case Routing

n_{lanes} lanes (including oncoming traffic), the number of vehicles n_{veh} can be estimated by

$$n_{veh} = \rho \cdot l \cdot n_{lanes} \tag{4.3}$$

In DRIVE, the number of transmitted messages is proportional to the number of IGWs transmitting the SA Announcements periodically. The SA Announcements are distributed in a geographical area l_{geo} of each IGW, which represents the size of its service area. Therefore, the number of transmitted messages is independent of the traffic density in this area. In order to completely cover an area, the distance between two neighbouring IGWs may not be larger than two times of their radio transmission range r_{radio}. Hence, on a street segment of l km the minimum number of IGWs n_{IGW} is determined by

$$n_{IGW} = \frac{l}{2 \cdot r_{radio}} + 1 \tag{4.4}$$

DRIVE versus Traditional Discovery

With these initial considerations the bandwidth requirements $Bw_{trad,opt}$ for traditional approaches like SLP using the optimal routing can be estimated. From equations 4.2 and 4.3 follows that the upper bound of the required bandwidth $Bw_{trad,opt}$ for traditional discovery protocols in case of optimal routing is defined by the following estimation:

$$
\begin{aligned}
Bw_{trad,opt} &= R_{trad,opt} \cdot P_{trad} \\
&= R_{trad,opt} \cdot P_{SrvRqst} \\
&= R_{opt}(S_{trad}) \cdot P_{SrvRqst}
\end{aligned}
$$

$$\leq \quad 2 \cdot S_{trad} \cdot P_{SrvRqst}$$
$$= \quad 2 \cdot n_{veh,geo} \cdot f_{SrvRqst} \cdot P_{SrvRqst}$$
$$= \quad 2 \cdot l_{geo} \cdot \rho \cdot n_{lanes} \cdot f_{SrvRqst} \cdot P_{SrvRqst} \tag{4.5}$$

Thereby, R_{opt} is the number of messages received per vehicle, S_{trad} is the overall number of messages transmitted, $P_{SrvRqst}$ is the size of a service request message, and $f_{SrvRqst}$ represents the frequency a vehicle transmits the service request messages. The estimation $R_{opt}(S_{trad}) \leq 2 \cdot S_{trad}$ follows from the fact that a vehicle may receive a transmitted message up to two times using the optimal routing. Equation 4.5 does not contain the service reply messages from the IGWs responding the the service requests.

Using DRIVE, the derivation of the bandwidth requirements in case of optimal routing is similar using equation 4.4. Thereby, R_{opt} is the number of received messages per vehicle, S_{DRIVE} is the overall number of transmitted messages using DRIVE, $P_{Announce}$ is the size of an SA Announcement message and $f_{Announce}$ represents the frequency an IGW transmits the SA Announcements. Hence, $Bw_{DRIVE,opt}$ has an upper bound of

$$Bw_{DRIVE,opt} \quad = \quad R_{DRIVE,opt} \cdot P_{DRIVE}$$
$$= \quad R_{DRIVE,opt} \cdot P_{Announce}$$
$$= \quad R_{opt}(S_{DRIVE}) \cdot P_{Announce}$$
$$\leq \quad 2 \cdot S_{DRIVE} \cdot P_{Announce}$$
$$= \quad 2 \cdot n_{IGW,geo} \cdot f_{Announce} \cdot P_{Announce}$$
$$= \quad 2 \cdot \left(\frac{l_{geo}}{2 \cdot r_{radio}} + 1 \right) \cdot f_{Announce} \cdot P_{Announce} \tag{4.6}$$

These estimations allow for a comparison of traditional discovery with DRIVE. In order to determine the overhead, table 4.6 summarises the values used for the different parameters. The packet size used for Service Requests and SA Announcements reflect realistic sizes [229]. The results are compared in figure 4.21, which shows the bandwidth requirements for SLP (upper figure) and DRIVE (lower figure) against the traffic density. For the ordinates in both figures, different scales are necessary to visualise the results appropriately. The different curves represent different frequencies used to transmit Service Requests ('SrvRqst' in case of SLP) respectively SA Announcements ('Announcement' in case of DRIVE). Using an optimal routing protocol, the bandwidth requirements of traditional discovery mechanisms increase with the number of vehicles whereas they remain constant with DRIVE. Another important observation is the difference regarding the effective bandwidth consumption. In case of one SA Announcement per second, the bandwidth requirements of DRIVE for, e.g., 20 vehicles is 10.56 kbit/s whereas SLP consumes 1.408 Mbit/s. The consumption of SLP is

Parameter	Description	Default Value
$f_{Announce}$	Frequency of SA Announcement Transmissions	(variable)
$f_{SrvRqst}$	Frequency of Service Request Transmissions	(variable)
l_{geo}	Size of Service Area	10 km
$n_{IGW,geo}$	Average Number of IGWs in Geocast Region	(variable)
n_{lane}	Number of Lanes (both Directions)	4 lanes
$n_{veh,geo}$	Average Number of Vehicles in Geocast Region	(variable)
$n_{veh,neigh}$	Average Number of Vehicles in Transmission Range	(variable)
ρ	Traffic Density	(variable)
$P_{SrvRqst}$	Packet Size for a Service Request	110 byte
$P_{Announce}$	Packet Size for an SA Announcement	110 byte
r_{radio}	Radio Transmission Range	1 km

Table 4.6: Default Values for the Evaluation

further multiplied with the number of IGWs in the service area, because each IGW has to respond to each Service Request with a Service Reply message.

The situation is different when flooding with duplicate detection is used to forward data packets. Thereby, a vehicle transmitting a message will receive this message from all neighboured vehicles, i.e. $n_{veh,neigh}$ times. Using the traditional discovery methods of SLP, the bandwidth requirements $Bw_{trad,flood}$ can be estimated by the following equation; the bandwidth required for the transmission of the service replies from the IGWs is not considered in this equation:

$$
\begin{aligned}
Bw_{trad,flood} &= R_{trad,flood} \cdot P_{trad} \\
&= R_{trad,flood} \cdot P_{SrvRqst} \\
&= n_{veh,neigh} \cdot n_{veh,geo} \cdot f_{SrvRqst} \cdot P_{SrvRqst} \\
&\leq 2 \cdot r_{radio} \cdot \rho \cdot n_{lanes} \cdot n_{veh,geo} \cdot f_{SrvRqst} \cdot P_{SrvRqst} \\
&= 2 \cdot r_{radio} \cdot (\rho \cdot n_{lanes})^2 \cdot l_{geo} \cdot f_{SrvRqst} \cdot P_{SrvRqst}
\end{aligned}
\tag{4.7}
$$

Similarly, the following coherences can be derived for DRIVE in case of flooding the vehicular ad hoc network:

$$
Bw_{DRIVE,flood} = R_{DRIVE,flood} \cdot P_{DRIVE}
$$

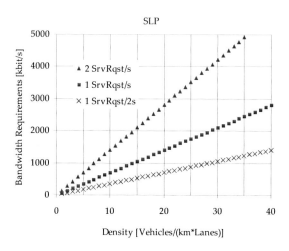

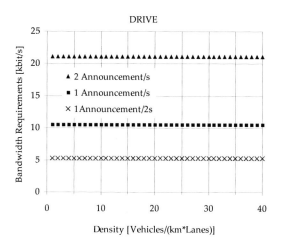

Figure 4.21: SLP vs. DRIVE (Optimal Routing)

$$
\begin{aligned}
&= R_{DRIVE,flood} \cdot P_{Announce} \\
&= n_{veh,neigh} \cdot n_{IGW,geo} \cdot f_{Announce} \cdot P_{Announce} \\
&\leq 2 \cdot r_{radio} \cdot \rho \cdot n_{lanes} \cdot n_{IGW,geo} \cdot f_{Announce} \cdot P_{Announce} \\
&= 2 \cdot r_{radio} \cdot \rho \cdot n_{lanes} \cdot \left(\frac{l_{geo}}{2 \cdot r_{radio}} + 1 \right) \cdot f_{Announce} \cdot P_{Announce} \qquad (4.8)
\end{aligned}
$$

In the worst-case scenario using flooding with duplicate detection, the traffic density ρ occurs as a quadratic factor in traditional discovery protocols, whereas it is a linear factor in the bandwidth estimation of DRIVE. Figure 4.22 visualises the dependency between the bandwidth requirements and the traffic density for both SLP and DRIVE. Similar to figure 4.21, different scales are necessary to visualise the differences. The parameters were set according to table 4.6. Like in the optimal routing scenario, the bandwidth required for DRIVE is significantly lower compared to SLP. For example, if the traffic density is 20 vehicles per km and lane, DRIVE requires 844.4 kbit/s whereas the consumption of SLP is 112.64 Mbit/s. This value is multiplied with the number of IGWs that respond to the service request. However, this example also illustrates the significant impact of the routing protocol. With the same parameters, the required bandwidth using DRIVE with an optimal routing algorithm is 10.56 kbit/s compared to 844.4 kbit/s in the worst-case.

The bandwidth requirements also depend on the size of the service area of an IGW. Figure 4.23 shows this coherence for a traffic density of 20 vehicles and a transmission rate for the Service Request and SA Announcement messages of $f_{SrvRqst} = f_{Announce} = 1\,\text{Hz}$. This figure also illustrates the impact of the radio transmission range r_{radio} for the DRIVE protocol using $r_{radio} = 1\,\text{km}$ and $r_{radio} = 0.5\,\text{km}$. This differentiation is not necessary for SLP using an optimal routing protocol, because r_{radio} does not affect the estimation of the bandwidth requirements in this case (equation 4.5). A noticeable result is that using DRIVE with flooding requires less bandwidth than SLP over an optimal ad hoc routing protocol for a service area of more than 2 km.

The comparison in this section shows that DRIVE requires significantly less bandwidth compared to traditional discovery concepts: At a traffic density of 20 vehicles/km, DRIVE requires only 0.75 % (flooding) respectively 7.5 % (optimal routing) of the overhead caused by traditional service discovery. The overhead of traditional discovery protocols increases with the number of vehicles, whereas the overhead in DRIVE is basically determined by the number of IGWs. This way, a general conclusion is that DRIVE provides a scalable mechanism to discover IGWs in VANETs. Without any knowledge about the availability of IGWs, the overhead caused by DRIVE can even be seen as the minimum overhead necessary for the discovery of IGWs. However, the comparison also showed the significant impact of the routing protocol deployed: Using DRIVE, an optimal routing strategy requires only 1.25 % of the overhead compared to flooding with duplicate detection. The overhead is also determined

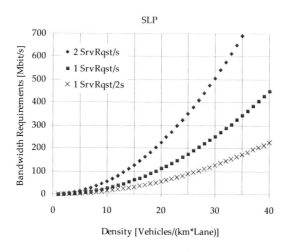

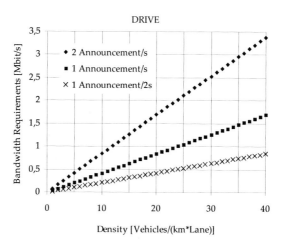

Figure 4.22: SLP vs. DRIVE (Flooding)

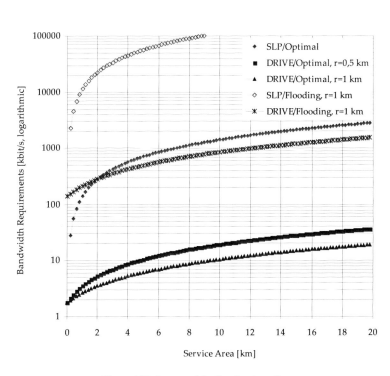

Figure 4.23: Impact of the Service Area Size

by the configuration parameters of DRIVE, namely the frequency of the SA Announcements, the radio transmission range, and the size of the service area. A general definition of suitable default values for these parameters is difficult since they need to be chosen carefully with respect to the capabilities of a real-word VANET scenario. These parameters should be chosen dynamically depending on other factors like, e.g., the traffic density on the road: For example, higher values for frequency, service area and radio transmission range may be advantageous for an empty motorway whereas in case of a congestion a reduction of these parameters would reduce the overhead without significant delays for the discovery of IGWs.

4.5.2 Mathematical Evaluation of MMIP6

MMIP6 produces additional overhead in the VANET, which is derived mathematically and evaluated qualitatively in this section. In addition, this evaluation investigates latency aspects of MMIP6 in two important situations: in case of a handover and the detection of a disconnection.

Besides the network traffic caused by DRIVE, the MMIP6 registration procedure produces additional signalling overhead. The registration procedure is triggered in the following situations:

▶ A handover to a new IGW is performed.

▶ The registration lifetime expires and needs to be renewed.

The average overhead for the registrations basically depends on the size of the registration messages, the routing protocol being deployed in the VANET, and the time interval between two consecutive registrations. Like in the previous section, the two routing protocols 'optimal' and 'flooding with duplicate detection' are used for the investigations. With the help of equation 4.4 for optimal routing and equation 4.3 for flooding, equation 4.9 estimates an upper bound for the required average bandwidth Bw_{Reg} of one vehicle for both ad hoc routing protocols. Table 4.7 describes the parameters used in this equation. Thereby, the function $fwd()$ specifies the average number of hops the respective message is forwarded within the VANET. In order to determine the frequency of the registrations $freq_{reg}$, equation 4.9 estimates this frequency by the inverse of the average time a vehicle requires to pass through the service area of the IGW, which is $\frac{v}{l_{geo}}$.

$$Bw_{Reg} = \left(P_{RegRqst} \cdot fwd(RegRqst) + P_{RegRply} \cdot fwd(RegRply) \right) \cdot freq_{reg}$$

Parameter	Description
$delay_{link}$	Transmission and Processing Delay per Link/Vehicle
$freq_{reg}$	Average Frequency of the Registrations
$fwd(msg)$	Number of relaying Vehicles for a Message
l_{geo}	Size of the Service Area
n_{lanes}	Number of Lanes
$P_{RegRply}$	Packet Size for a Registration Reply
$P_{RegRqst}$	Packet Size for a Registration Request
ρ	Traffic Density
r_{radio}	Radio Transmission Range
$t_{Announce}$	Time to the next Receipt of an SA Announcement
t_{FA}	Max. Processing Time in the FA for a RegRqst/RegRply
t_{HA}	Processing Time in the HA
$t_{locMissed}$	Timeout if an IPv6 address cannot be resolved to its Location
$t_{locQuery}$	Max. Time to resolve an IPv6 Address onto its Location
t_{relay}	Max. Relay Time between FA and HA for a RegRqst/RegRply
v	Average Vehicle Speed

Table 4.7: Parameters for the Evaluation of MMIP6

$$
\begin{aligned}
\leq \quad & \left\{
\begin{array}{ll}
\left(P_{RegRqst} + P_{RegRply} \right) \cdot \frac{l_{geo}}{2 \cdot r_{radio}} \cdot freq_{reg} & \text{(optimal routing)} \\
\left(P_{RegRqst} + P_{RegRply} \right) \cdot \rho \cdot n_{lanes} \cdot l_{geo} \cdot freq_{reg} & \text{(flooding)}
\end{array}
\right. \\
\approx \quad & \left\{
\begin{array}{ll}
\left(P_{RegRqst} + P_{RegRply} \right) \cdot \frac{v}{2 \cdot r_{radio}} & \text{(optimal routing)} \\
\left(P_{RegRqst} + P_{RegRply} \right) \cdot \rho \cdot n_{lanes} \cdot v & \text{(flooding)}
\end{array}
\right.
\end{aligned}
\tag{4.9}
$$

Equation 4.9 clearly shows the significant impact of the routing protocol being deployed in the VANET. The following numerical example clarifies this impact and gives an impression about the required bandwidth for the registration procedure in a real-world scenario. Assuming no extensions in the registration messages, a registration request has a length of 60 byte, and a registration reply is 44 byte long (cf. appendix B). Assuming a service area $l_{geo} = 10$ km, a radio transmission range of $r_{radio} = 1$ km, a traffic density of

$\rho = 20$ vehicles/km, four lanes, and an average speed of $v = 100$ km/h, the registration procedure consumes 11.57 bit/s when optimal routing is used whereas flooding requires 1,386.67 bit/s per vehicle. Multiplied with the traffic density, the overall bandwidth requirements are 0.17 kbit/s (optimal routing) respectively 20.8 kbit/s for flooding.

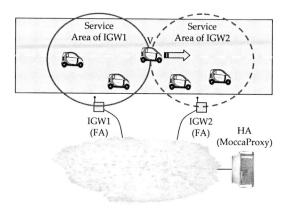

FA: Foreign Agent □ HA: Home Agent □ IGW: Internet Gateway

Figure 4.24: Worst-Case Scenario for a Handover without Disconnection

Besides the signalling overhead of MMIP6, the latency also plays an important role for the performance investigations. The derivation of delays caused by MMIP6 for the mobility management is based on a mathematical analysis similar to [238, 239, 240, 241]. An interesting aspect is the latency for the handover to a new IGW. In the worst-case scenario, the service area of two neighbouring IGWs is organised as illustrated in figure 4.24. Thereby, vehicle V moves out of the service area of IGW1 into the service area of IGW2. MMIP6 then has to wait until it receives the first SA Announcement of the new gateway, denoted as $t_{Announce}$. MMIP6 then starts the registration procedure, i.e. it sends a registration request to the FA via $fwd()$ hops with a transmission delay including a processing delay of $delay_{link}$ for each intermediate vehicle. The FA processes the request and relays it to the HA, which is represented by t_{relay}. After the processing time t_{HA}, the HA transmits the registration reply back to the FA, which itself processes the registration reply. The FA then has to find the position of the vehicle, which takes $t_{locQuery}$, and finally forwards the reply to the vehicle. Hence, the overall delay for a handover $delay_{HO}$ is calculated by adding the individual delays in the following way:

$$
\begin{aligned}
delay_{HO} \quad &\approx \quad t_{Announce} + fwd(RegRqst) \cdot delay_{link} + t_{FA,RegRqst} + t_{relay} + \\
&\qquad t_{HA} + t_{relay} + t_{FA,RegRply} + t_{locQuery} + fwd(RegRply) \cdot delay_{link} \\
&\leq \quad \frac{1}{f_{Announce}} + \frac{l_{geo}}{2 \cdot r_{radio}} \cdot delay_{link} + t_{FA} + t_{relay} + \\
&\qquad t_{HA} + t_{relay} + t_{FA} + t_{locQuery} + \frac{l_{geo}}{2 \cdot r_{radio}} \cdot delay_{link} \\
&= \quad \frac{1}{f_{Announce}} + \frac{l_{geo} \cdot delay_{link}}{r_{radio}} + 2t_{FA} + 2t_{relay} + t_{HA} + t_{locQuery} \qquad (4.10)
\end{aligned}
$$

Table 4.7 gives an overview for the parameters used in this equation. Thereby, the variable $t_{Announce}$ is limited by the inverse frequency of the SA Announcements. The delay between the targeted vehicle and the IGW can be estimated by the minimum number of hops between vehicle and IGW, i.e. by $\frac{l_{geo}}{2r_{radio}}$. This delay is basically independent of the routing protocol: in case of an optimal ad hoc routing protocol, the shortest route between vehicle and Internet Gateway is used, which can be assumed to provide the shortest delay. In case of flooding, the shortest route is implicitly included since all vehicles in the service area forward the messages. This way, the delay is also determined by the shortest route between vehicle and IGW.

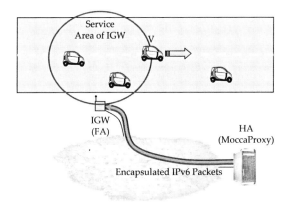

FA: Foreign Agent ∘ HA: Home Agent ∘ IGW: Internet Gateway

Figure 4.25: Worst-Case Scenario for a Disconnection

The second important time aspect is the delay until the MoccaProxy detects a disconnection of a vehicle from its IGW. Figure 4.25 depicts the worst-case situation for the delay estimations. Thereby, a vehicle V travels out of an IGW's service area after the MoccaProxy transmits an IPv6 packet to the vehicle. Hence, the IPv6 packet is first tunnelled from the HA to the FA and processed by the FA. Afterwards, the FA tries to resolve the IPv6 address of the targeted vehicle onto its current geographical position. In case of a successful resolution, the IGW will detect that the vehicle is outside of its service area. Otherwise, the location service of the location-based ad hoc routing protocol will respond with a failure message after a specified timeout. Hence, the delay for the location query is upper-bound to this timeout, i.e. $t_{locQuery} \leq t_{locMissed}$. After this time, the FA notifies the HA about the disconnection with an ICMP 'destination unreachable' message that is finally processed by the HA. Hence, the overall delay $delay_{Disc}$ to detect a disconnection is estimated as follows:

$$delay_{Disc} \approx t_{relay} + t_{FA} + t_{locQuery} + t_{relay} + t_{HA}$$
$$\leq 2t_{relay} + t_{FA} + t_{locMissed} + t_{HA} \tag{4.11}$$

4.5.3 Qualitative Evaluation

Table 4.4 summarises the qualitative evaluation of MMIP6. From its fundamental characteristics, MMIP6 belongs to the category of service discovery enhancements. This way, it has similar mobility support characteristics: MMIP6 supports both the mobility of vehicles and a mobile Internet access independent of the current location. MMIP6 also fulfils the 'Seamless Mobility' requirement since it provides the mobility support for vehicles similar to Mobile IPv4. If a vehicle has Internet access via an IGW, Internet hosts can communicate with the vehicle transparently and connections are handed over if a vehicle is able to communicate with a new IGW.

Approach	Mobility Support		VANET Networking		MOCCA Cooperation	Scalability & Efficiency
	Internet Access	Seamless Mobility	Ad Hoc Networks	Characteristics		
MMIP6	+ +	+ +	+ +	+ +	+ +	+

Table 4.8: Evaluation of MMIP6

An important property of MMIP6 is its focus on VANETs. The integrated DRIVE protocol discovers Internet Gateways in highly dynamical ad hoc networks even over multiple hops. Moreover, DRIVE is specifically tailored to the vehicular environment: The protocol mechanisms are independent of the routing protocol being deployed in the VANET and do not require multicast support. Hence, it can be easily implemented for prevalent location-based or IP-based ad hoc routing protocols. The intelligent selection of the most suitable IGW using fuzzy logic can improve the quality of service support dynamically for applications running on the vehicular platform. Hence, the two VANET networking requirements 'Ad Hoc Networks' and 'Characteristics' are both evaluated with '+ +'.

In contrast to application-specific enhancements, MMIP6 is seamlessly integrated into the MOCCA architecture. MMIP6 is based on IPv6, and modifications of components in the Internet infrastructure and in the end systems attached to the Internet are not necessary. The MMIP6 design ensures that IP packets in both directions are always routed through the MoccaProxy. As a result, the 'MOCCA Cooperation' requirement is completely fulfilled.

The scalability of a mobility management protocol is basically determined by the discovery of IGWs since the overhead caused by the registration procedure is negligible compared to the IGW discovery. The discussion in section 4.5.1 showed that the proactive DRIVE protocol scales well even with an increasing number of vehicles compared to traditional discovery protocols. Together with different optimisations, the evaluation of MMIP6 showed that the signalling overhead is low and communication is very efficient. Besides the overhead caused by the VANET routing protocol, the scalability is mainly determined by the number of IGWs, their service areas, and the frequency of the SA Announcements that must be carefully planned and configured to maintain the scalability and efficiency in a real-world deployment. Nevertheless, there is still optimisation potential if knowledge about the availability of gateways can be assumed. For example, the navigation unit of a vehicle may additionally comprise an overview about the available IGWs that is updated each time a vehicle passes an IGW. This information can be additionally used to reduce the overhead for the IGW discovery further on. Hence, the 'Scalability & Efficiency' requirement is evaluated with '+'.

4.6   Summary

Mobility management is a challenging task for the Internet integration of vehicular ad hoc networks. Besides the mobility support of the vehicles, the peculiarities of VANETs must be considered and it must be possible to integrate a suitable solution into the MOCCA architecture. Furthermore, vehicular networks typically show a highly dynamical network topology and may become very large. Hence, the mobility management of the vehicles must be scalable and efficient. An observation of related work for the Internet integration of ad hoc networks showed that none of the previously proposed solutions fulfils these requirements sufficiently.

In MOCCA, the mobility management is performed by MMIP6, the MOCCA Mobile IPv6. MMIP6 deploys basic protocol mechanisms from Mobile IPv4 but is designed to operate in IPv6-based ad hoc networking environments. For the discovery of Internet Gateways, MMIP6 implements a novel service discovery protocol called DRIVE. DRIVE features a proactive discovery approach suitable for being deployed in large-scale communication environments. Moreover, DRIVE is highly tailored to the characteristics of vehicular network scenarios: its services are specified independently of the ad hoc routing protocol and they can be easily implemented together with location-based and IP-based routing protocols. If several Internet Gateways are available simultaneously, a fuzzy logic engine in DRIVE is able to determine the most suitable gateway based on available information about the VANET and the gateways.

| Approach | Mobility Support | | VANET Networking | | MOCCA Coopera-tion | Scalability & Efficiency |
	Internet Access	Seamless Mobility	Ad Hoc Networks	Charac-teristics		
Mobile IPv6	+	++	--	--	o	--
Ad Hoc Routing Extensions	++	++	++	--	-	--
Application-Layer Mobile IP	++	++	++	--	--	--
Service Discovery Enhancements	++	++	++	-	o	--
MMIP6	++	++	++	++	++	+

Table 4.9: Evaluation Summary for Mobility Management

In order to determine the suitability of mobility management protocols, MMIP6 was evaluated and compared with existing related approaches for the mobility management of ad hoc networks. Table 4.9 summarises the results of this comparison. It shows that MMIP6 is a suitable candidate for the mobility management of vehicles: it provides a scalable and efficient mobility support for the vehicles, it takes the typical characteristics of vehicular ad hoc networks into consideration, and it is compatible to the MOCCA architecture. Due to the proactive discovery of DRIVE, scalability is maintained since the signalling overhead of MMIP6 is proportional to the number of gateways. In contrast, the overhead of related approaches depends on the number of vehicles. Therefore, these approaches do not provide the scalability for being deployed in large-scale VANETs. However, the evaluation of

MMIP6 also showed that there is a conflict of objective between the signalling overhead on the one hand and the responsiveness and convergence to the real-world situation on the other hand: The quicker the convergence, the more signalling overhead occurs. Another interesting observation of the evaluation is the significant impact of the routing protocol deployed in the vehicular ad hoc network. Investigations with an optimal routing protocol and a flooding approach with duplicate detection showed that the efficiency of both data delivery and data distribution is vitally important for a reduction of communication overhead.

The characteristics of MMIP6 are fundamental for the efficiency of the transmission of data at the transport layer, because it can provide useful information for the transport layer protocol. This aspect is seized in the following chapter, which describes the MOCCA transport layer.

Chapter 5

MCTP – MOCCA Transport Protocol

The transport layer resides between the network layer and the application layers. Therefore, it has to provide communication services to applications or application-based protocols running on different hosts. The most important transport protocols used in the Internet are the User Datagram Protocol (UDP) and the Transmission Control Protocol (TCP). UDP provides an unreliable and connectionless service whereas TCP provides a reliable and connection-oriented service. In the Internet, both protocols operate on top of the unreliable Internet Protocol IP. The consideration of the transport layer service is important for vehicular environments since transport protocols also implement several protocol mechanisms that highly determine the communication performance experienced by the applications.

The wide use of TCP and UDP also affects the Internet integration of VANETs: Since it is practically not possible to modify all hosts attached to the Internet, both TCP and UDP must be supported for communication with Internet hosts. Section 3 already introduced the basic architecture of the transport layer in MOCCA, which is segmented into two parts as illustrated in figure 5.1: Communication in the Internet (right hand side) and communication in the VANET cloud (left hand side). Communication in the Internet is still based on TCP and UDP. Thereby, the MoccaProxy acts as a performance enhancing proxy for TCP-based communication between vehicles and Internet hosts. This raises the need for a suitable transport protocol for communication between vehicles and the MoccaProxy.

This chapter introduces MCTP, an optimised transport protocol for the MOCCA architecture. MCTP combines several TCP enhancements in order to improve communication efficiency in the VANET scenario. It is highly integrated into the MOCCA architecture and operates in close interaction with the MOCCA communication protocols. The very basic idea of MCTP is to utilise available information and notifications from the network layer to distinguish between different communication states. MCTP therefore controls and configures TCP accordingly in order to improve its behaviour in these situations.

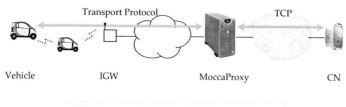

Figure 5.1: Transport Layer in MOCCA

This chapter begins in section 5.1 with a discussion of TCP, its congestion control mechanisms, and their suitability for communication in VANETs. Based on these investigations, section 5.2 derives the requirements for a transport protocol in MOCCA and discusses related work on improving the efficiency of TCP in mobile environments. MCTP, the transport protocol used in MOCCA, is introduced in section 5.3, which describes the basic principles of MCTP, its protocol state machine, and optional optimisations for further performance improvements. The qualitative evaluation of MCTP is addressed in section 5.4. Finally, section 5.5 concludes this chapter with a summary.

5.1 TCP in Vehicular Ad Hoc Networks

Originally, TCP was standardised in RFC 793 [242]. It provides a connection-oriented and reliable data delivery service for the application layers. After establishing a connection between two applications, TCP structures the byte stream into segments and ensures that the segments are delivered to their destination in a reliable manner. Therefore, TCP supports several protocol mechanisms [243]:

► Segmentation and reassembly to structure the byte stream into segments and vice versa.

► Timers and retransmissions for lost segments.

► Reordering of segments arriving out of order.

► Transmission error detection.

► Appropriate segment size discovery.

► Flow control and congestion control mechanisms.

Over the years, several enhancements and improvements were introduced that are already integrated in today's protocol stack implementations of most operating systems. The enhancements concerning the congestion control are described below.

TCP was developed and optimised for communication networks with a fixed topology. This way, it works well in wired networks and provides an acceptable performance in terms of data throughput. However, the characteristics of mobile networks in general and VANETs in particular differ fundamentally from wired networks as already discussed in section 2.1. This way, TCP provides a poor throughput in multi-hop ad hoc networks although a higher throughput might be possible in theory [244, 245, 246, 247]. This performance degradation mainly results from the flow and congestion control mechanisms deployed in TCP, which ultimately determine the amount of data in flight between a sender and a receiver and therefore the throughput of TCP.

5.1.1 Congestion Control in TCP

TCP implements a sliding window technique for the flow control algorithm. Thereby, the *window size* specifies the maximum number of unacknowledged bytes that can be sent into the network. TCP transmits segments into the network as long as it does not exceed the window size. Then, it has to wait until the communication peer acknowledges successfully received segments. TCP acknowledges segments cumulatively, i.e. an acknowledgement acknowledges all segments transmitted previously. The window size is determined by the currently computed congestion window from the sender and the advertised window from the receiver. The TCP flow control algorithm tries to mitigate congestion by controlling the window size. The congestion control consists of two dominant algorithms: *slow start* and *congestion avoidance*. Figure 5.2 illustrates the behaviour of both algorithms.

The slow start algorithm is specified in RFC 2001 [248]. It was developed to avoid congestion collapses in the network. The basic idea of the slow start is to control the data segments in the beginning of a data transfer as well as in case of segment losses. The slow start algorithm defines a *congestion window* (cwnd) to determine the number of segments that can be transmitted without waiting for an acknowledgement from the communication peer. In the beginning of the slow start phase, the congestion window is initialised with one segment. The slow start algorithm increases the value of cwnd at an exponential rate: If the communication peer acknowledges a segment before a retransmission timeout (RTO) expires, the size of the congestion window is doubled (see figure 5.2). The current value for the RTO is derived from the round trip time (RTT)[1] permanently measured while exchanging data [249]. The exponential growth of cwnd continues with each acknowledged segment until

---

[1] Actually, the RTO is equal to the sum of the smoothed RTT and four times its mean deviation

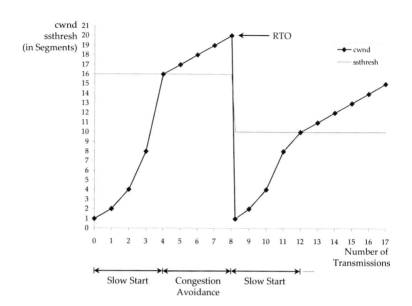

cwnd: Congestion Window ▫ ssthresh: Slow Start Threshold ▫ RTO: Retransmission Timeout

Figure 5.2: Congestion Control in TCP

the value of the congestion window reaches the *slow start threshold size* (ssthresh), which is at transmission number 4 in figure 5.2.

At this time, the slow start phase is followed by the congestion avoidance phase, which realises an "additive increase, multiplicative decrease" algorithm [250]. In the beginning, the value of cwnd increases linearly in order to probe for any spare capacity. The linear increase occurs approximately every RTT and will be continued until an RTO occurs (at transmission number 8 in figure 5.2). The congestion avoidance algorithm then sets the value of ssthresh to half of the current cwnd, and the cwnd itself is reset to one segment. Afterwards, TCP enters the slow start phase and communication continues as described previously. This behaviour causes a "sawtooth-like" behaviour of the window size.

The original flow control in TCP was improved over time. An example is the *fast retransmit/fast recovery* algorithm specified in RFC 2581 [251]. This algorithm is used when segments are dropped in the network, for example due to buffer overflows in intermediate routers. In this situation, the receiver of the missing segment transmits duplicate acknowledgements to inform the sender that the connection is still alive but that segments were not delivered to the receiver. If the sender receives three or more duplicate acknowledgements for one segment, it will retransmit the outstanding segments to the receiver without waiting for the expiry of the RTO. This mechanism is called fast retransmit. After the fast retransmit, the sender performs a fast recovery in the following way:

1. If three duplicate acknowledgements arrive at the sender, the value of ssthresh will be set to the minimum of cwnd and the window size.

2. For each acknowledgement received, the value of cwnd is increased by the segment size, and the sender transmits a new segment.

3. If an acknowledgement for the transmitted segment arrives at the sender, it also acknowledges the previous segments cumulatively. The value of cwnd will be set to the value of ssthresh and the congestion avoidance algorithm restarts as described previously.

Fast retransmit/fast recovery was first introduced in TCP Reno, the implementation currently integrated in common operating systems.

5.1.2 Impact of Vehicular Ad Hoc Networks

Originally, TCP was developed for wired networks with low bit error rates and low variances concerning bandwidth and delay. However, communication in multi-hop ad hoc networks in general and VANETs in particular is different compared to communication in the fixed Internet: On the one hand, vehicles are highly mobile and therefore the topology of the VANET is subject of a permanent reconfiguration or partitioning. On the other hand, communication is based on wireless radio technology resulting in variations of the transmission quality. Several studies investigated the impact of these aspects on the performance of TCP. For example, [252] studied the impact of the ad hoc routing protocol and [253, 254] examined the effects of the wireless transmission for the performance of TCP. Based on the investigations in this work, the following observations can be concluded with respect to the characteristics of VANETs:

▶ *Bandwidth:* Compared to wired networks, the available bandwidth in a VANET is rather low. Since radio propagation provides a shared medium, communicating vehicles have to compete for the available bandwidth. This way, the available data rate can vary heavily over time. The permanently changing number of communicating vehicles further aggravates this effect.

▶ *Delays and Jitter:* In general, VANETs exhibit higher transmission delays [255] due to the wireless communication. Moreover, the mobility of the vehicles introduces a potential jitter if the topology changes or if the underlying ad hoc routing protocol decides to use an alternative route for the IP packets.

▶ *Segment Losses:* Wireless transmission links are error-prone resulting in a higher rate of packet losses compared to fixed network technologies. Moreover, multi-hop communication further degrades the packet loss probability with each additional wireless hop between sender and receiver.

▶ *Temporary Disconnections:* The reconfiguration of the VANET topology also may partition the VANET resulting in a broken communication path between sender and receiver. Hence, communication may be interrupted until the ad hoc routing protocol finds an alternative path or until the separated network partitions are reconnected again. Moreover, vehicles will only have a temporary connection to the Internet as long as they travel into the service area of an IGW. Hence, vehicles may become disconnected even for a longer period of time if IGWs are not available.

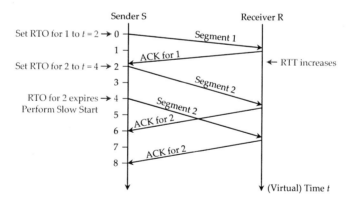

ACK: Acknowledgement ▫ RTO: Retransmission Timeout ▫ RTT: Round Trip Time

Figure 5.3: Impact of Varying Round Trip Times on the Retransmission Timeout

The conservative flow control used in TCP was not developed for such network characteristics resulting in performance degradations of TCP in mobile and wireless environments [9, 256]. As described in the previous section, TCP approximates itself to the available bandwidth using slow start and congestion avoidance. However, the varying bandwidth in VANETs requires a permanent adaptation, and TCP therefore has to perform the slow start frequently. Jitter has a similar impact on the congestion control since it causes high variations in the RTT. Yet the RTT is one of the fundamental parameters for the calculation of the RTO. The example given in figure 5.3 illustrates this impact where segment 1 is acknowledged in time. If the RTT between S and R increases, the RTO for segment 2 will expire at $t = 4$, segment 2 will be retransmitted, and TCP will enter the slow start. This way, a too small value for the RTO burdens the network with needless retransmissions and limits the number of simultaneous TCP segments in the network too restrictively. Vice versa, an overestimated RTO results in large latencies for lost segments, which also decreases the TCP throughput.

Another negative effect is that standard TCP is not able to distinguish between congestion in the network and transmission errors. In general, TCP interprets transmission errors as congestions in the network: The RTO expires and, thus, the slow start phase is activated. Even with the use of automatic request and repeat (ARQ) and forward error correction (FEC), the bit error rate in wireless networks is orders of magnitude higher compared to wired networks. Hence, TCP will hardly leave the slow start phase, which significantly reduces the data throughput although enough bandwidth is available. This effect is amplified by the long RTTs in VANETs. The rate at which a TCP sender increases its cwnd is directly proportional to the rate of the acknowledgements received. This way, the cwnd increases at a much lower rate due to the longer RTTs.

TCP also has problems with temporary disconnections, which might be caused by partitioned ad hoc networks or by the temporary Internet access provided by the IGWs. In order to reduce the overhead in case of congestions, TCP increases the RTO for a segment exponentially with each expiry. This exponential backoff is also known as "Karn's Algorithm". According to RFC 2988 [249], the retransmission timer may be limited at an upper bound of at least 60 s; in the Linux operating system, the maximum retransmission timer may increase up to 120 s. This way, it can take up to two minutes to detect a reconnection after a longer period of disconnection. In this time, TCP does not transmit any segments although the sender and receiver are able to communicate with each other.

5.2   Requirements and Related Work

Over the years, TCP evolved and was enhanced by several new protocol features. For example, TCP Reno introduced fast retransmit/fast recovery (cf. section 5.1.1), which was further improved in TCP New Reno according to RFC 2582 [257]. Furthermore, TCP was enhanced by selective acknowledgements (TCP SACK, RFC 2018 [258]) and forward acknowledgements (TCP FACK, [259]). These extensions are already integrated in current TCP implementations of common operating systems like Linux [260, 261].

However, such extensions do not solve the basic problems of TCP running in mobile and wireless environments. This way, TCP still provides a poor performance in the VANET scenario, i.e. for communication between a vehicle and the MoccaProxy [9, 262]. Based on the typical VANET characteristics described in section 2.1, an optimised transport protocol for MOCCA has to address the following aspects as summarised in figure 5.4:

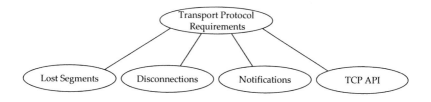

API: Application Programming Interface

Figure 5.4: Requirements for an Optimised Transport Protocol

► *Lost Segments:* An optimised transport protocol should be able to react efficiently to lost segments caused by transmission errors on the wireless link. In case of TCP, frequent slow starts should be avoided.

► *Disconnections:* An optimised transport protocol should be able to handle short-term or longer-term periods of disconnection caused by a partitioning of the VANET or in case an IGW is not available for Internet access.

► *Notifications:* The routing protocol or intermediate vehicles are typically able to notify the communicating peers about network or link characteristics. For example, if the routing protocol detects a partitioning of the VANET the optimised transport protocol should support such notifications in order to react quickly.

▶ *TCP API:* In order to alleviate the development and porting of applications for the VANET scenario, the transport protocol should provide a socket-like application programming interface (API) for the applications.

In order to improve the end-to-end communication efficiency at the transport layer, related work can be classified into the following three categories[2] [49, 263, 264]: (i) Pure congestion control modifications of TCP, (ii) utilisation of information from intermediate systems, and (iii) completely new transport protocols not based on TCP. The following sections introduce these three categories and finally discusses them with the requirements summarised in figure 5.4.

5.2.1 Congestion Control Modifications

The conservative congestion control mechanisms in TCP are the main reasons for the inefficiency of TCP in mobile environments. Hence, an obvious way to increase performance is to modify the congestion control in TCP. A noticeable amount of work tries to predict different situations based on local information. With the help of this information, the congestion control algorithms of TCP are modified to react accordingly depending on the current or predicted situation. The following examples give an impression about the variety of such approaches:

▶ Several approaches try to estimate the available bandwidth in an intelligent way. This estimation is used to optimise the flow control mechanisms of TCP. Examples are TCP Westwood (TCPW [265]), TCP Westwood with Bulk Repeat (TCPW-BR [266]), the approach proposed by Kao et al. [267], and the approach proposed by Tsukamoto et al. [268].

▶ TCP DOOR (Detection of Out-of-Order and Response [269]) and TCP Santa Cruz [270] modify the congestion control based on the arrival of out-of-order packets.

▶ TCP Probing [271] and the approach of Kao et al. [267] implement additional probe cycles to determine congestion in the network. In case of a congestion, the flow control in TCP is modified accordingly in order to increase TCP performance.

▶ Wireless TCP (W-TCP [272]) examines the inter-packet arrival times together with a rate-based congestion control mechanism. Other approaches like ADTCP [273] ad-

---

[2]The focus of this chapter is the communication between vehicles and the MoccaProxy and only discusses end-to-end solutions. The classification does not consider intermediate performance enhancing proxies since the MoccaProxy itself acts as a performance enhancing proxy in MOCCA. The discussion in section 3.4 shows that using a (mobile) proxy at the IGWs is not recommended for the VANET scenario.

ditionally measure short term throughput, packet loss ratio, and packet out-of-order delivery ratio, and use a modified TCP state machine to react appropriately.

▶ In Freeze-TCP [274], the receiver notifies the sender to stop transmission in case of an impending congestion. The receiver therefore transmits a zero window advertisement to force the sender to set cwnd to zero and to move into the zero window probing mode [260].

▶ Several approaches completely modify the algorithms used for slow start, congestion avoidance, and various timeout calculations. Example protocols are TCP Vegas [275, 276] and TCP Veno [277]. Other approaches like ATP (Ad Hoc Transport Protocol [137]) completely replace the congestion control of TCP by different algorithms.

The following section introduces TCP Vegas as a representative for a modified congestion control algorithm for TCP. A detailed discussion of these approaches can be found in [262, 278].

TCP Vegas

TCP Vegas [275, 276] modifies the sender-side of TCP. The basic goal is to improve the utilisation of the available bandwidth in order to increase the throughput of TCP. TCP Vegas does not introduce a more aggressive congestion control like, e.g. TCP Santa Cruz. Instead, it modifies the retransmission procedure of TCP as well as the slow start and congestion avoidance algorithm.

The basic principle of TCP Vegas is a more precise prediction of the RTO using information from the acknowledgements received. Thereby, TCP Vegas logs the system time between the transmission of a TCP segment and the receipt of the respective acknowledgement. In case of a duplicate acknowledgement, it additionally calculates the time difference between the current system time and the timestamp in the duplicate acknowledgement. If this difference is greater than the RTO, TCP Vegas does not wait for the three duplicate acknowledgements but retransmits the respective segment anew. TCP Vegas also calculates the time interval between the transmission of a TCP segment and an acknowledgement arriving after the RTO expired. If this difference is greater than the RTO, TCP Vegas will also retransmit the respective segment precautionary. Another optimisation is focused on the computation of the cwnd. TCP Vegas first tries to find out whether a reduction of the cwnd is necessary: the cwnd is only decreased if it was not decreased before the retransmission of a segment.

In contrast to standard TCP, TCP Vegas tries to detect congestion in the network. It therefore examines the expected data rate D_{exp} with the current (measured) data rate. D_{exp} is calculated as follows:

$$D_{exp} = \frac{WindowSize}{BaseRTT} \tag{5.1}$$

Thereby, *WindowSize* represents the current window size (see section 5.1.1) and *BaseRTT* is the measured RTT of a segment in case of a non-congested network. Similarly, the current data rate D_{cur} is measured by dividing the number of transmitted bytes by the RTT of the first acknowledgements of these data. Based on these coefficients, TCP Vegas defines two threshold values α and β ($0 < \alpha < \beta$). Both parameters specify whether the current network load is too high or too low. Hence, TCP Vegas distinguishes between three states of a connection. In each of these states, TCP Vegas reacts in the following way:

- ▶ $(D_{exp} - D_{cur}) < \alpha$. The network utilisation is too low and TCP Vegas increases cwnd linearly.

- ▶ $\alpha \leq (D_{exp} - D_{cur}) \leq \beta$. TCP Vegas assumes that the network utilisation is sufficient and does not modify cwnd.

- ▶ $(D_{exp} - D_{cur}) > \beta$. The network utilisation is too high and may cause congestion. Hence, TCP Vegas decreases cwnd linearly.

This mechanism only comes into operation in the congestion avoidance phase only; it is not used in the slow start phase. The detection of congestion requires modifications of the slow start algorithm, too. The cwnd still increases exponentially but only with every second RTT. This way, TCP Vegas is able to measure the current data rate and to compare it with the expected data rate since the cwnd is constant in the time between. If D_{cur} falls below D_{exp}, TCP Vegas moves from the slow start phase into the congestion avoidance phase.

Simulations showed that TCP Vegas outperforms standard TCP (TCP Reno) although it has a less aggressive congestion control mechanism. TCP Vegas is able to improve the data throughput between 40 % to 70 % with only one-fifth to one-half of the losses. It also provides a faster response time of up to 25 % compared to TCP Reno.

5.2.2   Utilising Information from Intermediate Systems

Communication efficiency also can be improved by considering information from intermediate systems, e.g. the relaying vehicles along the IP packet flow from the sender to the receiver. If intermediate systems are able to detect congestions, they can signal this information to the end systems. This way, an adapted TCP is able to use this information to optimise the communication efficiency.

Currently, several approaches are available to handle information from intermediate systems. The following examples illustrate the different kinds of information provided by intermediate systems:

▶ *Explicit Link Failure Notification (ELFN):* ELFN informs the sender about route changes in a mobile network. The sender can react appropriately to handle these changes [245, 279].

▶ *Explicit Loss Notification (ELN):* ELN is a mechanism that notifies a TCP sender about the reason for a packet loss. This way, appropriate mechanisms can be implemented for the different situations [280, 281].

▶ *Explicit Bad State Notification (EBSN):* EBSN notify the sender about bad states of a transmission link. Thus, the sender is able to carefully adjust its TCP timers [282].

▶ *Explicit Congestion Notification (ECN):* ECN notifies the sender about a pending congestion in the network [283].

The following section introduces ECN, which plays the most important role in practice among these approaches. Furthermore, many TCP enhancements use ECN to improve the TCP performance. Examples are the Ad hoc TCP (ATCP [136]), TCP Feedback (TCP-F [284]) and its extension "TCP with Buffering capability and Sequence information" (TCP BuS [285, 286]) and the Wireless Profiled TCP used in the Wireless Application Protocol (WAP). From these approaches, the Wireless Profiled TCP is introduced afterwards as a representative since it was specifically designed for mobile devices.

Explicit Congestion Notification

An important approach to signal pending congestion situations is the Explicit Congestion Notification (ECN). ECN is standardised by the Internet Engineering Task Force in RFC 3168 [283] and is already integrated in current Linux kernels. In order to detect pending congestions, ECN requires an active queue management in the intermediate communication systems, i.e. the routers between the communicating peers. RFC 3168 suggests the use of Random Early Detection (RED, RFC 2309 [287]) for the active queue management. ECN requires modifications in both the network layer and the transport layer, i.e. in IP and TCP. If a router detects a pending congestion in the network – i.e. on the network layer – it signals this information to the communicating end systems using two bits in the IP header reserved for ECN: the "ECN-Capable Transport" bit (ECT) and "Congestion Experienced" bit (CE). The combination of these bits has the following semantics:

▶ (ECT = 0, CE = 0): ECN is not supported by the intermediate system.

▶ (ECT = 0, CE = 1) or (ECT = 1, CE = 0): The sender supports ECN.

▶ (ECT = 1, CE = 1): A congestion occurred in the network.

The communication peers negotiate the ECN support in the connection establishment phase of TCP. Therefore, two reserved bits in the TCP header are used to signal ECN information in TCP: "ECN-Echo" (ECE) and "Congestion Window Reduced" (CWR). The receiver also uses these flags to signal pending congestions on the way from the sender to the receiver. Figure 5.5 shows an example illustrating the basic functionality of ECN in a congested multi-hop ad hoc network with three hops. This example assumes that a TCP connection already exists. The two boxes on each arrow represent the relevant flags set in IP (lower box) and TCP (upper box).

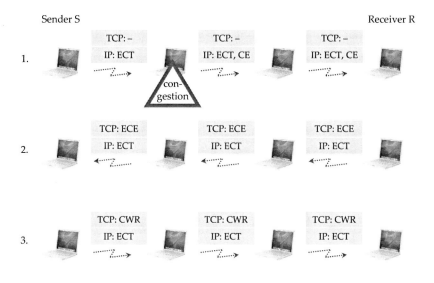

CE: Congestion Experienced ▫ CWR: Congestion Window Reduced ▫ ECE: ECN Echo
ECN: Explicit Congestion Notification ▫ ECT: ECN-Capable Transport

Figure 5.5: Example for ECN used in a Congested Network

In normal operation mode, the communication peers and the intermediate systems set the ECT flag in IP to signal that they support ECN. If an intermediate node detects a pending congestion, it will signal this information by setting the CE flag (step 1). This way, the receiver R recognises the experienced congestion and delivers this information to TCP. At this point, R has to notify sender S about the pending congestion. R therefore sets the ECE flag in the TCP acknowledgement transmitted to S (step 2). If S receives the acknowledgement, it decreases its congestion window in order to throttle the data rate. S also sets the CWR flag in the next segment to approve the receipt of the ECE to the receiver (step 3).

ECN shows a good performance in wireless networks, which was investigated in RFC 2884 [288]. It is implemented in current Linux kernels and ECN is also used by several TCP enhancements to react appropriately to congestions in the network. An example is the Wireless Profiled TCP introduced in the next section.

Wireless Profiled TCP

The Wireless Profiled TCP [289] is the connection-oriented communication protocol in the Wireless Application Protocol (WAP) version 2.0, which was originally specified by the WAP Forum (now Open Mobile Alliance, OMA [290]). Wireless Profiled TCP is also used for communication in i-mode [291]. In general, WAP enables mobile phones to access the Internet. The Wireless Profiled TCP can be used in two typical WAP scenarios as illustrated in figure 5.6. In the first scenario in figure 5.6 (a), the WAP-enabled device communicates with a WAP Proxy using the Wireless Profiled TCP. The WAP Proxy is an application layer proxy similar to WWW proxies or mail transfer agents (MTAs) used in the Internet. This way, WAP-enabled devices establish a TCP connection to the WAP Proxy using Wireless Profiled TCP, and the WAP Proxy then establishes a separate standard TCP connection with the origin server. The WAP Proxy will subsequently retrieve inbound data from either connection and send that data out through the other connection. Hence, the WAP Proxy allows for the optimisation of TCP over the wireless network. Wireless Profiled TCP implementations can also be used for end-to-end connectivity. Figure 5.6 (b) depicts this scenario, which does not deploy an intermediate WAP Proxy. This scenario requires the interoperability between the Wireless Profiled TCP and standard TCP.

Since Wireless Profiled TCP was developed for the Internet access of mobile phones, it also has to handle the wireless communication characteristics such as unreliable and error-prone wireless links. Besides the mandatory use of ECN, Wireless Profiled TCP follows a set of several recommendations summarised in RFC 2757 [49] for communication in wireless networks. These recommendations advise the implementation of the following standardised mechanisms for TCP:

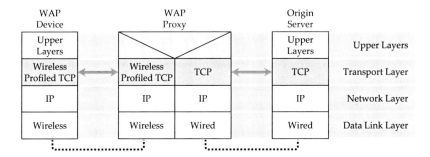

(a) Wireless Profiled TCP with WAP Proxy

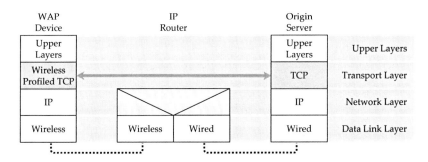

(b) Wireless Profiled TCP without WAP Proxy

Figure 5.6: Wireless Profiled TCP in the WAP Architecture

▶ *Large Window Size:* TCP should be able to utilise the available bandwidth efficiently. If the maximum window size is restricted, it could be possible that TCP will not exhaust the available bandwidth completely. Hence, Wireless Profiled TCP should support window sizes larger than 64 Kbyte.

▶ *Window Scale Option:* If a Wireless Profiled TCP implementation supports large window sizes, it must support the Window Scale Option as described in RFC 1323 [292].

▶ *RTT Measurement:* Wireless Profiled TCP supports measurements of the round trip times. It therefore has to support the timestamp option according to RFC 1323 [292].

▶ *Large Initial Window:* A Wireless Profiled TCP implementation may support RFC 2414 [293], which allows an increased initial window size of three or four segments (i.e. a maximum of 4380 byte).

▶ *Path MTU Discovery:* Another optional mechanism is the detection of the maximum transfer unit (MTU) as specified in RFC 1191 for IPv4 [294] and RFC 1981 for IPv6 [295]. If path MTU discovery is not supported, Wireless Profiled TCP may alternatively allow a MTU larger than the default IP MTU.

▶ *Selective Acknowledgement:* A mandatory feature is the support of selective acknowledgements according to RFC 2018 [258].

5.2.3   Non-TCP Transport Protocols

Although TCP is the most common communication protocol used in the Internet, there are a few alternative transport protocols not based on TCP. Examples are the original Wireless Application Protocol, which specifies a transaction-oriented communication scheme called Wireless Transaction Protocol (WTP) in addition to the Wireless Profiled TCP. Another protocol is the Stream Control Transmission Protocol (SCTP). This section briefly introduces SCTP since it is considered as one of the ten hottest information technology trends [296].

Stream Control Transmission Protocol

Besides TCP and UDP, SCTP is the third transport protocol standardised by the Internet Engineering Task Force in RFC 2960 [297]. SCTP is a connection-oriented transport protocol similar to TCP. In contrast to TCP, SCTP extends the term "connection" by an "association" providing an enhanced functionality. Associations may support several IP addresses on both peers called *multi-homing*. This way, communication between two peers is independent of the network interface currently used on each of the peers. Another important feature of associations is the *multi-streaming* capability as illustrated in figure 5.7. Multi-streaming enables SCTP to transmit several streams within one association. In figure 5.7 the SCTP association between the hosts contains n streams. Additional streams can be established within an existing association very quickly and existing streams can be removed from the association dynamically.

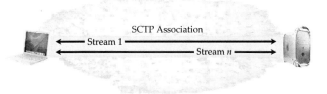

SCTP: Stream Control Transmission Protocol

Figure 5.7: Communication in SCTP

Besides the multi-homing and multi-streaming capability, SCTP provides additional important features:

▶ Message-orientation instead of byte-orientation used in TCP.

▶ Configuration of the required reliability.

▶ Four-way handshake to prevent denial-of-service attacks.

▶ Segmentation and reassembly similar to TCP.

▶ In-order delivery of data in several streams with an optional stream-independent delivery on arrival.

SCTP also implements flow control and congestion control mechanisms similar to TCP. The flow control of SCTP is based on each association whereas the congestion control is established within each transmission path. Further investigations on the SCTP flow control and congestion control including their evaluation in mobile environments can be found in [298, 299].

5.2.4 Discussion of Related Work

A collective evaluation of each proposed category is not possible. The numerous solutions of each category were developed and optimised for different communication scenarios and, thus, have different impacts on the TCP performance in the VANET scenario. This way, the categories cannot be evaluated with the help of the "plus/minus" scheme used in section 2.2. Instead, this discussion points out the strengths and weaknesses of the three categories in the VANET scenario.

A step towards a more efficient TCP in mobile environments is the use of different congestion control algorithms in TCP. In case of lost segments, these approaches try to estimate and predict whether the losses are the result of a congestion in the network or whether they are caused by transmission errors. Since these predictions are based on local information, they may not reflect the VANET characteristics resulting in a poor TCP performance. Moreover, the congestion control algorithms do not consider information and notifications from intermediate nodes within the ad hoc network and they do not provide additional mechanisms to handle both short-term and longer-term periods of disconnections.

The utilisation of information from intermediate systems is a promising approach to improve TCP efficiency in vehicular environments. With the help of this information, estimations about the situation in the network are more accurate compared to the predictions of pure congestion control modifications. This way, lost segments can be handled very efficiently depending on the reason of the loss. This concept implicitly includes the consideration of notifications, which enables TCP to react quickly to various situations in the network. However, TCP extensions like ECN basically do not solve the general problems of TCP in VANETs. For example, a detailed examination of the Wireless Profiled TCP showed that some of these extensions even reduce the performance whereas a combination of them improve the TCP performance [300]. Another interesting observation is that several approaches utilising information from intermediate systems are inherently able to handle periods of communication breakdowns. For example, Ad Hoc TCP, TCP Feedback and TCP BuS were designed to handle temporary disconnections. However, this feature relies on the exponential backoff implemented in TCP to calculate the retransmission timeouts. This mechanism is not suitable to handle long-term disconnections from the Internet appropriately since they may cause either a reset of the TCP connection or a long recovery phase after a reconnection to the Internet.

The deployment of transport protocols not based on TCP in the VANET scenario leaves ambivalent results. For example, the Wireless Transaction Protocol used in WAP was developed for transaction-oriented services like WWW and, thus, gives a two-edged result [262]:

▶ WAP outperforms TCP on lossy links if only few data is transmitted.

▶ The transmission of extensive data volumes degrades the data throughput to a few bytes per second.

In contrast, the concepts of SCTP like the multi-streaming capability are a promising alternative for being deployed in mobile networks [301] and especially in VANETs [298, 299]. However, applications explicitly have to utilise the multi-streaming capability in order to take full advantage of the SCTP concepts. This aggravates the cooperation between SCTP and MOCCA: Since the MoccaProxy communicates with the Internet using TCP, it cannot deploy the multi-streaming capabilities of SCTP natively, because both TCP and SCTP use port numbers to identify their connections and associations respectively. Hence, the MoccaProxy can only map a TCP connection to exactly one SCTP connection, which will likely cause an increased delay in the connection establishment phase due to the four-way handshake for the association establishment in SCTP. Moreover, SCTP – as well as other non-TCP transport protocols – do not provide a socket-like API. As a result, this category is not considered further on for being used in MOCCA.

5.3   MCTP

Vehicular environments require an optimised transport protocol based on TCP for an efficient Internet access. Such a protocol must be able to distinguish between error-prone links and network congestions in order to handle packet losses appropriately. Moreover, it must be able to utilise information from both intermediate systems and from other protocols. This is necessary for an efficient treatment of both short-term network partitions and longer-term periods of disconnections from the Internet. However, none of the existing related work fulfils these requirements sufficiently.

This way, MCTP (MOCCA Transport Protocol) was developed for communication between vehicles and the MoccaProxy in the MOCCA architecture. MCTP provides a core functionality that can be extended depending on the performance and characteristics of an inter-vehicle communication system used in a real-world deployment. The core functionality of MCTP is detailed in the following sections together with additional optimisation potentials, which might further improve the efficiency of MCTP in different deployment scenarios. Details about the MCTP implementation for the Linux operating system can be found in appendix D.

5.3.1 Protocol Functionality

MCTP combines several TCP enhancements proposed in the related work section. Its core functionality belongs to the category of utilising information from intermediate systems, which is extended by modifications of the congestion control mechanisms used in TCP. In general, MCTP is based on the principles of Ad Hoc TCP (ATCP [136]), which relies on information on pending congestions in the network. This idea is combined with an approach similar to TCP Feedback [284] and TCP Stop-and-Go proposed by Ritter [302]. Like ATCP, MCTP implements a sublayer between TCP and IP from a conceptual point of view as depicted in figure 5.8. The basic principle of MCTP is that it observes the IP packet flow between sender and receiver in order to react appropriately. Therefore, MCTP considers additional notifications from protocols on the underlying communication layers as well as from intermediate systems:

▶ ECN indicates pending congestions detected by intermediate systems (cf. section 5.2.2).

▶ Intermediate systems indicate a partitioned network using ICMP messages of type "destination unreachable". This information is relevant for the local communication between vehicles only, i.e. for communication without accessing the Internet.

▶ The DRIVE protocol in MMIP6 notifies MCTP in case of disconnections from the Internet (i.e. in case it does no longer receive any SA Announcements from the IGWs).

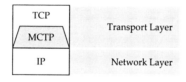

MCTP: MOCCA Transport Protocol

Figure 5.8: MCTP in the TCP/IP Model

This available information enables MCTP to distinguish between link errors, congestions, network partitions, and disconnections from the Internet. Figure 5.9 summarises the information processing in MCTP. Besides the available information from underlying communication layers and from intermediate systems, MCTP also takes into account events caused by TCP itself. Such events are the retransmission timeouts for segments and the arrival of (duplicate) acknowledgements for successfully transmitted segments. Based on this knowledge, MCTP controls the transmission procedure of TCP in the different situations by controlling retransmissions and timeouts, and by probing for the network characteristics. MCTP therefore implements its own protocol state machine, which comes into operation after TCP established a connection between the end systems[3].

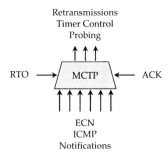

Retransmissions
Timer Control
Probing

RTO   →   MCTP   ←   ACK

ECN
ICMP
Notifications

ACK: Acknowledgement ▫ ECN: Explicit Congestion Notification
ICMP: Internet Control Message Protocol ▫ RTO: Retransmission Timeout

Figure 5.9: MCTP Information Processing

5.3.2 MCTP Protocol State Machine

The MCTP protocol state machine is based on a modified ATCP state machine, which was extended by connection freeze mechanisms similar to TCP Stop-and-Go. This state machine implements the core functionality of MCTP that may be enhanced by further optimisations as described in section 5.3.4. The MCTP protocol state machine comprises the following five states[4]:

▶ *NORMAL:* The normal operation mode.

▶ *LOSS:* The operation mode in case of unreliable, i.e. lossy, communication links.

---

[3]Applied to the TCP protocol state machine [303], MCTP comes into operation after TCP enters the "ESTABLISHED" state.

[4]The original ATCP state uses the four states NORMAL, LOSS, CONGESTED, and PARTITIONED only.

▶ *CONGESTED:* MCTP enters this state in case of a congested network.

▶ *PARTITIONED:* The operation mode for a partitioned network.

▶ *DISCONNECTED:* This state represents a disconnection from the Internet.

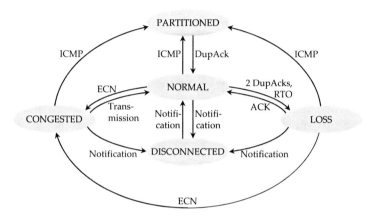

ACK: Acknowledgement ▫ DupAck: Duplicate Acknowledgement
ECN: Explicit Congestion Notification ▫ ICMP: Internet Control Message Protocol
RTO: Retransmission Timeout

Figure 5.10: MCTP Protocol State Machine

Figure 5.10 shows the transition diagram between these states in the MCTP protocol state machine. A basic feature of this state machine is that it explicitly differentiates between segment losses caused by congestion and segment losses caused by single transmission errors for ongoing connections. Moreover, MCTP distinguishes between a partitioned network and a disconnection from the Internet in case of a temporary communication breakdown. The first situation only occurs if a vehicle communicates with another vehicle via multi-hop ad hoc communication. It therefore does not include the Internet for its communication. In the second situation, it is assumed that the vehicle communicates with an Internet host. This way, both states can be seen as orthogonal from each other – except for the home address forwarding optimisation implemented in MMIP6 (cf. section 4.4.4). The states NORMAL, LOSS, and CONGESTED are the common operation modes of MCTP in case a data flow is possible. PARTITIONED and DISCONNECTED are only entered when a communication flow is not possible. These situations are detailed in the following sections.

Normal Operation, Congestions and Losses

An important goal of MCTP is to minimise the number of slow starts in an ongoing connection. As described in section 5.1.1, segment losses activate the slow start algorithm, which degrades the TCP performance in terms of throughput. A TCP sender considers a segment as being lost in the following two situations:

▶ The sender receives three consecutive duplicate acknowledgements for one segment (DupAck).

▶ A retransmission timeout (RTO) occurred for one segment at the sender side.

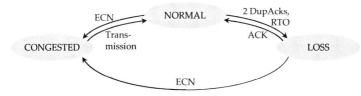

ACK: Acknowledgement ▫ DupAck: Duplicate Acknowledgement
ECN: Explicit Congestion Notification ▫ RTO: Retransmission Timeout

Figure 5.11: MCTP State Machine for Congestions and Losses

An important feature is that MCTP performs a situation-based handling of lost segments. MCTP therefore classifies losses caused by congestions in the network and losses caused by transmission errors. The MCTP protocol state machine therefore implements the two states CONGESTED and LOSS where segment retransmissions are handled differently. Figure 5.11 depicts the respective part of the MCTP protocol state machine, which works in the following way: After TCP established a connection successfully, MCTP initially operates in the NORMAL state and observes the IP packet flow in the end system. This way, TCP initially starts communication with a slow start phase to determine the initially available bandwidth. In order to detect a congestion in the network, MCTP relies on ECN (see section 5.2.2). This way, activated ECN flags in the header of arrived IP packets indicate a pending congestion in an intermediate system. In this situation, MCTP switches into the CONGESTED state and does nothing: it ignores DupAcks as well as the expiry of RTOs. This way, MCTP leaves the congestion control completely to TCP and does not interfere with the normal congestion behaviour of TCP. After the TCP sender transmits a new segment, MCTP returns to the NORMAL state.

In the NORMAL state, MCTP counts the number of DupAcks received for a segment. If ECN does not indicate a pending congestion in the network, a segment loss was likely caused by a transmission error. If MCTP receives two DupAcks for a segment in this situation, it enters the LOSS state in order to handle the segment loss appropriately. Since the TCP congestion control reacts only after the third DupAck, it is not affected by the second DupAck and does not interfere with MCTP in this situation. Similarly, MCTP enters the LOSS state if an RTO expires for a segment and ECN does not indicate a pending congestion in the network. In the LOSS state, MCTP forces TCP to enter the persist mode by shrinking the congestion window (cwnd) to zero and by freezing the retransmission timers. This way, TCP does not invoke the congestion control, which would be the wrong thing to do in this situation. Instead, MCTP itself retransmits the unacknowledged TCP segment. It therefore controls the retransmission timers accordingly to retransmit the segment in case that the acknowledgements are not forthcoming. If an acknowledgement for the segment arrives from the peer, MCTP forwards the acknowledgement to TCP, which also removes TCP from the persist mode. MCTP then returns to the NORMAL operation mode.

There is one exception in this processing as illustrated in figure 5.11. If arriving IP packets indicate a pending congestion while MCTP is in LOSS state, MCTP restores the congestion window and the RTOs and switches to the CONGESTED state. This way, it does not perform further retransmissions but leaves the retransmission procedure to the congestion control of TCP.

This operation mode is similar to ATCP. Differences occur in the handling of DupAcks: Whereas ATCP waits for three consecutive DupAcks before switching into LOSS mode, MCTP only waits for two DupAcks. Furthermore, ATCP is based TCP Reno whereas MCTP is based on TCP New Reno using an improved fast retransmit/fast recovery mechanism and selective acknowledgements.

Partitioned and Disconnected Mode

The mobility of the vehicles may stall ongoing connections in the VANET for a temporary period of time. These communication disruptions are typically caused in the following two situations:

► *Network Partitioning:* The vehicular ad hoc network may be partitioned if communication links between vehicles break. If the ad hoc routing protocol for inter-vehicle
communication does not find an alternative route, communication between two vehicles is no longer possible.

► *Disconnection from the Internet:* Due to the temporary availability of IGWs, vehicles
may become disconnected from the Internet, for example, if the vehicle is currently
not located within the service area of an IGW.

MCTP considers these two situations and controls TCP appropriately in order to improve
the recovery after a connection breakdown. Therefore, MCTP comprises the two states PAR-
TITIONED and DISCONNECTED. The PARTITIONED state represents a network partitioning that is relevant for inter-vehicle communication. In contrast, the DISCONNECTED state
is entered when the vehicle becomes disconnected from the Internet, i.e. it is only used for
connections between a vehicle and the MoccaProxy in the Internet. This differentiation is
very important for MCTP, because it allows the deployment of optimised strategies in the
respective situation[5].

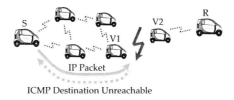

ICMP: Internet Control Message Protocol

Figure 5.12: Example for a Network Partitioning

A partitioning of the ad hoc network occurs if an intermediate link between two communicating vehicles breaks, which is exemplified in figure 5.12. In this example, the communication link between vehicle V1 and V2 breaks. If the ad hoc routing protocol realises the
breakdown and is, thus, not able to forward an IP packet of the sending vehicle S towards
the receiving vehicle R, it will send an ICMP destination unreachable message back to S. This

---

[5]Since all vehicles form one logical IPv6 subnet, the decision whether or not the communication peer is a
vehicle is simple: a sender has to compare the subnet of both the IPv6 source and destination address. If both
subnets are equal, the communication peer is located in the VANET (see section 3.1.2).

DupAck: Duplicate Acknowledgement ▫ ICMP: Internet Control Message Protocol

Figure 5.13: MCTP State Machine for Partitioning and Disconnections

way, S is notified about the partitioning in the network. If MCTP receives a "destination un-reachable" ICMP message from an intermediate vehicle, it moves into the PARTITIONED state as illustrated in figure 5.13. In this state, MCTP forces TCP to enter the persist mode and freezes the retransmission timers as described in the previous section. In addition, MCTP performs a window probing mechanism similar to the zero window probing used in TCP [260]. Thereby, MTCP probes the connection periodically with acknowledgements. MTCP therefore uses a constant period for sending the probe packets using the last value of the RTO before MCTP switched to the PARTITIONED state. This is in contrast to the zero window probing implemented in TCP, which exponentially backoffs the probing period. If MCTP receives a DupAck from the receiver, the connection is apparently re-established and communication can be continued. In this case, MCTP removes TCP from the persist mode, activates the slow start phase of TCP without reducing ssthresh, and moves itself back to the NORMAL operation mode. The PARTITIONED state is also entered from the LOSS state and the CONGESTED state upon receiving an ICMP destination unreachable message as illustrated in figure 5.10. The explicit probing of the connection in case of a network par-titioning is necessary since it cannot be assumed that the ad hoc routing protocol is able to detect the re-establishment of the end-to-end route between the communicating peers. This way, the probing forces the routing protocol to check for the re-establishment of a route. If the connection cannot be restored after a pre-defined period of time, MCTP assumes that the connection cannot be re-established and advices TCP to reset the connection.

The PARTITIONED mode is of relevance for inter-vehicle communication only. This mode is similar to ATCP; differences between MCTP and ATCP are the probing, which is based on the TCP zero window probing in ATCP, and the unmodified ssthresh after returning to the NORMAL operation mode. The PARTITIONED mode is not used when a vehicle communicates with a host in the Internet. This situation is not supported by ATCP. In this scenario, a vehicle must be located within the service area of an IGW and it must be able to communicate with the gateway either directly or using multi-hop communications. If the vehicle moves out of the service area, communication within the Internet host will break down. However, this situation is different compared to a partitioning of the network, because MCTP can be notified about the presence of an IGW. MCTP therefore interacts with the mobility management protocols deployed in MOCCA, namely MMIP6 and DRIVE (cf. section 4). In MMIP6, the DRIVE protocol announces the availability of an IGW by the periodical transmissions of SA Announcement messages in the service area of the IGW. These messages can be used to indicate the presence of an IGW to MCTP in the following three ways:

▶ If the vehicle receives SA Announcements, it has access to the Internet and, thus, the vehicle can communicate with the Internet host.

▶ If the SA Announcements fail to appear for a certain period of time, MCTP assumes a disconnection from the Internet.

▶ If the vehicle receives SA Announcements after a period of disconnection, MCTP assumes a reconnection to the Internet and communication with the Internet host can be continued.

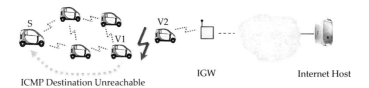

ICMP: Internet Control Message Protocol ▫ IGW: Internet Gateway

Figure 5.14: Disconnection from the Internet due to Network Partition

These assumptions also include the situation when a vehicle becomes disconnected from the Internet due to a network partitioning. Figure 5.14 depicts this situation for a link loss between vehicle V1 and V2 (for a better clarification, this figure does not show the part between the IGW and the Internet). In this case, vehicle S will be notified from its MMIP6 implementation about the disconnection since it does not receive further SA Announcements from the IGW. S will also receive an ICMP destination unreachable message about the network partitioning from intermediate vehicle V1. Since S communicates with a host in the Internet, it discards the ICMP message and moves into the DISCONNECTED operation mode in the common way upon receiving the notification.

In MOCCA, MMIP6 notifies MCTP about the events of disconnections and reconnections. When MCTP receives a notification for a disconnection while communicating with Internet hosts, it switches into the DISCONNECTED state, as illustrated in figure 5.13. The disconnected mode will also be activated if MCTP operates in the CONGESTED state or the LOSS state (cf. figure 5.10). In this mode, MCTP completely stops the TCP transmissions and freezes the RTO timers. Both TCP and the MCTP sublayer remain in this state until MMIP6 notifies MCTP about a reconnection to the Internet through a new IGW. MCTP then restores TCP and moves itself back to the NORMAL operation mode. In addition, MCTP activates the slow start phase of TCP without modifying the threshold for the slow start. This allows TCP to converge its data rate to the new situation. Finally, MCTP triggers TCP to retransmit queued segments immediately. If such segments are not available, MCTP sends two acknowledgements in order to generate a duplicate acknowledgement.

The notification is also performed in case MMIP6 decides to handover its connections to a new IGW. As described in section 4.5.2, the handover to a new IGW typically causes a short period of disconnection, in which packets are likely being lost. Before the vehicle starts the handover procedure, it notifies MCTP about the pending disconnection. This way, TCP does not try to send any segments as long as the handover is performed. After the handover is completed, MMIP6 notifies MCTP about the reconnection and communication will be continued.

5.3.3   Protocol Interactions in MOCCA

The communication protocols deployed in the MOCCA architecture collaborate in an integrated fashion, i.e. they highly interact with each other. Interaction is not only restricted to the MOCCA protocols, it also may include communication protocols that are not an integral part in MOCCA.

MOCCA Protocols

As described in the previous section, MCTP relies on information from the mobility management protocol MMIP6 implemented in MOCCA. MMIP6 notifies MCTP about the availability of IGWs. The respective information is provided by the DRIVE protocol implemented in
MMIP6 for the discovery of IGWs. If the state of the availability changes, MMIP6 will notify
MCTP about the following events:

▶ Beginning and ending of a handover procedure if MMIP6 decides to perform a handover.

▶ Disconnection from the Internet if the connection to the current IGW is lost and an
   alternative IGW is not available.

▶ Reconnection to the Internet if the vehicle travels into the service area of a new IGW
   after a disconnection.

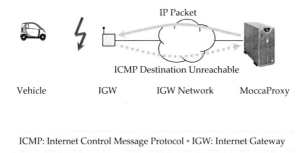

ICMP: Internet Control Message Protocol ▫ IGW: Internet Gateway

Figure 5.15: Notification of the MoccaProxy

These events are of relevance for communication between the vehicle and the Internet
only – it is not used for local inter-vehicle communications. Moreover, the events are signalled only for the MCTP implementation in the vehicles. The information is not available
for the MCTP implementation in the MoccaProxy since it is up to the vehicle to decide about
handovers and the availability of IGWs. Instead, the MoccaProxy relies on information generated by ICMP as depicted in figure 5.15. If an IP packet cannot be delivered to the vehicle
after a disconnection, the IGW is not able to resolve the current location of the vehicle. In
this case, the IGW sends an ICMP destination unreachable message back to the MoccaProxy.
This way, the MCTP implementation in the MoccaProxy moves into the PARTITIONED

mode (cf. figure 5.10) and activates the probing, whereas the MCTP implementation in the vehicle switches to the DISCONNECTED mode. Thereby, the probing messages of the MoccaProxy are not distributed in the VANET since the IGW is not able to resolve the location of the addressed vehicle. After the notification about the reconnection, the MCTP state machine in the vehicle immediately retransmits the queued segments. If such segments are not available, MCTP sends a duplicate acknowledgement to the MoccaProxy. This indicates the MoccaProxy that the connection is re-established and communication can be continued. Thus, the MCTP implementation in the MoccaProxy moves back from the PARTITIONED state into the NORMAL operation mode and continues communication.

Further Communication Protocols

The MCTP state machine requires additional information from the communication protocols implemented in the underlying network layer for a proper operation. This way, the network layer has to support the following two features:

▶ *ICMP Support:* ICMP is required to notify a sender about a network partitioning.

▶ *ECN Support:* ECN is used to distinguish between congestions and transmission errors.

Both ICMP and ECN have to interact with the routing protocol used in the VANET. Thus, the routing protocol must be able to detect broken links as well as pending congestions. Therefore, the forwarding algorithm within the vehicles has to provide an active queue management like Random Early Detection (RED [287]). These mechanisms are already integrated in the protocol stack implementations of common operating systems like Linux and are, thus, acceptable for being deployed in vehicles. The interaction with the routing protocol is not discussed further on since it depends on the routing and forwarding strategies implemented in the routing protocol used in the VANET, which it is not included in scope for the Internet integration of VANETs.

5.3.4   Improvement Potentials of MCTP

The raw MCTP functionality can be improved in several ways depending on the capabilities and the performance of the protocols used in the underlying communication layers, the characteristics of a real inter-vehicle communication system, and the communication patterns of applications. The optimisations introduced in this section address aspects of the MOCCA architecture, integration aspects, and the MCTP protocol itself.

Architectural Improvements

An important issue is the way the IGWs communicate with the MoccaProxy. In the MOCCA architecture, the IGWs are connected to the MoccaProxy via the IGW network as illustrated in figure 5.16 (see also section 3.1.1). The IGW network can be realised in several ways:

▶ Dedicated ATM network providing high data rates at low delays.

▶ IGWs can be connected to an ISP via xDSL technology providing higher delays and lower data rates compared to ATM.

▶ The Internet can connect the IGWs to the MoccaProxy. The delays may be high compared to both ATM and xDSL[6].

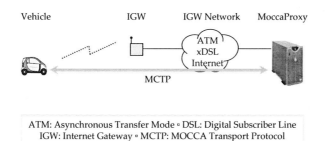

ATM: Asynchronous Transfer Mode ▫ DSL: Digital Subscriber Line
IGW: Internet Gateway ▫ MCTP: MOCCA Transport Protocol

Figure 5.16: Connection of the Internet Gateways to the MoccaProxy

If the Internet is used for communication between IGWs and MoccaProxy, an architectural optimisation is to reduce the latency of retransmissions by "shortening" the communication path between the vehicle and the MoccaProxy. This could be achieved with caching mechanisms in the IGW. A possible solution is the use of snooping techniques like TCP Snoop [304, 305]. Figure 5.17 shows the combination of MCTP and TCP Snoop in the VANET scenario for communication between the vehicle and the MoccaProxy. A Snoop Agent located at the IGW preserves a cache for unacknowledged segments transmitted in either direction. The Snoop Agent performs local retransmissions according to timeouts and the policy of unacknowledged packets. Therefore, it monitors the TCP segments exchanged through the IGW. It caches each segment for the vehicle that passes the IGW and keeps track of the last sequence number acknowledged by the vehicle. If the Snoop Agent does

---

[6]As stated in sections 2.1 and 3.1, the transmission delays in the Internet are still expected to be low compared to the delays in vehicular ad hoc networks.

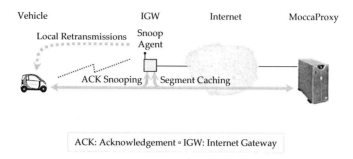

ACK: Acknowledgement ▫ IGW: Internet Gateway

Figure 5.17: Integration of TCP Snoop into MCTP

not receive an acknowledgement from the vehicle within a certain period of time, either the segment or the acknowledgement was lost. Alternatively, the Snoop Agent could receive duplicate acknowledgements from the vehicle, which also indicate a segment loss. In this situation, the Snoop Agent retransmits the segment directly from its cache resulting in a faster retransmission compared to retransmissions from the MoccaProxy. Additionally, the Snoop Agent filters duplicate acknowledgements to avoid unnecessary retransmissions of segments from the MoccaProxy.

In the reverse direction from the vehicle to the MoccaProxy, the Snoop Agent also monitors the segment stream to detect gaps in the sequence numbers of MCTP. As soon as the Snoop Agent detects a missing segment, it returns a negative acknowledgement (NACK) to the vehicle. Thus, the vehicle can quickly retransmit the missing segment.

TCP Snoop does not cover situations where a vehicle gets involved in handovers. In this case, the cache in the Snoop Agent with the monitored segments remains unused since the vehicle changes its IGW. This way, it does not reduce the latency of the handover procedure in MMIP6. Moreover, TCP Snoop requires the support of NACKS in MCTP as well as some slight modifications in the MCTP protocol state machine. Further details can be found in [306], which proposes the use of TCP Snoop together with Ad Hoc TCP, the basis of MCTP.

Integration Improvements

The integrated MOCCA protocols used in the underlying network layer may provide additional useful information. This information can be utilised to optimise MCTP further on. An example could be an improved estimation of the retransmission timeout RTO. In the core MCTP functionality, the RTO is predicted by Karn's algorithm implemented in TCP. This algorithm can be extended to consider the available information in order to reduce retransmission timeouts further on. For example, the calculation of the RTO may additionally comprise the distance to the IGW and the speed the vehicle travels. Such improvements are highly related to the VANET deployment, i.e. they require comprehensive investigations and measurements of the MOCCA protocols in a real VANET environment. Therefore, they are not included in the core functionality of MCTP.

Protocol Improvements

Besides the architectural and integration optimisations of the transport layer in MOCCA, MCTP itself can also be optimised further on. In general, the congestion control in MCTP is left to the TCP slow start and congestion avoidance algorithms in case of network congestion. An interesting solution would be the combination of MCTP with TCP Vegas (see section 5.2.1). TCP Vegas tries to avoid changes in the slow start phase by predicting time-outs in order to increase TCP efficiency. Such optimisations must be carefully adjusted and fine-tuned since they highly depend on the communication characteristics of a real inter-vehicle communication system. This way, optimisations of the TCP congestion control are not included in the core functionality of MCTP.

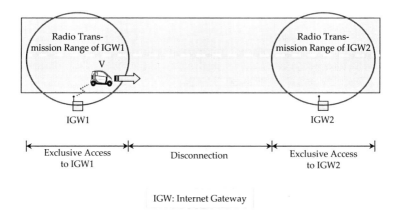

Figure 5.18: Example Scenario for MCTP Optimisation

The available information can also be used to optimise the MCTP protocol state machine, e.g. to improve the approximation of the available bandwidth after a period of disconnection or after a partitioning of the VANET. In the core functionality of the protocol state machine, MCTP forces TCP to approximate the available bandwidth by resetting the congestion window to activate the TCP slow start. This approximation can be replaced by a more intelligent algorithm that takes into account the TCP state before the disconnection or partitioning as well as available information from MMIP6. Figure 5.18 depicts an example scenario where such an intelligent algorithm can be useful. In this example, the traffic density on a road is very low and a vehicle V has exclusive access to an Internet Gateway IGW1. This way, V can completely utilise the available bandwidth to communicate with an Internet host. If V gets disconnected after leaving the radio transmission range of IGW1, MCTP moves into the DISCONNECTED mode until V is able to communicate with IGW2. In this situation, DRIVE provides additional information about IGW2, such as an expected low traffic density and a low utilisation of IGW2. Based on this information, MCTP may not decide to force the TCP slow start but to continue communication with the configuration before the disconnection. This optimisation would increase the TCP performance after a period of disconnection or partitioning. However, it is not implemented in the core functionality of MCTP since the configuration depends on many factors of a real VANET environment that cannot be derived in theory.

5.4   Qualitative Evaluation

In order to determine the suitability of MCTP for the VANET scenario, this section evaluates MCTP in a qualitative way. Therefore, MCTP is discussed in the context of the requirements identified in section 5.2, namely lost segments, disconnections, notifications, and TCP API. Since several principles of MCTP are based on Ad Hoc TCP (ATCP) proposed by Li et al., the simulation and measurement results published in [136] are also considered for the qualitative evaluation of the requirements. A quantitative evaluation of the MCTP performance in typical vehicular communication scenarios on the road is subject of chapter 6.

5.4.1   Handling Segment Losses

An important characteristic of MCTP is the situation-based handling of segment losses. Losses are treated in two ways:

► On lossy communication links, MCTP retransmits the unacknowledged segment autonomously while TCP is frozen in the persist mode. This way, TCP does not perform congestion control in case of lost segments.

► In case of an indicated congestion, the standard TCP congestion control ensures that TCP throttles back the current transmission rate.

Measurements showed that ATCP, the basis of MCTP, completely avoids the slow start of TCP on lossy communication links with a bit error rate of 10^{-5} [136]. Depending on the transmission delay per hop, ATCP requires about 50 % to 25 % of the transfer time to download a 1 Mbyte file compared to TCP Reno. In combination with a periodic congestion every 5 s, the transfer time of ATCP was about 40 % to 15 % compared to the transfer time of TCP.

These results are also valid for MCTP since MCTP implements the basic principles of ATCP for handling segment losses. Thereby, the differences between MCTP and ATCP are marginal: A major difference is that MCTP enters the LOSS state after two consecutive DupAcks whereas ATCP waits for three DupAcks. This way, MCTP expects a more spontaneous handling of segment losses indicated by three DupAcks. A second difference is that ATCP is based on TCP Reno, whereas MCTP uses TCP New Reno and, thus, an improved fast retransmit/fast recovery mechanism. Moreover, MCTP implicitly supports selective acknowledgements not used in ATCP. As a result, MCTP efficiently handles segment losses and, thus, fulfils the 'Lost Segments' requirement.

5.4.2 Handling Disconnections and Network Partitioning

The MCTP protocol state machine was designed to react appropriately to temporary communication breakdowns. It therefore differentiates the following two situations:

▶ A partitioning of the VANET while two vehicles communicate with each other.

▶ A disconnection from the Internet while a vehicle communicates with an Internet host.

In case of a VANET partitioning, the sending vehicle is notified by ICMP about an unreachable communication peer. In this situation, MCTP puts TCP into persist mode and probes the TCP connection periodically for a reconnection. In contrast to ATCP, MCTP does not perform an exponential backoff of the probing period; instead, it uses the value of the last round trip time. This is due to the fact that the routing protocol of the sending vehicle is expected to drop IP packets if it cannot find a valid route to the destination vehicle. This way, the probing does not waste any bandwidth. After a reconnection, it may take up to the last round trip time until MCTP realises the reconnection and communication is continued.

Disconnections from the Internet are not implemented in ATCP. In MCTP, disconnections are handled more efficiently since the DRIVE protocol directly notifies MCTP if it does no longer receive any SA Announcements from IGWs. In this situation, communication with the Internet is no longer possible and MCTP forces TCP to enter the persist mode until DRIVE notifies MCTP about a newly available IGW. TCP does not send any probe packets during this time. This way, MCTP can handle disconnections from the Internet very efficiently.

As a result, MCTP provides a quick convergence of TCP in case of network partitioning and disconnections from the Internet. Since the disconnections are a very important aspect of the Internet integration of VANETs, they are examined and evaluated further on in chapter 6.

5.4.3 Support of Notifications

The MCTP protocol state machine basically processes information and events generated either locally or by intermediate systems. Local events may be caused by the MOCCA protocols on the underlying network layer such as the notification of a disconnection when IGWs are not available for Internet access. Moreover, the MCTP protocol state machine can be extended by further notifications. An example could be the notification of changing network conditions in order to improve communication efficiency further on (see the improvements described in section 5.3.4).

MCTP also considers notifications generated by intermediate systems. Examples are notifications about potential congestions using ECN and notifications about the partitioning of the VANET using ICMP. The protocol state machine also interferes with indirect notifications caused by TCP such as timeouts or duplicate acknowledgements. Hence, MCTP is able to process these events in order to react quickly to sudden changes in the network conditions.

5.4.4 TCP Application Programming Interface

An important feature of MCTP is its implementation as a sublayer between TCP and IP. This sublayer does not modify the semantics of standard TCP. MCTP is therefore interoperable with TCP New Reno, the commonly used TCP in the Internet. This way, MCTP can be mixed up with standard TCP, i.e. an MCTP-enabled host can communicate with a common TCP host. In this case, the performance of MCTP generally corresponds to the performance of standard TCP.

The implementation as a sublayer of TCP also leaves the service access point of TCP untouched. This way, MCTP can be used similar to TCP using the socket API, which facilitates the porting of existing IP-based applications as well as the development of future applications for the VANET scenario. This way, MCTP completely fulfils the 'TCP API' requirement.

5.5 Summary

The transport layer is of vital importance for the performance of a communication system. The communication protocol on this layer hides the typical characteristics of the underlying networking technologies to the application-based protocol layers. This way, the transport protocol significantly affects the communication performance experienced by the applications. In the MOCCA architecture, the MoccaProxy segments the end-to-end transport layer connection into two parts: communication with Internet hosts, and communication with vehicles. Whereas communication in the Internet is based on TCP, an optimised transport protocol can be used for communication between vehicles and the MoccaProxy. Such a transport protocol has to face several challenges: efficient and situation-based handling of segment losses, a quick convergence in case of disconnections, the consideration of notifications about changing network conditions, and a programming interface similar to TCP. TCP is not a suitable solution since its conservative congestion control provides poor performance in vehicular environments. Moreover, an observation of related work on TCP improvements for mobile and wireless environments showed that none of the existing solutions fulfils the transport protocol requirements for vehicular ad hoc networks sufficiently.

This chapter introduced MCTP, the transport protocol integrated into the MOCCA protocol architecture. MCTP can be used for communication between vehicles as well as communication between vehicles and the MoccaProxy. MCTP is based on the principles of Ad Hoc TCP but was enhanced in several ways to take into account the typical characteristics of vehicular environments. MCTP operates in a sublayer between IP and TCP, which processes available information and events in order to control TCP appropriately in different situations. This way, it is able to classify segment losses by congestions or transmission errors and it is able to handle temporary network partitioning and disconnections from the Internet very efficiently. This core functionality can be extended by further improvements considering additional notifications from the underlying MOCCA protocols in an integrated manner. Hence, MCTP is a suitable solution for being deployed in the MOCCA architecture. A qualitative evaluation showed that MCTP fulfils the transport protocol requirements for VANETs. Measurements from the authors of Ad Hoc TCP [136] – the basis of MCTP – in a typical ad hoc network scenario showed that Ad Hoc TCP reduces the time to transfer a certain amount of data between two hosts in the ad hoc network to one third compared to standard TCP. MCTP will improve this performance further on since it provides a better handling of network partitioning. The following chapter evaluates MCTP for the Internet integration of VANETs.

Chapter 6

Evaluation

The previous chapters proposed the different communication protocols of the MOCCA architecture and evaluated them in the context of the related work in the respective areas. The goal of this chapter is to evaluate the MOCCA architecture as a whole in two ways: a quantitative evaluation and a qualitative evaluation. The *quantitative* evaluation determines the performance of MOCCA by measurements in a testbed, which emulates different vehicular communication situations: a crossway in a city, an empty motorway at night, a motorway with a high traffic flow, and a congested motorway. For these scenarios, this chapter proposes communication models for four typical vehicular scenarios on the road. These models reflect the characteristics a vehicle experiences while travelling in the respective scenario. The results of the measurements are discussed and compared with measurements using a split TCP approach and an end-to-end TCP approach in the same testbed. The *qualitative* measurements evaluate MOCCA in the context of the requirements for the Internet integration of VANETs. With these investigations, MOCCA is compared with the related work on Internet integration.

This chapter begins with a description of the approach used for the evaluation of MOCCA in section 6.1. Section 6.2 introduces four vehicular communication scenarios together with the communication models for a vehicle in each scenario. This section is followed by the quantitative evaluation in section 6.3, which attends to the methods used for the measurements, the results of the evaluation, and a discussion of the results. The qualitative evaluation is subject of section 6.4 that evaluates the suitability of MOCCA for the Internet integration of VANETs. Finally, section 6.5 summarises this chapter with the key results of the evaluation and a comparison of MOCCA with related work.

6.1   Goals and Used Approach

The movement of a vehicle and the traffic flow on the road depends on many factors. Examples are the type of the road (e.g., a motorway, a rural road, or a street in a city), daytime, day of the week, weather and road conditions, macro-mobility patterns, and micro-mobility movements. Even a driver's preference, mood, and schedule influence the traffic on the road. As a result, the traffic on a road is very heterogeneous and the modelling of realistic traffic scenarios is a very complex matter due to the amount of parameters affecting the traffic flow and the mobility of individual vehicles. For example, an analysis of the observed traffic on a motorway at night showed that it is almost impossible to model the traffic flow in this situation [307]. An exact specification of the network conditions in the VANET is not possible, too. Many parameters immediately depend, e.g., on the number of communicating vehicles, their distribution, and the communication patterns of the applications being used. Moreover, environmental and physical aspects affect the performance characteristics further on such as the radio wave propagation that only can be considered by having detailed geographical information. This way, exact assertions on the available bandwidth, packet delays, packet losses and jitter are very difficult to model in a realistic way.

The goal of this evaluation is to determine the performance of MOCCA under typical conditions on the road using the FleetNet communication system for inter-vehicle communication. An evaluation in a real-world test environment is not practical since many vehicles are needed and the results are not reproducible due to permanently changing conditions. Moreover, FleetNet hardware and software is currently not available for the tests. An alternative approach is a pure simulation of realistic network conditions with existing network simulators like ns-2 [308]. This is also not suitable since these tools cannot process the amount of data that are necessary for the simulation runs. Moreover, simulation tools are based on abstract end system models that further may adulterate the measurements.

For these reasons, the evaluation of MOCCA follows a hybrid approach: For the evaluation, an MCTP prototype was implemented to measure the performance of MCTP using real end systems. The measurements are performed in a testbed that emulate the lower communication layers in an abstract way. The emulation reflects abstract models for the performance characteristics of the FleetNet communication system as well as for the characteristics of the MOCCA protocols operating on the network layer, namely MMIP6 and DRIVE. This approach is justified by the fact that MCTP provides an interface to the MOCCA architecture hiding the lower protocol layers to the applications. The emulation used for the evaluation models the different "segments" in the MOCCA architecture as depicted in figure 6.1:

▶ Communication in the VANET, i.e. between vehicles and IGW, which is based on the FleetNet communication system.

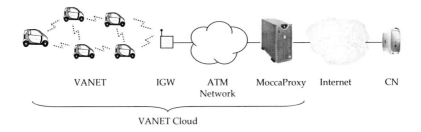

VANET   IGW   ATM   MoccaProxy   Internet   CN
                             Network

VANET Cloud

ATM: Asynchronous Transfer Mode ∘ CN: Correspondent Node
IGW: Internet Gateway ∘ VANET: Vehicular Ad Hoc Network

Figure 6.1: VANET Scenario used for the Evaluation

► Communication between the IGW and the MoccaProxy, which assumes an ATM network (Asynchronous Transfer Mode) [309, 310].

► Communication between the MoccaProxy and the CN using the Internet.

Since an exact model of these situations cannot be developed with arguable efforts, sim-
plifications and abstractions are necessary to model the communication behaviour of the
road communication scenarios. Although such abstractions reflect a rather unrealistic im-
age of the real world, they allow assertions about the usefulness of communication protocols, their efficiency and improvement potentials, and their performance in expected environments and situations.

6.2   Vehicular Communication Scenarios

Since traffic on the road is highly heterogeneous, one scenario cannot cover all facets of existing road situations. This evaluation is based on four different scenarios reflecting "typical"
communication scenarios in different road traffic situations:

► A crossway in a city.

► A motorway at night.

► A motorway with a high traffic flow.

► A congested motorway.

In order to model the network layer characteristics, all scenarios assume the FleetNet communication system for inter-vehicle communications (see section 2.1.1). The FleetNet air interface is based on a modified UTRA-TDD scheme[1] using Code Division Multiple Access (CDMA) to separate the communication channels of the vehicles [27]. In order to model inter-vehicle communication, parameters for the link layer performance of FleetNet are necessary, which can be found in [255]: The maximum net link layer bandwidth[2] of the FleetNet communication system is $Bw_{net} = 588$ kbit/s. The digital modulation deploys a Quatenary Phase Shift Keying (QPSK) scheme, which is able to transmit 2 bit per 1 Hz. Typical transmission delays for one link are in the magnitude of three to four transmission frames whereby the duration of a frame is 10 ms. Hence, the resulting delay for one hop in the worst case is $delay = 4 \cdot 10$ ms $= 40$ ms, which is assumed in the following scenarios.

The wireless transmission causes a rather high packet error rate compared to wired networks. At higher noise levels, the frame error rate of FleetNet can be up to 10^{-3} [255]. An average IP packet of $1,500$ byte is, thus, split up into 29 link layer frames each having a length of 420 bit. Therefore, the resulting IP packet error rate would be up to 2.9 % in this case. In the following scenarios, an IP packet error rate of $err = 1$ % is assumed, which is in accordance with the results proposed in [311]. Hence, the overall IP packet loss probability depends on the number of hops and can be calculated using the following equation:

$$loss(hops) = 1 - (1 - err)^{hops} = 1 - 0.99^{hops} \tag{6.1}$$

On the network layer, the DRIVE protocol requires additional bandwidth for the discovery of the IGWs. In order to distribute the SA Announcements of DRIVE in the VANETs (cf. section 4.4.2), a simple flooding mechanism is assumed for this purpose. Since this overhead also depends on the topology of the VANET, more precise estimations are used for the respective scenarios in order to determine the overhead caused by DRIVE.

Further abstractions are necessary for the protocols on the network layer and the transport layer. In general, the additional overhead of these layers is not considered since this overhead varies with packet sizes and configurations. The models also do not consider the overhead of the location-based routing protocol, which is basically determined by the protocol mechanisms used as well as the protocol implementation. Furthermore, the overhead for the registration of MMIP6 is neglected since it is rather small and it also depends on the configuration of MMIP6. Although these limitations may represent a simplification of the scenarios, they are acceptable to investigate the MOCCA performance in "typical" situations.

---

[1]UTRA TDD: UMTS Terrestrial Radio Access – Time Division Duplex.

[2]This value considers a spreading factor of 1 and a code rate for the convolution code of $\frac{1}{3}$. The usage of a higher code rate will lead to a higher bandwidth but also to a higher bit error rate. Choosing a higher spreading factor will cause a reduction of the useable data rate.

Further relevant parameters vary between the scenarios and are introduced in the respective scenario description.

6.2.1 City Crossway

The first scenario represents a crowded crossway in a city, which combines four street segments as illustrated in figure 6.2. Each segment consists of one lane per direction. The traffic flow is controlled by traffic lights for each street segment. An IGW mounted at a corner of the crossing provides access to the Internet for the vehicles at the crossway. The traffic flow in this scenario can be subdivided into two phases for each street segment. While the traffic lights are red for one street segment, the vehicles on this segment have to wait and do not move. If the light switches to green, the vehicles will start moving to pass the crossway. In the following, the first case is called "red phase" and the second case is called "green phase".

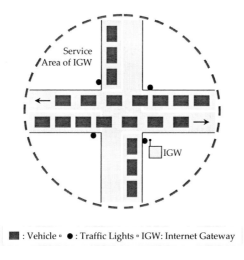

■ : Vehicle □ ● : Traffic Lights □ IGW: Internet Gateway

Figure 6.2: An Urban Crossway

The crossway scenario shows the following characteristics for one street segment:

▶ The movement of the vehicles during the green phase is very smooth. The vehicles drive at low speeds and typically do not overtake each other – except when a vehicle turns off at the crossway. As a result, the mobility of the vehicles is low and the reconfiguration rate of the VANET is also very low.

▶ During the red phase, there is no movement of the vehicles on the respective street segment. Thus, the mobility is static and the topology of the VANET does not change for the vehicles on the respective lane.

▶ The Internet access is provided by one IGW only covering the whole crossway. All vehicles have to share the available bandwidth. In this scenario, there will not be any handovers to other IGWs. Hence, vehicles are no longer able to access the Internet when leaving the service area of the single IGW.

The traffic in a city mainly consists of cars and small busses. In Germany, the average length of these vehicles is $l_{veh} = 4.5\,$m with an average distance of $\Delta x = 2\,$m between two consecutive vehicles waiting in front of the traffic lights [312]. For simplicity reasons, this scenario assumes that all vehicles start on one segment to move at the same time when the traffic lights switch to green. Therefore, the average distance between the vehicles can be supposed to be almost constant. The diameter of the geographical service area (dotted circle in figure 6.2) indicates the area where the IGW can be used by the vehicles. Hence, this diameter represents the area wherein the vehicles forward the SA Announcements of the IGW as described in section 4.4.2. In this scenario, the diameter of the service area is assumed with $l_{geo} = 800\,$m to supply the whole crossway. The adaptive radio transmission range r_{radio} depends on the number of vehicles taking part in the VANET, because every communicating vehicle causes additional interference. In this scenario, $r_{radio} = 100\,$m seems to be a suitable value as shown later in this section. The penetration φ specifies the share of communicating vehicles participating in the VANET. It has to be assumed that only a certain percentage of cars will be equipped with VANET-capable technology. It can be expected that more luxury cars and trucks will be the first deployment candidates. In urban areas, there will be many compact cars or lower-equipped cars that predominantly will not have the necessary communication hardware. Here, a penetration of $\varphi = 8\,\%$ is assumed for the crossway scenario. Table 6.1 summarises the micro-mobility parameters used for the crossway scenario. As described in the previous section, the FleetNet communication system has an expected net bandwidth of $Bw_{net} = 588\,$kbit/s with a delay of $delay = 40\,$ms per link and an IP packet error rate of $err = 1\,\%$. The expected jitter of the transmission delay is set to $\pm10\,$ms.

With the help of these micro-mobility parameters, it is possible to determine several important macro-mobility statistics. The first estimation considers the minimum number of hops between a vehicle at the border of the service area and the IGW. Having optimum conditions, the distance between two communicating vehicles is as large as the radio transmission range. Hence, the minimum number of hops can be derived in the following way:

$$hops_{min} = \frac{\frac{1}{2} \cdot l_{geo}}{r_{radio}} = \frac{400\,\text{m}}{100\,\text{m/hop}} = 4\,\text{hops} \tag{6.2}$$

Parameter	Description	Default Value
l_{veh}	Average Length of a Vehicle	4.5 m
Δx	Distance between two Vehicles	2 m
l_{geo}	Diameter of the IGW's Service Area	800 m
r_{radio}	Radio Transmission Range	100 m
φ	Penetration of communicating Vehicles	8 %
Bw_{net}	Available Bandwidth (net)	588 kbit/s
$delay$	Transmission Delay per Link	40 ms
err	Packet Error Rate per Link	1 %
$jitter$	Variation of Transmission Delay	±10 %

Table 6.1: Micro-Mobility Parameters for the Crossway Scenario

The second important factor is the traffic density ρ representing the number of vehicles per lane and km. The traffic density is a measure for the average utilisation of the road. According to [307], the traffic density can be estimated from the lengths of the vehicles, the distance between two vehicles, and the number n of vehicles that pass one lane in a time period as follows:

$$\rho = \left(\frac{1}{n} \cdot \sum_{i=1}^{n} (l_{veh(i)} + \Delta x_i) \right)^{-1} \approx \left(\frac{1}{n} \cdot \sum_{i=1}^{n} (l_{veh} + \Delta x) \right)^{-1} = \frac{1}{l_{veh} + \Delta x} \qquad (6.3)$$
$$= \frac{1}{(4.5 + 2)\,\text{m/vehicle}} \approx 154\,\text{vehicles/km}$$

A third important parameter is the number of vehicles n_{veh} in the service area of the IGW. In the crossway scenario, the service area consists of four street segments, each with a length of 400 m and one lane per direction. The vehicles occupy at maximum six lanes simultaneously since the traffic lights are usually green for at most two street segments at the same time. This way, the number of vehicles in the service area is $n_{veh} = (0.4 \cdot 6 \cdot 154)$ vehicles $=$ 370 vehicles. Considering the penetration of $\varphi = 8\,\%$, the service area comprises about 30 communicating vehicles that compete for the available bandwidth of the IGW. In this model, it is assumed that the communicating vehicles are distributed equally on the six lanes. This means that there are $\frac{30}{6} = 5$ vehicles on each of the six lanes. Thus, the average distance between two neighboured communicating vehicles is $\frac{400}{5} = 80$ m. This shows that $r_{radio} = 100$ m is an appropriate configuration to make inter-vehicle communication possible.

For simplification, this scenario assumes that all vehicles access the Internet simultaneously and do not communicate locally except for the forwarding of IP packets from other vehicles towards the IGW. Hence, the available bandwidth per vehicle is solely determined by the last hop to the IGW, because all vehicles have to share the bandwidth of this hop. A small share of the available net bandwidth is needed for the transmission of the SA Announcements inside the direct transmission range of the IGW. The average number of vehicle in the immediate transmission range of the IGW can be derived by dividing r_{radio} by the average distance between two communicating vehicles. In the worst case, the announcements are forwarded by all vehicles located in the immediate transmission range of the IGW. Hence, on average $100/80 = 1.25$ vehicles per street segment forward the SA Announcements from the IGW in addition to the transmission of the IGW itself. The overhead Bw_{DRIVE} caused by DRIVE (equation 4.6) in the immediate transmission range of the IGW can be specified more accurately by equation 6.4. Assuming an average size for the SA Announcements of $P_{Announce} = 110$ bytes (as derived in section 4.5.1) and a frequency of $f_{Announce} = 2\,\text{Hz}$, the overhead caused by DRIVE is determined in the following way:

$$\begin{aligned} Bw_{DRIVE} &= \text{\# transmissions} \cdot f_{Announce} \cdot P_{Announce} \\ &= (1 + 6 \cdot 1.25) \cdot 2\,\text{Hz} \cdot 110\,\text{byte} = 14.96\,\text{kbit/s} \end{aligned} \tag{6.4}$$

If all vehicles access the Internet simultaneously, the available bandwidth Bw for each vehicle is determined by equation 6.5. Thereby, a simplified assumption can be made that the available bandwidth is distributed equally among the communicating vehicles; measurements with competing TCP flows in [313] showed that these flows share the available bandwidth almost fairly.

$$Bw = \frac{Bw_{net} - Bw_{DRIVE}}{\text{\# communicating vehicles}} = \frac{588 - 14.96}{30}\,\text{kbit/s} = 19.1\,\text{kbit/s} \tag{6.5}$$

The effect of packet duplicates caused by the location-based routing protocol in FleetNet is negligible for this scenario, because there is no more than one communicating vehicle in the transmission range of any other vehicle that forwards data packets towards the IGW. Furthermore, the routing protocol has only little impact on the communication: The position of the IGW is included in the first SA Announcement received by the vehicle (see section 4.4.4). According to section 4.4.4, an additional location query to determine the position of the IGW is not necessary in this case.

Mobility Model for One Vehicle

An important requirement for the evaluation is the observation of a vehicle V passing the crossway. When V enters the service area of the IGW, it will receive the SA Announcements of the IGW. With the help of these announcements, V identifies the IGW and MMIP6 registers itself with the Foreign Agent running on the IGW. After that, the vehicle is able to access the Internet. The initial distance between the IGW and V at the border of the service area is 5 hops, which corresponds to the number of communicating vehicles on each lane. For simplicity reasons, this scenario supposes that traffic is only forwarded by communicating vehicles on the same direction. No packets are routed to the IGW by vehicles on the oncoming traffic. Hence, the initial transmission delay between V and the IGW is $5 \cdot 40\,\text{ms} = 200\,\text{ms}$ with a jitter of $\pm 10\,\%$ (see table 6.1).

In the beginning, the traffic lights for the street segment are red and the vehicles do not move. If the traffic lights switch to green, the vehicles start up and pass the crossway slowly. Without the loss of generality, it is assumed that all vehicles start moving at the same time with the same speed of $15\,\text{km/h}$. While V approaches the IGW, the number of hops is decremented every $80\,\text{m}$, i.e. the average distance between two communicating vehicles. Therefore, the number of hops is reduced every $80\,\text{m}/15\,\text{km/h} \approx 19\,\text{s}$.

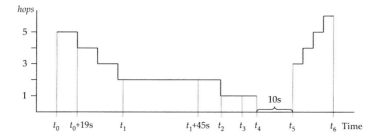

Figure 6.3: Mobility Impact on the Number of Hops

Figure 6.3 shows the distance (in hops) between V and the IGW over time when V drives through the service area of an IGW. At t_0, V enters the service area of the gateway and is now able to access the Internet whereby four vehicles between V and the IGW forward the IP packets of V. The number of hops is reduced every $19\,\text{s}$ until t_1. At this time, the traffic lights switch to red for this segment. Hence, V does not move for the next $45\,\text{s}$ and the distance to the IGW is constant during this period. Afterwards, the traffic lights again switch to green and V continues its movement. At t_2, V enters the radio transmission range of the IGW at a distance of $r_{radio} = 100\,\text{m}$ to the IGW. Within this area, the vehicle is in a position to communicate with the IGW directly. Thus, delay and the packet loss rate are minimal during this period. At time t_3, V passes the traffic lights. Therefore, it speeds up to

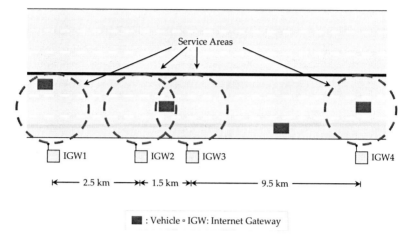

Figure 6.4: A Motorway at Night

an assumed speed of 30 km/h. The whole period of having direct access to the IGW is, thus, $\frac{100\,m}{15\,km/h} + \frac{100\,m}{30\,km/h} = 36\,s$. In this example, the following communicating vehicle is assumed to turn off at the crossing. Hence, V becomes disconnected at t_4 for a period of 10 s until t_5 when a following communicating vehicle moves into the transmission range of V and re-establishes the Internet connection. This gap might be bridged by considering the ability of the oncoming traffic to forward data packets, which is not considered in this model. From this time, the number of hops increases every $80\,m/30\,km/h = 9.6\,s$. The connection is lost after a distance of 5 hops when V leaves the service area of the IGW at time t_6.

6.2.2   Motorway at Night

The second scenario represents an almost empty motorway at night. Figure 6.4 depicts this motorway consisting of three lanes per direction. Thereby, four IGWs provide Internet access for the passing vehicles. The characteristics and assumptions of this scenario are the following:

▶ The vehicles are driving at high speeds. Hence, the duration of a connection with an IGW is rather short.

▶ The distance between the first and the second IGW is larger than the diameter of the IGW's service area. For this reason, communication is not possible in a small area of 500 m between the two IGWs resulting in a short-term disconnection from the Internet.

▶ The radio transmission areas of the second and the third IGW overlap each other for 500 m. Hence, a vehicle has to perform a handover to make continuous communication possible while passing IGW2 and IGW3.

▶ The distance between IGW3 and IGW4 is assumed to be 9.5 km, which causes a long period of disconnection. This is justified by the assumption that especially at an early deployment phase the IGWs will not have an area-wide coverage.

Parameter	Description	Default Value
l_{veh}	Average Length of a Vehicle	4.5 m
Δx	Distance between two Vehicles	1,000 m
l_{geo}	Diameter of the IGW's Service Area	2,000 m
r_{radio}	Radio Transmission Range	1,000 m
φ	Penetration of communicating Vehicles	15 %
Bw_{net}	Available Bandwidth (net)	588 kbit/s
$delay$	Transmission Delay per Link	40 ms
err	Packet Error Rate per Link	1 %
$jitter$	Variation of Transmission Delay	±5 %

Table 6.2: Micro-Mobility Parameters for the Motorway at Night

In this scenario, it is assumed that cars or small busses travel on the motorway only. The average length of these vehicles is $l_{veh} = 4.5$ m [312]. Due to the low traffic density at night, the average distance between two neighboured vehicles is assumed with $\Delta x = 1$ km and the diameter of the service area of an IGW is supposed to be $l_{geo} = 2,000$ m. According to [314], the adaptive radio transmission range in FleetNet might be up to 1,000 m. Since only few vehicles drive on the motorway, the radio transmission range r_{radio} is set to this maximum value, which is much higher than in the other scenarios. The penetration φ of communicating vehicles is also likely higher than in the crossway scenario, because on a motorway there might be a higher number of better-equipped cars than in a city. A penetration rate of $\varphi = 15$ % is assumed to be suitable for this scenario. The following parameters are chosen as in the crossway scenario: $Bw_{net} = 588$ kbit/s, $delay = 40$ ms (per link), and $err = 1$ % per link. The jitter is assumed to be lower compared to the previous scenario, because a vehicle always has a direct and exclusive access when communicating with the IGW; it does not have to forward any data packets of other vehicles. This way, *jitter* = ±5 % seems to be suitable for this purpose. Table 6.2 summarises the micro-mobility parameters used for the motorway at night scenario.

From these micro-mobility parameters, several macro-mobility observations can be derived. According to equation 6.3, the traffic density per lane is $\rho \approx \frac{1,000}{1,000+4.5} \approx 1$ vehicle/km, which reflects the emptiness on the motorway. The total number of vehicles n_{veh} within the service area of one IGW is calculated by

$$n_{veh} = \rho \cdot \# \text{lanes} \cdot l_{geo} = 6 \text{ vehicles} \tag{6.6}$$

Considering the penetration of $\varphi = 15$ %, there is no more than one communicating vehicle inside the service area of an IGW. Under these circumstances, a vehicle driving through the service area has the full available bandwidth of this gateway for 2 km. This bandwidth is slightly reduced by the transmission of SA Announcements in the radio transmission diameter of the IGW. Like in the crossway scenario, a frequency of two SA Announcements per second is assumed. In the worst case, the communicating vehicle forwards the SA Announcements resulting in two transmissions for each SA Announcement. Hence, the overhead caused by DRIVE for the motorway at night model is determined as follows:

$$Bw_{DRIVE} = \# \text{transmissions} \cdot f_{Announce} \cdot P_{Announce} = 2 \cdot 2 \text{ Hz} \cdot 110 \text{ byte} = 3.52 \text{ kbit/s}$$

According to equation 6.5, the average available bandwidth in this scenario for a vehicle passing the first IGW is $Bw_{IGW1} = 584.48$ kbit/s. This value is only valid for the case that the vehicle is in the transmission range of a single IGW. Between IGW2 and IGW3, there is a small area where the vehicle has direct access to both gateways as illustrated in figure 6.4. Although a vehicle can only have a connection to one of the gateways, the SA Announcements from both gateways need to be forwarded. As a result, the overhead caused by DRIVE is doubled in this area, resulting in an available bandwidth of $Bw_{IGW2,3} = 580.96$ kbit/s.

Since no other communicating vehicles are travelling in the transmission range of a vehicle, communication with the IGW is only possible if the gateway can be accessed directly. This is why the number of hops and, therefore, the delay for a connection is always constant as long as an IGW is available. Like in the crossway scenario, duplicates can be neglected since inter-vehicle communication does not occur with the assumed parameters.

Mobility Model for One Vehicle

On empty motorways, drivers usually travel at high speeds. According to [307], the average speed of cars on motorways with a low traffic density is 150 km/h. In the following, it is assumed that a vehicle V passes the four IGWs with this speed (cf. figure 6.4). The examined motorway segment has a total length of 15.5 km. The distance between the first and the second IGW is assumed to be 2.5 km. Thus, the service areas of both gateways are separated and a coverage gap of 500 m occurs between IGW1 and IGW2. The distance between IGW2 and IGW3 is assumed to be 1.5 km, which means that the transmission ranges of the gateways overlap each other for a distance of 500 m. When leaving the service area of IGW3, V becomes disconnected from the Internet for a longer period of time before it reconnects to the Internet via IGW4. Thereby, the distance between IGW3 and IGW4 is assumed to be 9.5 km, resulting in a gap of 7.5 km where V has no Internet access.

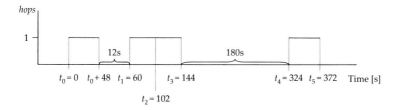

Figure 6.5: Impact of the Vehicle's Mobility on the Number of Hops

In this scenario, figure 6.5 shows the variation of the number of hops for vehicle V against the time. The first IGW gets accessible at time t_0. Vehicle V can communicate with IGW1 over a distance of 2 km, which corresponds to $2 \cdot r_{radio}$. At a speed of 150 km/h, the contact to this gateway will be lost after 2 km/150 km/h $= 48$ s. Hence, at $t_0 + 48$ s there is no other IGW available and the Internet access becomes temporarily unavailable. For simplicity reasons, the use of the oncoming traffic for Internet access to one of the gateways is not considered. Afterwards, V passes a distance of 500 m without having Internet access, i.e. V is temporarily disconnected from the Internet for 500 m/150 km/h $= 12$ s.

The next event occurs at $t_1 = t_0 + 48$ s $+ 12$ s $= t_0 + 60$ s, where V enters the radio transmission range of the IGW2 and again gets access to the Internet. Since the transmission areas of IGW2 and IGW3 overlap each other, the Internet connection of V with the second IGW can be handed over to IGW3. The handover occurs at $t_2 = t_1 + \frac{1.75\,\text{km}}{150\,\text{km/h}} = t_1 + 42$ s. The latency caused by the processing of the handover is assumed with $t_{HOlat} = 24$ ms that corresponds to the measurements in [315]. During this time, all packets are assumed as being lost due to a "hard" handover. In this example, the handover occurs at t_2 when the vehicle is located in the middle of both IGWs. After the handover to IGW3 at $t_2 + t_{HOlat}$, V is able to continue with its communications. IGW2 and IGW3 together cover a service area of 3.5 km. With the assumed speed of 150 km/h, V has connectivity to the Internet for 3.5 km/150 km/h $= 84$ s while passing both gateways. The vehicle leaves the transmission range of IGW3 at $t_3 = t_1 + 84\,\mathrm{s}$ and V becomes disconnected from the Internet until it travels into the service area of IGW4 at t_4. Since the coverage gap between IGW3 and IGW4 is 7.5 km, the reconnection to the Internet via IGW4 occurs at $t_4 = t_3 + \frac{7.5\,\mathrm{km}}{150\,\mathrm{km/h}} = t_3 + 180\,\mathrm{s}$. Finally, V becomes disconnected from the Internet when leaving the service area of IGW4 at $t_4 + 48\,\mathrm{s}$.

6.2.3 Motorway with high Traffic Flow

The third scenario used for the evaluation models a motorway with a high traffic flow, e.g. during day time, as shown in figure 6.6. Corresponding to the previous scenario, the motorway has three lanes per direction. The features and assumptions for this scenario are the following:

▶ The traffic flow is high and is slightly disturbed by overtaking manœuvres. The mobility of the vehicles is also high and differs between the individual lanes. Vehicles on the left lane will drive at higher speeds than, e.g., trucks on the right lane.

▶ Faster vehicles often overtake slower ones. Therefore, the topology of the VANET is subject to a frequent reconfiguration rate.

▶ Two gateways IGW1 and IGW2 mounted at the roadside provide Internet access for the motorway segment considered. The service areas of the IGWs do not overlap each other. This way, communication is not possible in an area between the IGWs.

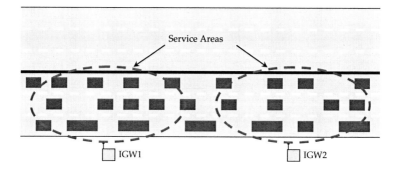

Figure 6.6: A Motorway with high Traffic Flow

The specification of the average length of a vehicle is more complex than in the previous scenarios, because the motorway traffic is characterised by many different kinds of vehicles like cars, trucks, or semi-trailer trucks. The middle and the left lane are mainly occupied by cars and small transporters with an average length of $l_{veh} = 4.5\,\text{m}$ [312]. The average length at the right lane is higher, because trucks basically travel on the right lane. The average length of a truck is assumed with their maximum permissible length of 12 m as defined in [316]. Assuming trucks to have a share of 10 % of the total road traffic, the average length of vehicles on all three lanes of the motorway is $l_{veh} = 5.3\,\text{m}$ [307]. Furthermore, the average distance Δx between two neighboured vehicles can be assumed with 28 m. The following parameters are chosen as in the motorway at night scenario: Diameter of the service area $l_{geo} = 2,000\,\text{m}$, penetration $\varphi = 15\,\%$, net bandwidth $Bw_{net} = 588\,\text{kbit/s}$, and packet error rate $err = 1\,\%$ per link. The radio transmission range is set to $r_{radio} = 100\,\text{m}$ and the transmission delay is at 40 ms per link with an assumed jitter of $\pm 20\,\%$. This higher value for the jitter considers the increased frequency of reconfigurations in the ad hoc network caused by the higher mobility of the vehicles. Table 6.3 summarises the micro-mobility parameters of this model.

Parameter	Description	Default Value
l_{veh}	Average Length of a Vehicle	5.3 m
Δx	Distance between two Vehicles	28 m
l_{geo}	Diameter of the IGW's Service Area	2,000 m
r_{radio}	Radio Transmission Range	100 m
φ	Penetration of communicating Vehicles	15 %
Bw_{net}	Available Bandwidth (net)	588 kbit/s
$delay$	Transmission Delay per Link	40 ms
err	Packet Error Rate per Link	1 %
$jitter$	Variation of Transmission Delay	$\pm 20\,\%$

Table 6.3: Micro-Mobility Parameters for the Motorway with high Traffic Flow

Based on these assumptions, the minimum number of hops needed to communicate with the IGW from the border of the service area is $hops_{min} = (0.5 \cdot 2,000/100)\,\text{hops} = 10\,\text{hops}$ (according to equation 6.2).

According to [307], the traffic flow on a motorway is colloquial designated as "high" if the traffic density ρ exceeds 30 vehicles/km (per lane). The density in this example can be assumed with $\rho = 30$ vehicles/km, which corresponds to the result using equation 6.3. This result shows that the assumption for Δx is a suitable distance between two vehicles. Obviously, the traffic density on the right lane may be lower than on the other lanes, because this lane is mainly occupied by longer vehicles that in addition might observe a higher safety distance than the driver of cars[3]. Under these conditions, the total number of vehicles in the service area are derived with the help of equation 6.6: $n_{veh} = 2$ km $\cdot$ 3 lanes $\cdot$ 30 vehicles/km $= 186$ vehicles. With a penetration of $\varphi = 15\%$, there are about 27 communicating vehicles in the service area of the IGW. Hence, the average distance between two communicating vehicles is 2,000 m/27 vehicles ≈ 74 m/vehicles. The other way round, there are

$$n_{neighbours} = \frac{2 \cdot r_{radio}}{\text{avg. communication distance}} \tag{6.7}$$

$$= \frac{200\,\text{m}}{74\,\text{m/vehicle}} = 2.7 \,(\text{communicating}) \text{ vehicles} \tag{6.8}$$

in the radio transmission range of each communicating vehicle. This way, packet duplications may occur since a node has more than one forwarding node in its immediate communication range [318]. In this example, a duplication rate of $dup = 1\%$ per link was chosen. The following equation determines overall duplication probability dependent on the number of hops:

$$dup(hops) = 1 - (1 - dup)^{hops} = 1 - 0.99^{hops} \tag{6.9}$$

The transmission and forwarding of the SA Announcements from an IGW causes additional overhead that reduces the available bandwidth for Internet access. Using equation 6.4, the overhead in this model is $Bw_{DRIVE} = (2.7 + 1) \cdot 2\,\text{Hz} \cdot 110\,\text{byte} = 6.512\,\text{kbit/s}$. Like in the previous scenarios, it is assumed that all vehicles access the Internet simultaneously. According to equation 6.5, the average available bandwidth for each communicating vehicle is, thus,

$$Bw = \frac{588 - 6.512}{27}\,\text{kbit/s} = 21.57\,\text{kbit/s} \tag{6.10}$$

Mobility Model for one Vehicle

The mobility analysis in this scenario is more complex due to the different characteristics on the three lanes. In this model, the examined motorway segment has a length of 5 km. Two gateways IGW1 and IGW2 provide Internet access for the passing vehicles, as depicted in

---

[3]In Germany, the minimum safety distance for vehicles having a payload of more than 3.5 t and driving at a speed of minimum 50 km/h should be at least 50 m (StVO, §4,3 [317]).

figure 6.6. The service area of each IGW is 2,000 m with an assumed gap of 1,000 m between the service areas of IGW1 and IGW2. Under the assumption that all communicating vehicles are distributed equally, the minimal distance of a vehicle at the border of a service area is $hops_{min} = 10$ hops. Hence, the overall delay between the gateway and a vehicle at this position is $10 \cdot 40$ ms $= 400$ ms with a jitter of $\pm 20\%$. For simplicity reasons, this scenario distinguishes between two situations: A vehicle that drives on the right lane, and a vehicle travelling on the left lane, which drives at higher speed and overtakes other vehicles.

Vehicle on the Right Lane

The traffic on the right lane is usually very smooth. The vehicles drive at an almost constant speed of 85 km/h. In the beginning, the reduction of the number of hops is dominated by the influence of approaching the IGW. If a faster vehicle on another lane forwards the IP packets of a vehicle V in the direction of the IGW, it may occur that this vehicle leaves the radio transmission range of V. Thus, the Internet access becomes temporarily unavailable for V if no other vehicle is available to forward the data. This does not only interrupt the communication of V but also of other following vehicles that use V as a forwarding hop towards the IGW. For simplicity reasons, this scenario assumes that all lanes are equally used by communicating vehicles. Since the radio transmission range of V is larger than the average distance between two communicating vehicles, it is supposed that there will be a communication path between V and the IGW in most situations. Considering the average distance of 74 m between two communicating vehicles, the number of hops to the IGW will be reduced every 74 m$/85$ km/h ≈ 3 s. From the border of the service area, $1,000$ m$/(74$ m$/$hop$) = 14$ hops are needed to communicate with the IGW. Figure 6.7 illustrates the impact of the mobility of the observed vehicle V to the number of hops experienced for communication.

At t_0, V moves into the service area of IGW1 and discovers the gateway by receiving its SA Announcements. The number of hops is decremented periodically every 3 s until t_1, when the connection is lost for a short period of 1 s since other communicating vehicles are not available to forward the IP packets towards the IGW. This model only considers vehicles moving in the same direction; vehicles in the oncoming traffic are not taken into account for the Internet access. At t_2, V communicates directly with IGW1. As long as the vehicle is located in the radio transmission diameter of IGW1, i.e. $2 \cdot r_{radio} = 200$ m, both delay and packet losses will be minimal. This period takes until $t_3 = t_2 + 200$ m$/85$ km/h $\approx t_2 + 9$ s. At this time, Internet access again becomes unavailable for 2 s since the contact to the gateway is assumed to be lost when leaving the radio transmission range of the IGW. After the reconnecting to the IGW via three hops at $t_3 + 2$ s, the number of hops between V and IGW1 increases every 3 s. The next event occurs at t_4 when V leaves the service area

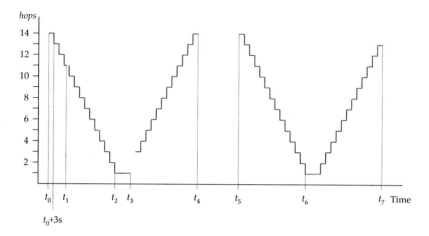

Figure 6.7: Effect of Vehicle's Movement on the Number of Hops (Right Lane)

of IGW1 after 14 hops and therefore further communication with the Internet is no longer possible.

The second gateway IGW2 becomes accessible at $t_5 = t_4 + 1,000\,\text{m}/85\,\text{km/h} \approx t_4 + 42\,\text{s}$. Here, a similar behaviour can be observed: The distance to the IGW is decremented periodically every 3 s. At t_6, V drives into the radio transmission range of IGW2 and, thus, has again direct Internet access for a period of 9 s. Afterwards, the distance increases every 3 s. Finally, V becomes disconnected from the Internet at t_7 after 13 hops instead of 14 hops, because the communication path to a following vehicle is assumed to be lost. The communication path cannot be re-established until V leaves the service area of the second gateway.

Vehicle on the Left Lane

The second situation examines a vehicle W driving on the left lane of the motorway. Therefore, W travels at a much higher speed, which is assumed to be 120 km/h on average. A velocity of 100 km/h can be considered for vehicles on the middle lane corresponding to the measurements in [307]. Hence, the duration of the Internet access is much shorter than for vehicles on the right lane. Additionally, a vehicle on the left lane will overtake vehicles on the other lanes. If the overtaken vehicle was used as next hop for the data packets, an additional reduction of the number of hops occurs. Similar to the vehicles on the right lane, it is assumed that W has a rather continuous Internet access. For vehicles on the left lane, the distance (in hops) to the IGW is decremented every $74\,\text{m}/120\,\text{km/h} \approx 2.2\,\text{s}$. Actually, this period may vary between 3 s and 2.2 s since vehicles on other lanes also can be used to forward the IP packets. Here, a reduction is assumed every 2.5 s for simplicity reasons. It is also assumed that only vehicles driving in the same direction forward the data towards the IGW. The reduction period will be shorter if the vehicle overtakes its "forwarding" vehicle. Thereby, only overtaking manœuvres of W are considered. Assuming a distance to the next-hop vehicle of 74 m when using it as a forwarding hop, the overtaking manœuvre of a communicating vehicle on the middle lane will take $74\,\text{m}/(120 - 100)\,\text{km/h} \approx 13.3\,\text{s}$. If the next-hop vehicle is located on the right lane, the overtaking procedure will last only $74\,\text{m}/(120 - 85)\,\text{km/h} \approx 7.6\,\text{s}$ due to the higher speed difference.

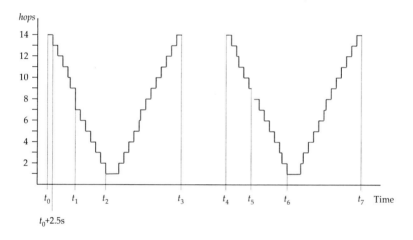

Figure 6.8: Effect of Vehicle's Movement on the Number of Hops (Left Lane)

Figure 6.8 depicts the distance (in hops) between W and the gateways IGW1 and IGW2 against the time. It can be assumed that the change of the number of hops is quite irregular due to the overtaking manœuvres. At t_0, W enters the service area of IGW1, and IP packets from W pass 14 hops to IGW1. The number of hops is reduced on average every 2.5 s while W approaches to IGW1. At time t_1 the number of hops is decremented by 2 since an assumed overtaking manœuvre overlaps the reduction. At t_2, W reaches the radio transmission range of IGW1 and W can communicate directly with the IGW for $200\,\text{m}/120\,\text{km/h} = 6\,\text{s}$. Afterwards, the number of hops increases when leaving the radio transmission range of IGW1 and following vehicles forward the IP packets of W back towards IGW1. At t_3, W leaves the service area of IGW1 and, thus, becomes disconnected from the Internet.

After travelling a distance of 1 km, W discovers IGW2. At t_4, the connection to the Internet is re-established and communication can be continued similar to the beginning of this scenario. The next event occurs at t_5 where the connection is lost for 1 s since no other communicating vehicle is within reach during this period. Direct communication with the gateway becomes possible at t_6. This period takes 6 s as derived above. Afterwards, the number of hops again increases until t_7. Here, the geographical distance between W and IGW2 exceeds 1 km and W leaves the service area of the IGW.

6.2.4 Congested Motorway

The last scenario models a congestion on a motorway with three lanes per direction. Figure 6.9 depicts this situation, which shows the following characteristics and assumptions:

► The congestion on the motorway occurs in one direction only.

► The vehicles do not move. Hence, the topology of the VANET is static and communication with an IGW is of long-term nature. Furthermore, the transmission characteristics are almost constant.

► Internet access is provided by a single IGW. Therefore, all communicating vehicles have to share the available bandwidth of this gateway.

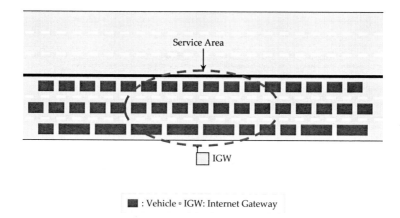

Figure 6.9: A Congested Motorway

Similar to the previous scenario, the average length of a vehicle l_{veh} is 5.3 m with an average distance between two consecutive vehicles of $\Delta x = 2$ m [312]. The diameter of the IGW's service area is set to $l_{geo} = 900$ m, which is rather short compared to the other motorway scenarios. However, this configuration proved as suitable as derived below. In addition, the radio transmission range is reduced to $r_{radio} = 50$ m in order to minimise the interference in the VANET due to the higher traffic density. The remaining micro-mobility parameters are chosen like in the previous motorway scenario (section 6.2.3): The net bandwidth is $Bw_{net} = 588$ kbit/s, the delay is $delay = 40$ ms per link with a jitter of $jitter = \pm20\%$, a packet error rate of $err = 1\%$, and a penetration of $\varphi = 15\%$. Table 6.4 gives a summary of the micro-mobility parameters.

Parameter	Description	Default Value
l_{veh}	Average Length of a Vehicle	5.3 m
Δx	Distance between two Vehicles	2 m
l_{geo}	Diameter of the IGW's Service Area	900 m
r_{radio}	Radio Transmission Range	50 m
φ	Penetration of communicating Vehicles	15 %
Bw_{net}	Available Bandwidth (net)	588 kbit/s
$delay$	Transmission Delay per Link	40 ms
dup	Packet Duplication Rate per Link	2 %
err	Packet Error Rate per Link	1 %
$jitter$	Variation of Transmission Delay	±20 %

Table 6.4: Micro-Mobility Parameters for the Congested Motorway

In this model, the minimum number of hops required for communication between a vehicle at the border of the service area and the gateway is $hops_{min} = 450\,\text{m}/(50\,\text{m/hop}) = 9$ hops (according to equation 6.2). This result justifies the decision to reduce the value of l_{geo} in this scenario. Otherwise, $hops_{min}$ would be twice as large as in the crossway scenario. Measurements showed that communication is practically impossible for distant vehicles in high density VANETs [313]. Such vehicles would suffer from high packet loss rates and delays.

According to [307], congestion occurs if the traffic density ρ reaches a maximum $\rho_{max} \approx$ 140 vehicles/km per lane. This corresponds to the result using equation 6.3 and the micro-mobility parameters in table 6.4. In this scenario, the congestion covers all three lanes of the motorway. Therefore, the total number of vehicles located in the service area of the IGW is $n_{veh} = 900\,\text{m} \cdot 3\,\text{lanes} \cdot 140\,\text{vehicles/km} = 378\,\text{vehicles}$. Considering the penetration of $\varphi = 15\%$, there are about 57 communicating vehicles in the service area of the IGW, which have to share the available bandwidth of this IGW. Based on this result and the assumption that the communicating vehicles are equally distributed over the service area of the IGW, the average distance between two neighboured communicating vehicles is $l_{geo}/50\,\text{vehicles} \approx 16\,\text{m}$. This way, there are on average $n_{neighbours} = 2 \cdot r_{radio}/16\,\text{m} = 6.3$ communicating vehicles in the radio transmission diameter of each vehicle. This justifies the reduction of the transmission range to $r_{radio} = 50\,\text{m}$ as stated above.

In this situation, a location-based routing protocol may cause duplicates while forwarding an IP packet over several hops. This duplication rate cannot be modelled exactly, because it basically depends on the routing protocol being deployed. Hence, a duplication rate of $dup = 2\%$ per link is assumed in this scenario and the total duplication rate depending on the number of hops is determined by the following equation:

$$dup(hops) = 1 - (1 - dup)^{hops} = 1 - 0.98^{hops} \tag{6.11}$$

In order to determine the available bandwidth per vehicle, the overhead caused by the discovery of the IGW has to be determined. According to equation 6.4, the overhead caused by the SA Announcements is:

$$\begin{aligned} Bw_{DRIVE} &= \#\,\text{transmissions} \cdot f_{Announce} \cdot P_{Announce} \\ &= (6.3 + 1) \cdot 2\,\text{Hz} \cdot 110\,\text{byte} = 12.848\,\text{kbit/s} \end{aligned} \tag{6.12}$$

Similar to the previous examples, it is assumed that all vehicles access the Internet simultaneously. According to equation 6.5, the available bandwidth for each vehicle is

$$Bw = \frac{588 - 12.848}{50}\,\text{kbit/s} = 11.503\,\text{kbit/s} \tag{6.13}$$

Mobility Model for one Vehicle

In contrast to the other scenarios, the vehicles do not move in a congestion. Therefore, the network topology is static and does not change over time. The individual transmission delay and link quality depends on the position of a vehicle within the congestion. Hence, this communication model considers the transmission of vehicles at different distances to the IGW.

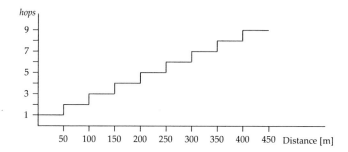

Figure 6.10: Distance against the Position of a Vehicle

This model represents a motorway segment of 2 km length. As derived in the previous section, a vehicle located at the border of the service area has a minimum distance of 9 hops to the IGW. Here, the transmission delay is $9 \cdot 40$ ms $= 360$ ms with a jitter of $\pm 20\%$ (see table 6.4). Figure 6.10 shows the dependency of the number of hops against the distance of a vehicle to the IGW. The representation in figure 6.10 is idealised and assumes that all vehicles are distributed equally in the service area of the IGW. Additionally, it considers only the situation when IP packets are forwarded by the neighboured vehicle that is closest to the IGW. Therefore, the number of hops needed to communicate to the IGW might exceed clearly a value of nine dependent on the real situation and the routing protocol being used. In the worst case, a vehicle at the border of the service area requires $l_{geo}/2$hop distance $= (450/16)$ hops ≈ 28 hops to communicate with the gateway when all vehicles are distributed equally. In this case, the vehicle will suffer from a packet error rate of 24.5 % and an average packet delay of 1.12 s.

6.3 Quantitative Evaluation

The goal of the quantitative evaluation is to determine the performance of MOCCA in the typical vehicular scenarios described in the previous section. Thereby, the transport protocol MCTP is of particular interest, because it basically determines the performance characteristics experienced by the applications. The characteristics of the MOCCA protocols at the network layer as well as the inter-vehicle communication system are hidden to the applications. The quantitative evaluation is based on measurements using the prototype implementation of MCTP for the Linux operating system, which is described in appendix D. The measurements were performed in a testbed emulating the different vehicular scenarios described in section 6.2.

6.3.1 Testbed Setup and Tests

The testbed for the evaluation consists of five Linux hosts connected via standard 100 Mbit/s
Ethernet with each other as depicted in figure 6.11. Thereby, two connected hosts form one
IP subnet in order to route the data appropriately. On the left-hand side, the mobile node
(MN) represents the vehicle that communicates via the MoccaProxy (middle) with a correspondent node (CN) in the Internet on the right-hand side. A VANET emulator between
the MN and the MoccaProxy emulates the vehicular communication scenarios. A second
network emulator between the MoccaProxy and the CN models the communication characteristics in the Internet. For the emulations, the NISTNet network emulator [319] was used
that allows the definition of network conditions for IP packet flows passing the emulator.
Therefore, NISTNet shapes the network traffic flows according to configurable parameters
like bandwidth, delay, jitter, packet drop rate, and packet duplication rate.

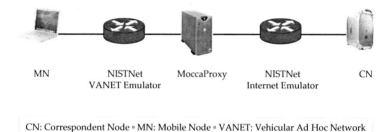

MN   NISTNet   MoccaProxy   NISTNet   CN
          VANET Emulator   Internet Emulator

CN: Correspondent Node ▫ MN: Mobile Node ▫ VANET: Vehicular Ad Hoc Network

Figure 6.11: Distance against the Position of a Vehicle

The VANET emulator reflects the communication characteristics between MN and MoccaProxy. It therefore implements the models of the four vehicular communication scenarios
using shell scripts, which reconfigure the NISTNet parameters over time. The shell scripts
model the network conditions a vehicle experiences when driving through one of the scenarios, i.e. the mobility of one vehicle. The VANET emulator covers the inter-vehicle communication only; it does not consider the impact of the IGW network that connects the IGWs
to the MoccaProxy. This limitation can be accepted since the evaluation assumes an ATM-
based network to connect the gateways to the MoccaProxy (see section 6.1) and packet error
rate, transmission delay, jitter and packet duplication rate in ATM networks are negligible
compared to the communication characteristics in the VANET. Moreover, the ATM network
is not considered to limit the bandwidth provided by the IGWs.

In practice, the communication characteristics in the Internet are highly complex and heterogeneous, which makes the definition of a realistic model almost impossible for the Internet emulator. Therefore, the following parameters are used, which are derived from several investigations and measurements carried out in [320, 321, 322]:

▶ The available bandwidth between MoccaProxy and CN is assumed to be higher compared to the bandwidth in the VANET. This way, the bandwidth specified for the Internet emulator was not limited.

▶ The delay is assumed to be 200 ms with a jitter of ±10 ms. These values were measured in [320, 321].

▶ The IP packet error rate is specified with 0.2 %, which was the average packet error rate measured in [322]. IP packet duplicates are not assumed in the Internet emulator.

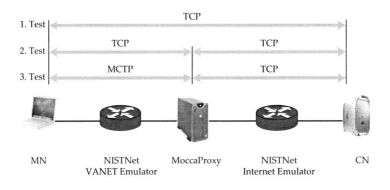

CN: Correspondent Node ▫ MN: Mobile Node ▫ VANET: Vehicular Ad Hoc Network

Figure 6.12: Evaluation Tests

The quantitative evaluation was performed for the four scenarios developed in section 6.2, namely crossway in a city, motorway at night, motorway with high traffic flow, and congested motorway. In order to compare MOCCA with traditional approaches, three different tests were performed for each scenario as depicted in figure 6.12:

1. The goal of the "no proxy" test is to determine the performance of a traditional end-to-end TCP connection between the MN and the CN. Thereby, the host in the middle does not segment the TCP connection.

2. In the "TCP split" test, the MoccaProxy segments the end-to-end TCP connection into two separate TCP connections. This test allows evaluating the use of split performance enhancing proxies in vehicular communication scenarios.

3. The "MOCCA" test evaluates the MOCCA architecture. In contrast to the TCP split test, MCTP is used for communication between the MN and the MoccaProxy.

A suitable measurement for the evaluation is the data throughput at the transport layer from the MN to the CN. This traffic flow direction was chosen since the NISTNet emulator did not transmit ICMP destination unreachable messages in case of a simulated disconnection. A sender application at the MN transmits a byte stream to the CN via the VANET emulator, the MoccaProxy, and the Internet emulator. A receiver application at the CN receives the segments and logs their arrival time. This way, the log files give information about the effective data throughput over time. Each test comprises three measurements of the data throughput in order to determine deviations of the measurements. This is necessary since NISTNet implements a statistical network emulator, i.e. jitter, packet losses and duplicates occur statistically. Hence, several measurements under identical emulations typically generate different results. The measurements themselves were performed with a maximum transfer unit of $MTU = 1,500$ byte and both ECN (Explicit Congestion Notification) and SACK (Selective Acknowledgements) were activated for TCP. The results are represented by a mean value of the three measurements. Therefore, the received segments were averaged within intervals of one second: If (x, y) represents the total amount of data y received at the arrival time x and S_i ($1 \leq i \leq n$) represents the results of measurement i, then the set M of the mean values is defined in the following way:

$$\overline{M} = \{(\bar{t}, \overline{m}) \ \mid \ \bar{t} \in \mathbb{N}_0 \ \wedge \ \forall(\bar{t}, m_i) \in M_i, \ 1 \leq i \leq n : \ \overline{m} = \frac{1}{n} \cdot \sum_{j=1}^{n} m_j\} \quad (6.14)$$

Thereby, M_i represents the set of the total amount of data in measurement i received every second, i.e.

$$M_i = \{(t, m) \ \mid \ t \in \mathbb{N}_0 \ \wedge \ \exists(x, y) \in S_i \ \wedge \ \forall(a, b) \in S_i, \ a \neq x : \ a < x \leq t \ \wedge \ m = y\}$$

The mean value for the representation of the average data throughput reflects the "typical" behaviour of a test in different communication scenarios. This way, the evaluation compares the results of the three tests 'no proxy', 'TCP split', and 'MOCCA'. These charts show the received kilobytes of data (ordinate) over time (abscissa). In addition to the three measurements, each chart contains the development of the number of hops between MN and MoccaProxy over time at the scale on the right-hand side. This allows pointing up the dependency between the hops delays and the data throughput.

6.3.2   Measurements for the Crossway

The chart in figure 6.13 shows the comparison of the averaged measurements for the three tests. The three graphs are close together with some slight advantages for the MOCCA test in the beginning of the emulation. The similarity of the results in this phase is obvious since all tests use the same TCP implementation and decreasing delays cause less retransmission timeouts. This avoids slow starts in TCP, and MCTP operates in the NORMAL mode for most of the time. Significant differences between the graphs occur at the disconnection at about 160 s. Due to the higher round trip time in the no proxy test, it takes a long time until TCP realises the reconnection an continues the transmission of data segments. The split approaches perform better in this situation whereas MOCCA clearly takes advantage from the notification about the disconnection and the re-connection. After the reconnection, MOCCA recovers very quickly whereas no proxy and TCP split show a moderate increase of the data throughput.

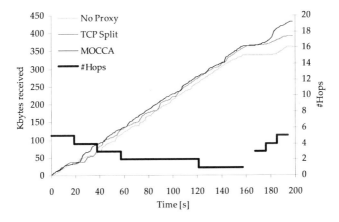

Figure 6.13: MOCCA Test for the Crossway

In order to examine the impact of the disconnection, figure 6.14 presents the details for the measurements. The measurements in this figure show the three measurements of the throughput for the end-to-end TCP test (no proxy test in the upper chart) and the TCP split test (lower chart). The measurements of the no proxy test are very smooth. The reduction of the number of hops has a minor impact on the data throughput; only after the first reduction of the number of hops at about 20 s, variations in the communication flow can be detected.

Crossway, No Proxy

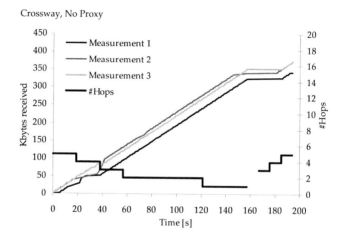

Crossway, TCP Split

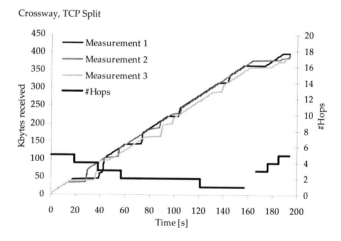

Figure 6.14: Comparison for the Crossway Scenario

However, the impact of the disconnection of 10 s at about 160 s is noticeable in the no proxy measurements: After the re-connection, it takes more than 10 s until TCP continues with the transmission of segments. In contrast to the no proxy test, the TCP split measurements show more discontinuous graphs; the discontinuity can be explained by transmission errors, which forced TCP to retransmit a segment after several other segments were transmitted. This effect does not occur in the no proxy measurements since the higher delays of the end-to-end connection absorbs the variations in the delay more easily. The TCP split graphs also exhibit a faster convergence after the disconnection. It takes less than 10 s until TCP detects the re-connection and continues its transmission.

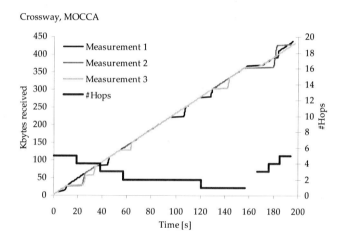

Figure 6.15: No Proxy and TCP Split Tests for the Crossway

Figure 6.15 depicts the three measurements using MOCCA. The graphs increase smoothly and are close together during the decreasing number of hops in the beginning. The measurements also showed a minor "stairs-like" increase of the data throughput caused by segment losses, which also occurred in the TCP split measurements. At about 160 s, the disconnection is noticed and MCTP is notified accordingly to switch into the DISCONNECTED state. The re-connection was also signalled to MCTP with a delay of 200 ms. Afterwards, MOCCA shows a quick convergence to the re-connection and continues the transmission of data segments efficiently. An interesting behaviour shows 'Measurement 2', which demonstrates the usefulness of selective acknowledgements. In this measurement, packet losses occurred immediately after the re-connection but succeeding segments were received correctly. This way, it takes some time to retransmit the lost segments before MCTP delivered the segments en bloc.

After the emulation run of 195 s, the no proxy test transmitted 363.448 Kbyte, the TCP split test transmitted 393.373 Kbyte, and the MOCCA test was able to transfer 432.469 Kbyte of data on average. Figure 6.16 summarises the percentage differences in the overall throughput using the throughput of the no proxy test as the reference value of 100 %.

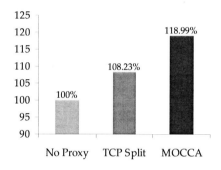

Figure 6.16: Throughput Comparison (Crossway Scenario)

6.3.3 Measurements for the Motorway at Night

The investigation of the motorway at night scenario is interesting since a vehicle exclusively uses the available bandwidth of the IGW. Figure 6.17 depicts the comparison of the averaged measurements for the three tests. This chart shows clearly the advantages of split connection approaches in this scenario. Although a rather high bandwidth is available for the vehicle, the no proxy test has apparent problems to transfer data during the whole emulation time. The measurements also show the impact of the different periods of disconnections from the Internet. Whereas the handover at about 110 s does not affect the TCP throughput significantly, it takes a longer time for TCP to realise the re-connection to the second IGW after the disconnection at about 50 s. The long disconnection (starting at about 160 s) of three minutes between the third and the fourth IGW cannot be handled sufficiently by the no proxy test: TCP was not able to realise the reconnection while the vehicle travels through the service area of IGW4. In contrast, the split connection approaches exhibit different performance characteristics: The throughput increases while connectivity is available by the first three

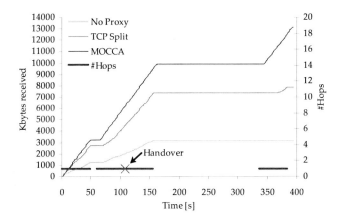

Figure 6.17: Comparison for the Motorway at Night Scenario

IGWs. However, the TCP split test also has problems with the longer period of disconnection. It takes on average more than 70 s until the re-connection to IGW4 is realised and TCP continues its transmission. Figure 6.17 also demonstrates the advantage of the optimised transport protocol MCTP. While connected to an IGW, the throughput increases continuously and steep. The chart also shows that MOCCA is able to handle even longer periods of disconnections very efficiently compared to the other tests.

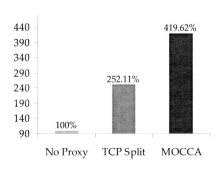

Figure 6.18: Throughput Comparison (Motorway at Night)

In the motorway at night scenario, MOCCA outperforms the other two tests. Figure 6.18 summarises the percentage improvement of TCP split and MOCCA over the end-to-end

TCP connection without a proxy. After the emulation runs, the following averaged amount of data was transmitted in the different tests:

► No proxy transmitted 3.132 Mbyte.

► TCP split transmitted 7.897 Mbyte, which is more than twice the throughput of the no proxy measurements.

► MOCCA transmitted 13.144 Mbyte, which is more than four times as much as achieved in the no proxy test.

6.3.4   Measurements for the Motorway with High Traffic Flow

The scenario of a motorway with a high traffic flow is very heterogeneous and covers several typical communication situations in vehicular environments. Examples are frequent variations of the delay and both short-term and long-term disconnections from the Internet. Similar to the mobility observations in section 6.2.3, the evaluation for this scenario was carried out separately for vehicles driving on the right lane and vehicles driving on the left lane.

Right Lane

The averaged results of the measurements for the right lane are are depicted in figure 6.19. A general observation is that the averaged graphs show similar characteristics in the beginning whereas TCP split has slight advantages. This behaviour can be expected since decreasing error rates and packet delays are advantageous reduce RTTs and, thus, avoids slow starts in TCP (and MCTP). The statistical nature of NISTNet additionally affects the results of the measurements further on. The throughput of the three tests decreases slightly when the number of hops increases in the time interval between 50 s and 80 s. Similar to the crossway scenario, this chart depicts the effects of a longer period of disconnection between 90 s and 130 s: After the reconnection to the Internet through the second IGW, it takes a long time until TCP detects the reconnection and continues with its transmission. Interestingly, the no proxy test had a slightly quicker response time, which is explained by statistical deviations of the NISTNet emulator during the measurements where one of the measurements continues the transmission 20 s after the reconnection. On average, it took about 35 s until no proxy and TCP split recover after the reconnection.

The MOCCA measurements in figure 6.19 show a smooth and continuous behaviour over the total simulation run. An interesting observation is that MCTP is able to transmit data until the disconnection from IGW1 occurs (at about 90 s) whereas the communication in case

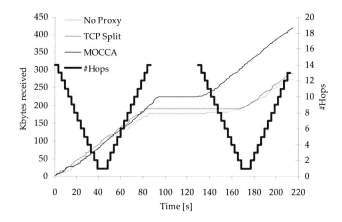

Figure 6.19: Comparison for the Motorway with High Traffic Flow (Right Lane)

of no proxy and TCP split stalled about 10 s before the disconnection from IGW1 occurs. This effect can be explained with the high packet error rates at this distance, which reduces the TCP throughput significantly. After the re-connection to IGW2 at 130 s, MOCCA reacts quickly and MCTP continues its transmission in the same way than in the beginning of the emulation. In this phase, the graph also increases continuously.

Left Lane

Whereas the differences in the throughput on the right lane for the no proxy and the TCP split tests are rather small, the measurements in figure 6.20 for the left lane show a different behaviour. The graph of the no proxy test is rather smooth but TCP seems to have problems especially in the beginning. It takes on average 20 s until the no proxy test is able to transmit a noticeable amount of data. The no proxy test for the left lane also illustrates the problem of TCP with longer periods of disconnections. It takes about 35 s until TCP recovers after the reconnection to the second IGW at about 95 s. In contrast, TCP split has a significantly better performance since the data throughput increases more steadily in the beginning. The TCP split measurements also converge more quickly after the re-connection to the Internet via IGW2, which takes on average 25 s. However, in both tests TCP was not able to recover from the long-term disconnection before the short-term disconnection at about 105 s occurred.

The behaviour of the MOCCA measurements in figure 6.20 shows a characteristic similar to the measurements for the right lane. Thereby, the transmission of data segments continues until the disconnection from IGW1 at about the same rate as TCP split. After the

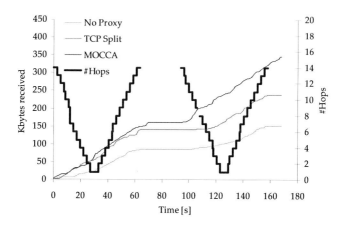

Figure 6.20: Comparison for the Motorway with High Traffic Flow (Left Lane)

reconnection to the second IGW, MOCCA reacts quickly and the transmission is continued with a very short delay but suffers from the high packet losses in the beginning. However, the averaged graph shows a rather discontinuous behaviour after the reconnection. The MOCCA measurements also reflect the limitations of NISTNet. In this test, NISTNet delivered the data packets with a reproducible brief delay that cumulated to several seconds over the emulation run resulting in a "stretched" average curve. This way, a small amount of data was delivered after the reconnections from both IGW1 and IGW2 although the emulator was configured with a packet loss rate of 100 % to emulate the disconnection.

Comparison

The two comparisons showed that the frequency of variations for the delay affects the throughput negatively for all three tests: The effective throughput in the left lane scenario was significantly lower compared to the right lane. The high frequency of variations results in a reduced throughput and a more discontinuous data transfer. A general observation is that the results show a different behaviour on the left lane and on the right lane. Whereas the throughput of no proxy and TCP split on the right lane scenario is similar, TCP split outperforms no proxy in the scenario on the left lane. However, no proxy and TCP split show a similar behaviour in case of disconnections and reconnections. It takes a long time until TCP reacts to a reconnection whereas MOCCA provides a very quick convergence. In both scenarios, the performance of MOCCA is significantly higher compared to the other tests: Over the simulation time, the no proxy test transmitted 274.155 Kbyte, TCP split trans-

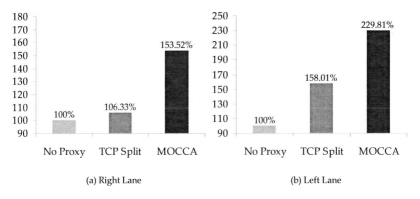

(a) Right Lane   (b) Left Lane

Figure 6.21: Throughput Comparison (Right and Left Lane)

mitted 291.531 Kbyte, and MOCCA was able to transfer 420.885 Kbyte of data in the right lane scenario. In the left lane scenario, the following amounts of data were transferred: 150.592 Kbyte (no proxy), 237.955 Kbyte (TCP split), and 346.072 Kbyte (MOCCA). Figure 6.21 illustrates the percentage differences between the three tests for the right lane (figure (a)) and the left lane (figure (b)).

6.3.5 Measurements for the Congested Motorway

The congested motorway scenario models a static network topology of the VANET. This allows a direct comparison of the different tests in the absence of mobility. As described in section 6.2.2, the congested motorway scenario provides a continuous Internet access at a rather low data rate. The communicating vehicles in the service area of an IGW have different distances to the gateway resulting in different network characteristics experienced by the vehicles located at different positions. For the evaluation of the congested motorway scenario, two distances were investigated in order to determine the impact of different positions: The minimum distance when a vehicle is located in the direct radio transmission range of the IGW (i.e. one hop distance), and the maximum distance of nine hops a vehicle is away from the IGW.

One Hop

In the one hop scenario, MCTP has a noticeable advantage compared to the no proxy and the TCP split measurements as depicted in figure 6.22. In the beginning, the no proxy test shows a continuous and smooth growth of the data transmission until about 55 s, which was

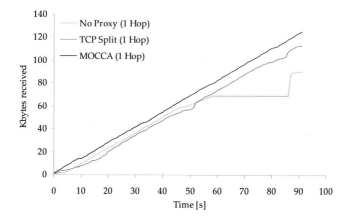

Figure 6.22: Comparison for the Congested Motorway (1 Hop)

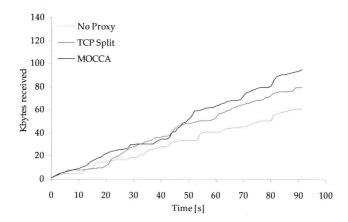

Figure 6.23: Comparison for the Congested Motorway (9 Hops)

even slightly higher compared to TCP split. Afterwards, the situation changed and the data throughput stalled for about 30 s. In contrast, the TCP split test exhibits a more robust result with a steady increase of the data throughput over the simulation run. The MOCCA test shows a similar behaviour but the data throughput was at any time higher compared to the other two tests.

Nine Hops

The comparison of the three tests for the nine hops distance in figure 6.23 shows the impact of high delays and packet errors paired with a low bandwidth. At this distance, the vehicle experiences a delay of 1.12 s and a packet loss rate of 24.5 % for the communication with the IGW. The graphs show that the throughput is apparently lower for all three tests compared to the one hop scenario. Moreover, they exhibit high variations caused by stalled connections. Again, MCTP has noticeable performance advantages compared to the no proxy test and the TCP split test. This is an interesting result since the high error rates do not allow to increase the congestion window in TCP as well as in MCTP. This behaviour can be explained with the quick retransmissions of MCTP in the LOSS state, which handles segment losses caused by transmission errors very efficiently.

Comparison

The static topology of a congested motorway allows an investigation of the MCTP protocol mechanisms that are not related with disconnections and network partitions. In general, MOCCA has apparent performance advantages in the congested crossway measurements. For the one hop measurements, the three tests provide acceptable results that are very close to the theoretical maximum. The measurements of TCP split in the nine hops scenario are close to the MOCCA test. This result can be expected since high error rates also result in many congestion notifications and MCTP thus advises TCP to control the congestion. The differences in the discontinuity of the tests in the two scenarios also occur in the measurements performed for each test. For example, the three measurements for the MOCCA measurements depicted in figure 6.24 are very smooth and increase continuously in the one hop scenario. Moreover, they show an almost identical behaviour. In contrast, figure 6.25 shows the MOCCA measurements in the nine hop scenario. Here, the three graphs are very discontinuous and have a high variance due to the high packet losses, delays, and jitter. This chart also shows that the data throughput of all measurements stalled frequently during the emulation.

Figure 6.26 summarises the percentage differences of the three tests in the one hop scenario (left) and the nine hop scenario (right) using the no proxy result as the reference

Congested Motorway (1 Hop), MOCCA

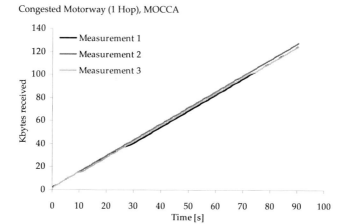

Figure 6.24: MOCCA Test for the Congested Motorway (1 Hop)

Congested Motorway (9 Hops), MOCCA

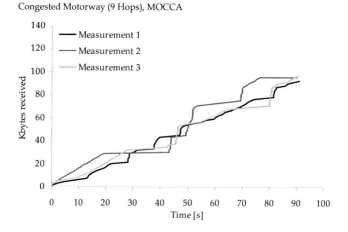

Figure 6.25: MOCCA Test for the Congested Motorway (9 Hops)

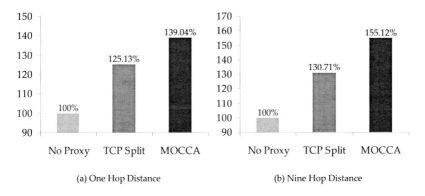

(a) One Hop Distance					(b) Nine Hop Distance

Figure 6.26: Throughput Comparison (Congestion Scenario)

value of 100 %. In the one hop scenario, the overall average data throughput of the no proxy test was 90.259 Kbyte, TCP split transmitted 112.944 Kbyte of data, and MOCCA was able to send 125.493 Kbyte. Nevertheless, the comparison shows that all tests perform well in this scenario and are very close to the theoretical maximum throughput of about 130 Kbyte (according to equation 6.13). In the nine hop scenario, the no proxy test transmitted 61.299 Kbyte, TCP split had an average throughput of 80.123 Kbyte, and MOCCA was able to transfer 95.085 Kbyte of data on average.

6.3.6 Discussion of the Results

A general observation of the quantitative evaluation is that MOCCA improved the communication efficiency in the proposed vehicular communication scenarios. In all measurements, MOCCA achieved the highest throughput in terms of transmitted data segments followed by TCP split and the end-to-end TCP approach without a proxy. The low performance of the no proxy test was basically caused by the higher delays of the end-to-end TCP connection. This way, the characteristics of the VANET scenarios were propagated into the fixed part of the network, which aggravated an efficient handling of transmission errors. The measurements of the motorway at night scenario showed that this property could be harmful in vehicular environments. Another observation was the insufficient handling of disconnections in TCP. For example, in the motorway at night scenario several measurements of no proxy and TCP split were not able to detect the availability of the last IGW within the 48 s the vehicle travels in the radio transmission range of this gateway.

The strengths of MOCCA and its transport protocol MCTP is that it addresses these defi-

ciencies of TCP. The proxy-based architecture avoids the propagation of the VANET characteristics into the fixed Internet part and MCTP handles segment losses caused by transmission errors efficiently. In addition, the notification mechanisms in MOCCA enable MCTP
to react quickly to disconnections from and re-connections to the Internet. Although the
measurements apparently show the advantages of MOCCA compared with other solutions,
there is still potential for performance improvements in MOCCA:

▶ The MCTP prototype implemented for the measurements has a high dependency on
   the capabilities of the operating system. This way, several protocol mechanisms in
   MCTP are performed not in an optimal way: For example, the notifications are handled by Linux with an additional delay of at least 50 ms. Hence, an optimised implementation will additionally improve the performance results.

▶ The improvements introduced in section 5.3.4 are not implemented in the MCTP prototype. They may further improve the performance of MOCCA.

The expressiveness of the evaluation results are slightly limited by some deficiencies of
the NISTNet emulator. The measurements were performed for IPv4 since NISTNet supports
IPv4 only. However, measurements with IPv6 are expected to provide similar results. During the emulation runs, the queuing of packets in NISTNet showed some indeterministic
inconsistencies in the data delivery, which sometimes results in an additional delay of the
delivery. Another deficiency of NISTNet is that it can emulate network characteristics for
one direction only. This way, the directions to and from the vehicle were emulated separately
using the same communication parameters. Finally, the emulations are based on vehicular
communication models with an assumed VANET communication system. Yet, this may
likely have different characteristics in a real-world deployment. However, these limitations
can be accepted since the quantitative evaluation revealed the differences between MOCCA
and existing solutions under different network characteristics.

As a summary, the quantitative evaluation showed that MOCCA is able to improve communication in the VANET scenario. The proxy-based MOCCA architecture together with
the optimised transport protocol MCTP handles different communication characteristics
very efficiently. As a result, MOCCA increases the throughput between a vehicle and a
host in the Internet significantly compared to existing solutions like end-to-end TCP and
split TCP approaches.

6.4   Qualitative Evaluation

The goal of the qualitative evaluation is to determine the suitability of MOCCA for the Internet integration of VANETs. Therefore, MOCCA is discussed in the context of the Internet

integration requirements introduced in section 2.2. The four requirements are the mobility support of the vehicles, the consideration of vehicular aspects, transport layer issues, and scalability. This way, MOCCA can be compared with the related work for the Internet integration as evaluated in section 2. Table 6.5 summarises the qualitative evaluation results of MOCCA.

Project	Mobility Support		Vehicular Aspect		Transport Layer		Scalability	
	Hetero-geneity	Seamless Mobility	Ad Hoc Network.	Vehicular Charact.	Efficien-cy	Applica-bility	Addres-sing	Architec-ture
MOCCA	+ +	+ +	+ +	+ +	+	+ +	+ +	+ +

Table 6.5: Qualitative Evaluation of MOCCA

The mobility management in MOCCA is handled by MMIP6 providing a seamless and transparent mobility support for the vehicles in heterogeneous communication environments. Together with the MoccaMuxer, MMIP6 is able to switch communication flows between different communication systems in order to utilise the heterogeneity. Moreover, the MoccaMuxer is able to find out the most suitable alternative communication system. Together with the use of global and permanent IPv6 addressing of the vehicles, the connection establishment can be initiated either by a vehicle or by a correspondent node in the Internet. As a result, the requirements 'Heterogeneity' and 'Seamless Mobility' are both fulfilled.

The MOCCA architecture was developed specifically for vehicular environments based on ad hoc networks. The 'Ad Hoc Networking' requirement is completely fulfilled since MMIP6 supports the mobility of VANETs in the following way:

► With the help of the DRIVE protocol, MMIP6 is able to discover the IGWs efficiently even over multiple hops.

► DRIVE also select the "most suitable" IGW if several gateways are available simultaneously.

► The MOCCA protocols are basically independent from underlying communication protocols used in the VANET. For example, MMIP6 can be easily adapted to different routing protocols without fundamental modifications of the routing protocol itself. Nevertheless, the evaluation of MMIP6 showed that the routing protocol deployed in the VANET has a significant impact on the overhead caused by the Internet integration protocols.

The MOCCA protocols are also designed with respect to vehicular environments. They consider information from the vehicular environment for their optimisation strategies and MOCCA is able to handle the high mobility of vehicles as well as temporary disconnections from the Internet. This way, the 'Vehicular Characteristics' requirements is evaluated with '++'. Nevertheless, there is still potential for further improvements using additional information, which could be available in the vehicular environments and in the VANET protocols.

MOCCA also addresses transport layer issues. The MoccaProxy segments an end-to-end TCP connection between vehicle and correspondent node in the Internet into two connections. Thereby, the optimised transport protocol MCTP is used for communication between the vehicle and the MoccaProxy. The quantitative evaluation in section 6.3 showed that this approach outperforms both traditional end-to-end TCP and split TCP solutions. The 'Efficiency' requirement is evaluated with '+' since highly optimised transport protocols not based on TCP may improve the communication performance further on. However, such protocols would require modifications of the vehicular applications since they come along with a loss of the TCP semantics. This way, the 'Applicability' requirement is completely fulfilled in MOCCA since the MoccaProxy does not require any modifications of TCP used for communication in the Internet. The proxy-based approach enables the deployment of MCTP for communication with the vehicles. MCTP itself is based on TCP concepts and provides the same semantics and a socket-based application programming interface. This alleviates the deployment of existing applications and the development of further applications for vehicular environments.

Concerning the addressing issues in the VANET, the vehicles are identified by global and unique IPv6 addresses in MOCCA. These addresses are static and permanent, which makes an automatic configuration of the IPv6 addresses dispensable. This approach ensures the scalability of the addressing resulting in a '++' for the 'Addressing' requirement. The MOCCA architecture itself provides the required scalability, too. Potential bottlenecks like the MoccaProxy are located in the fixed Internet and, thus, can be designed in a scalable way. For example, several MoccaProxies may connect the VANET cloud to the Internet and the MoccaProxies themselves may be realised by powerful cluster farms. The protocols used for the mobility management, i.e. MMIP6 and DRIVE, also showed their scalability and efficiency in vehicular environments. This way, the 'Architecture' requirement is also completely fulfilled.

The qualitative evaluation showed that MOCCA fulfils the Internet integration requirements. Hence, MOCCA is a highly suitable solution for the integration of vehicular ad hoc networks into the Internet.

6.5 Summary

The goal of this chapter is the evaluation of MOCCA in a quantitative and a qualitative way. Therefore, this chapter proposes communication models for typical vehicular scenarios: a crossway in a city, a motorway at night, a motorway with a high traffic flow, and a congested motorway. The four scenarios have different characteristics and, thus, cover different aspects of communication.

An important quantitative assessment factor for the Internet integration is the effective data throughput for communication between a vehicle and a host in the Internet. For the measurements of the data throughput, a testbed emulates the communication characteristics for the Internet access from vehicles in the four scenarios. In this testbed, MOCCA is compared with two alternatives: a split TCP approach and an end-to-end TCP approach. The results apparently shows the deficiencies of TCP in vehicular environments: TCP was not able to handle periods of disconnections efficiently and the conservative congestion control reduced the performance in the different scenarios. In contrast, MOCCA shows an appropriate behaviour in such situations: MOCCA outperforms both the split TCP approach and and the end-to-end TCP approach in all measurements.

Project	Mobility Support		Vehicular Aspect		Transport Layer		Scalability	
	Hetero-geneity	Seamless Mobility	Ad Hoc Network.	Vehicular Charact.	Efficien-cy	Applica-bility	Addres-sing	Architec-ture
(Over)DRiVE	+	+ +	– –	–	–	– –	+ +	+ +
COMCAR	+	+	– –	o	– –	– –	– –	–
IPonAir	+	+ +	(+)	– –	?	?	+ +	(– –)
InfoFueling	(+)	?	– –	+ +	– –	o	(– –)	?
CarNet	– –	(o)	+ +	+ +	– –	– –	– –	–
MOCCA	+ +	+ +	+ +	+ +	+	+ +	+ +	+ +

Table 6.6: Comparison of Internet Integration Approaches

A qualitative evaluation determines the suitability of MOCCA for the Internet integration of vehicular ad hoc networks. Table 6.6 summarises the evaluation results of MOCCA and the related work discussed in chapter 2. In addition to the mobility support of the vehicles, MOCCA is able to determine the most suitable alternative communication network using fuzzy logic. This feature is only supported in a completely different way in COMCAR and IPonAir. The support for vehicular ad hoc networks is an inherent strength of MOCCA. Except for CarNet, none of the remaining solutions takes vehicular aspects into account. A remarkable feature of MOCCA is the transport layer, which is not yet addressed in other Internet integration solutions. The importance of this feature is illustrated in the quantitative evaluation, which shows that the optimised transport protocol MCTP improves the communication performance and, thus, the communication efficiency. Finally, the MOCCA architecture and its protocols are scalable, which is very important for a large-scale deployment. Besides the DRiVE/OverDRiVE approach, this aspect is not considered in related solutions.

This chapter clearly shows that MOCCA is an eminent approach for the Internet integration of vehicular ad hoc networks. Besides the deployment of MOCCA in the testbed, it also proves its relevance in practice: In the FleetNet project, the MOCCA concepts are used to integrate the FleetNet communication system for inter-vehicle communication into the Internet [323].

Chapter 7

Conclusion and Outlook

Vehicular ad hoc networks become very important for future vehicular-centred applications. With a successive deployment of network technologies for inter-vehicle communication, the demand grows to integrate these networks into the Internet. The goal of the Internet integration is that the vehicular ad hoc network appears as a transparent extension of the Internet, which opens up the vehicular network for the Internet. This is a challenging task since communication in vehicular networks differs fundamentally from the Internet. Communication in the Internet requires a static network topology, whereas vehicular networks are highly mobile: Vehicles communicate with each other in a multi-hop ad hoc fashion and they change their gateway to the Internet permanently. Therefore, the Internet integration has to solve the mobility support of vehicles. It also has to consider typical characteristics of vehicular ad hoc networks and the transport layer has to ensure an efficient communication between vehicles and the Internet. Moreover, a solution for the Internet integration must be highly scalable since vehicular ad hoc networks may become very large, comprising potentially thousands of vehicles.

7.1 Contribution

This thesis proposes MOCCA, a novel proxy-based mobile communication architecture for the Internet integration of vehicular ad hoc networks. A MoccaProxy located in the Internet bridges the differences between the vehicular network and the Internet. The MoccaProxy also hides the mobility of the vehicles. This way, the vehicular ad hoc network appears as a static IP-based network to the Internet. The MOCCA architecture comprises several communication protocols and protocol mechanisms at the network layer and the transport layer, which enable an efficient Internet integration:

▶ *MMIP6:* The mobility management is handled at the network layer by the MMIP6 protocol. MMIP6 provides a scalable mobility support for large vehicular networks. The protocol is based on the concepts of Mobile IPv4, but it is optimised for the mobility support in IPv6-based vehicular multi-hop ad hoc networks.

▶ *DRIVE:* In MMIP6, the DRIVE protocol discovers Internet Gateways in vehicular ad hoc networks very efficiently even over multiple hops. DRIVE is based on service discovery concepts, but works in a proactive manner. Moreover, a fuzzy logic engine in DRIVE determines the most suitable Internet Gateway if several gateways are available simultaneously.

▶ *MoccaMuxer:* The MoccaMuxer performs vertical handovers in heterogeneous overlay networks. A fuzzy logic engine in the MoccaMuxer is able to determine the most suitable alternative communication system. This way, the heterogeneity can be utilised to improve connectivity and communication further on.

▶ *VehicleProxy:* A VehicleProxy within the vehicle enables common applications on mobile devices within a vehicle to use MOCCA without any modifications. Therefore, the VehicleProxy bridges the differences in the communication protocols at the network layer and at the transport layer in a transparent way.

▶ *MCTP:* The MOCCA transport layer uses MCTP, a modified and enhanced version of TCP. MCTP is designed for communication in vehicular environments and provides the semantics and programming interface of TCP. The proxy-based nature of MOCCA allows the introduction of MCTP for communication between vehicle and MoccaProxy, whereas the communication between the MoccaProxy and the Internet host is based on standard TCP.

An important feature of MOCCA is the integrated approach of the architecture where the communication protocols highly cooperate with each other. This interaction is used to harmonise and to optimise the different communication protocols even over the borders of the communication layers. For example, MMIP6 uses DRIVE for the discovery of alternative Internet Gateways, and the mobility management notifies MCTP in case of disconnections from the Internet. Moreover, available information from the vehicular environment is considered for protocol optimisations. For example, DRIVE uses this information to find the most suitable Internet Gateway.

For the evaluation of Internet integration approaches, this thesis provides communication models for four typical vehicular scenarios: Communication at a crossway in a city, on an empty motorway at night, on a motorway with a high traffic flow, and on a congested motorway. The evaluation is based on measurements in a testbed that emulates the characteristics of the Internet access one vehicle experiences in the four scenarios. During this evaluation, MOCCA was compared with an end-to-end approach using TCP and a splitted TCP approach. The measurements showed that MOCCA outperforms the two other approaches. The effective data throughput of MOCCA in the emulation runs was apparently higher compared to end-to-end TCP and splitted TCP. The performance enhancement can be traced back to the features of MCTP to handle transmission errors and disconnections appropriately. A qualitative comparison of MOCCA with related work showed that MOCCA completely fulfils the Internet integration requirements. The results of the evaluation revealed that MOCCA is a very suitable solution for the Internet integration of vehicular ad hoc networks that improves the communication performance between vehicles and hosts in the Internet.

7.2 Future Work

The MOCCA architecture was proved as a comprehensive solution for the Internet integration of vehicular ad hoc networks. However, there is still potential for further improvements. An important aspect of future work is the consideration of additional information to optimise the MOCCA communication protocols further on. For example, the DRIVE protocol for the discovery of suitable Internet Gateways may consider additional parameters of the vehicular network to improve its decision strategies. Further investigations are also useful to determine the impact of routing protocols for vehicular ad hoc networks. These investigations are necessary to improve the interaction and therewith the efficiency between MOCCA and the routing protocol being deployed.

MOCCA can be used as a basis for further extensions. The following examples give a notion of these extensions:

▶ *Transport Layer for Inter-Vehicle Communication:* MCTP is optimised for the Internet integration, i.e. the communication between vehicles and Internet hosts. A transport protocol for inter-vehicle communication may require further optimisation strategies not included in MCTP.

▶ *Quality of Service:* MOCCA does not address any quality of service issues. The mobility management could be extended appropriately to support the necessary quality of service. This is important, e.g., for safety-related applications between vehicles.

▶ *Security:* A general problem of proxy-based architectures is that commonly used security methods at the network layer are not supported. Since the MoccaProxy splits the end-to-end connection, the communication peers cannot be authenticated appropriately. The integration of such security methods in MOCCA is a difficult task and requires new (and potentially weakened) trust models. Such models rely on a trusted relationship between the service provider of the proxy and the user where the trustworthy service provider has to ensure the privacy of user data.

► *Seamless Mobile Applications:* Although MOCCA is able to handle disconnections from the Internet efficiently, existing applications will time out in case of a stalled data transfer. These application-specific aspects must be handled accordingly, e.g. by modified applications or by an appropriate middleware solution.

► *Demonstration of Applications:* With the help of MOCCA, vehicular applications can be developed in order to demonstrate the usefulness of MOCCA in practice.

Future work may also comprise enhanced evaluations of MOCCA. Therefore, further vehicular communication scenarios can be developed in order to improve the performance of MOCCA in vehicular environments. Another open topic is the investigation of the impact caused by the network that connects the Internet Gateways to the MoccaProxy. Furthermore, detailed performance investigations can also be achieved by a simulation of MOCCA in simulated vehicular environments. The simulations will provide further results about the dependencies of communication in cases where several vehicles communicate simultaneously. Finally, measurements in a real vehicular ad hoc network are necessary to determine the deviations between the communication characteristics of the models and in practice.

Appendix A

MoccaMuxer Fuzzy System

This appendix describes the decision process implemented in the MoccaMuxer (see section 3.3.2). This decision process is based on fuzzy logic [160, 161]. The fuzzy controller developed for the optimisation of the dynamic handover between available communication systems is based on a two-tiered decision process, as illustrated in figure A.1. The first tier is the *Abstraction Controller*, which calculates a number of generic parameters from a set of basic parameters provided by the operating system. The second step is a *Decision Controller*, which determines the "most suitable" communication system among the available communication systems.

Figure A.1: Fuzzy Controller for the Decision Process

These parameters are by no means complete, but can be extended easily by further parameters and quality of service requirements of the applications [324]. However, this basic parameter set shows the feasibility of this approach for the VANET scenario.

A.1   Basic Parameters

The Abstraction Controller is fed with various basic parameters, which are usually provided by the operating system in a more ore less direct way. A detailed description of the generation of these basic parameters for the Linux operating system can be found in [148]. In the following description of the basic parameters, the mnemonic 'rx' represents the receiving state, 'tx' the transmission state. For the decision process, the following basic parameters were used:

▶ *Device State:* The parameter devState represents the state of a network device, which indicates whether the network device is active or inactive. It can be used for a simple handover when a network device gets deactivated.

▶ *Packet and Byte Statistics:* These parameters provide statistical information about the transmitted and received packets or bytes. This way, the parameters rxPacketCount and txPacketCount denote the packet counters, rxDevDataRate and txDevDataRate the data rate of the network device, rxIpDataRate and txIpDataRate the respective data rates on an IP basis.

▶ *Maximum Data Rate:* The maximum data rate is necessary for the interpretation of the statistical data. Therefore, the following parameters are used: maxRxDevDataRate and maxTxDevDataRate represent the maximum data rate of the interfaces. On the IP basis, the maximum data rate is often assumed as constant, which is represented by maxDataRate. For network devices with a shared medium, this value has to be used with caution.

▶ *Output and Input Queue:* Another important parameter are the number of bytes in the output and input queue. Therefore, the parameters rxQueue, txQueue, maxRxQueue and maxTxQueue specify the current utilisation of these queues and their maximum length.

▶ *Error Counters:* Errors are also a very useful information source. The decision process takes into account the number of transmission errors (rxErrorCount, txErrorCount).

▶ *Incoming Tunnels:* Usually, tunnels are symmetrical. Hence, the decision process has to consider incoming tunnels, which are represented in the parameters hasTunnel and tunnel.

A.2   Abstraction Controller

Usually, basic parameters are rather unreliable, so they cannot be used immediately for the decision process. Moreover, it is sometimes unknown whether their value is meaningful or not. Hence, the first step of the decision process maps the basic parameters onto a set of generic and hardware-independent parameters. This way, the Abstraction Controller maps the basic parameters to generic parameters in the following way:

► Relative error counter: `relTxErrorCount` = `txErrorCount` / `txPacketCount`

► Queue utilisation: `relTxQueue` = `txQueue` / `maxTxQueue`

► Relative device data rate: `relTxDevDataRate` = `txDevDataRate` / `maxTxDevDataRate`

► Relative IP data rate: `relTxIpDataRate` = `txIpDataRate` / `maxDataRate`

The 'rx' parameters are calculated respectively. Based on these generic parameters, the fuzzyfication process can be specified. The Abstraction Controller therefore deploys a fuzzy set with five states with a triangular pattern, as illustrated in figure A.2. The five states are `verylow`, `low`, `medium`, `high`, and `veryhigh`.

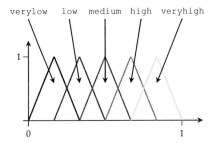

Figure A.2: Fuzzy Set for the Fuzzyfication

The very basic result of the first calculation is to determine the load of a network device and its link quality. Figure A.3 depicts the dependency graph for the load, represented by the abstract `load` parameter. The emphasised parameters are basic parameters, the others are the generic parameters.

The load measures the utilisation of the underlying network. Therefore, the following fuzzy rules sets are optimised to detect high loads. The first fuzzy rules set determines the load of a network device `txDevLoad` for transmissions.

```
if relTxDevDataRate is veryhigh or relTxQueue is veryhigh
  then txDevLoad is veryhigh;
if relTxDevDataRate is veryhigh or relTxQueue is high
  then txDevLoad is veryhigh;
```

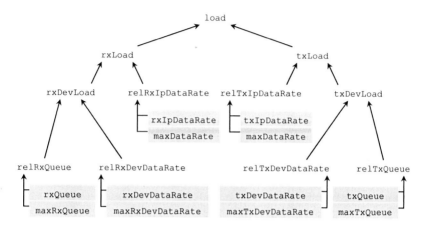

Figure A.3: Dependency Graph for load

```
if relTxDevDataRate is high or relTxQueue is medium
  then txDevLoad is high;
if relTxDevDataRate is medium or relTxQueue is low
  then txDevLoad is medium;
if relTxDevDataRate is low
  then txDevLoad is low;
end;
```

If a tunnel is used for communication, the data rate used by the IP address has to be added to estimate the load without a tunnel. This results in the parameter txLoad in the following way:

```
if (hasTunnel) then
  txLoad = txDevLoad + relTxIpDataRate;
else
  txLoad = txDevLoad;
end;
```

A similar calculation is performed for the 'rx' parameters, which results in the rxLoad parameter respectively. The overall load is determined by the maximum of these two parameters, i.e.

```
load = max(txLoad, rxLoad);
```

Another important generic parameter is the link quality, represented by the quality parameter. Therefore, the fuzzy system applies the following fuzzy rules, as depicted in figure A.4. It first calculates the transmission quality txQuality as follows:

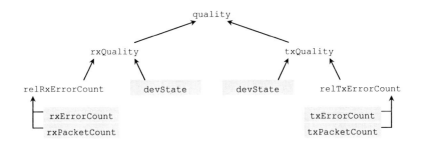

Figure A.4: Dependency Graph for `quality`

```
if (devState == inactive) then
  txQuality is verylow;
else
  if relTxErrorCount is veryhigh then txQuality is verylow;
  if relTxErrorCount is high then txQuality is low;
  if relTxErrorCount is medium then txQuality is medium;
  if relTxErrorCount is low then txQuality is high;
  if relTxErrorCount is verylow then txQuality is veryhigh;
end;
```

The rx parameters are calculated accordingly. With these results, the fuzzy system determines the overall link quality by the minimum of the results, i.e.

```
quality = min(txQuality, rxQuality);
```

A.3   Decision Controller

The difference between calculating the generic parameters (see previous section) and the decision process is that the decision process uses the parameters of two IP addresses in order to find the best available network. The parameters of the IP address that might be tunneled are denoted as 'other.xxx' to distinguish the parameters of the two IP addresses. The decision process distinguishes two situations:

► If the connectivity is lost, the decision process determines the best suited IP address to be used for further communications.

► Incoming tunnels are treated in a different way, because in this situation the communication peer already determined its most suitable network interface.

A.3.1   Basic Decision Process

Figure A.5 depicts the dependency graph to calculate the overall rating if the decision process has to find the best suited network device. In the first step, the decision process calculates the estimated relative data rates `estRelTxIpDataRate` and `estRelRxIpDataRate` that would be generated on the alternative device if a tunnel is created:

```
estRelTxIpDataRate = other.txIpDataRate / maxDataRate;
estRelRxIpDataRate = other.rxIpDataRate / maxDataRate;
```

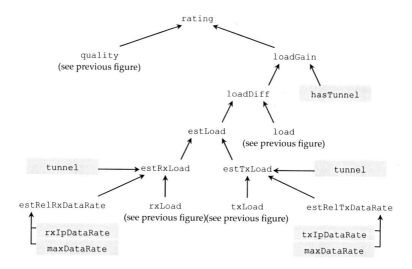

Figure A.5: Dependency Graph for the Decision Process

Together with the generic parameters `txLoad` and `rxLoad` (see figure A.3) the decision process calculates the estimated load for both transmission and receipt according to the following calculations:

```
if (other.tunnel != ipAddress) then
  estTxLoad = txLoad + estRelTxIpDataRate;
else
  estTxLoad = txLoad;
end;
```

The `estRxLoad` parameter is calculated accordingly. The final estimated load `estLoad` for the network device depends on the medium, i.e. whether it is used in simplex or duplex

mode. In the simplex mode the load is additive, whereas in duplex mode the estimated load
is the maximum of transmission and receipt load:

```
estLoad = estTxLoad + estRxLoad;        // simplex mode
estLoad = max(estTxLoad, estRxLoad);    // duplex mode
```

In the next step, the `loadDiff` parameter determines whether a handover would allow to
send the packets for the IP address through a network interface with a lower load. This parameter only differentiates situations with a decreasing load; all situations with an increasing load are mapped to `verylow`. Hence, the following fuzzy rules calculate the parameter
`loadDiff`:

```
switch other.load:
  case verylow:
    loadDiff is verylow;
  case low:
    if estLoad is verylow then loadDiff is low;
    if estLoad is in (low,medium,high,veryhigh) then loadDiff is verylow;
  case medium:
    if estLoad is verylow then loadDiff is medium;
    if estLoad is low then loadDiff is low;
    if estLoad is in (medium,high,veryhigh) then loadDiff is verylow;
  case high:
    if estLoad is verylow then loadDiff is high;
    if estLoad is low then loadDiff is medium;
    if estLoad is medium then loadDiff is low;
    if estLoad is in (high,veryhigh) then loadDiff is verylow;
  case high:
    if estLoad is verylow then loadDiff is veryhigh;
    if estLoad is low then loadDiff is high;
    if estLoad is medium then loadDiff is medium;
    if estLoad is high then loadDiff is low;
    if estLoad is veryhigh then loadDiff is verylow;
end;
```

In order to prefer the device currently used, an existing tunnel must be taken into consideration to reduce the number of handovers. The result is a new parameter `loadGain`, which
is determined by the following fuzzy rules:

```
if (other.tunnel != ipAddress) then
  loadGain is loadDiff;
else
  if loadDiff is verylow then loadGain is low;
  if loadDiff is low then loadGain is medium;
  if loadDiff is medium then loadGain is high;
  if loadDiff is high then loadGain is veryhigh;
end;
```

Finally, the fuzzy system determines the overall rating using the parameters quality (as illustrated in figure A.4) and loadGain. The rating parameter is calculated as follows:

```
switch quality:
  case verylow:
    rating is verylow;
  case low:
    if loadGain is in (verylow,low) then rating is verylow;
    if loadGain is in (medium,high) then rating is low;
    if loadGain is veryhigh then rating is medium
  case medium:
    if loadGain is verylow then rating is verylow;
    if loadGain is in (low,medium) then rating is low;
    if loadGain is in (high,veryhigh) then rating is medium;
  case high:
    if loadGain is verylow then rating is verylow;
    if loadGain is low then rating is low;
    if loadGain is in (medium,high) then rating is medium;
    if loadGain is veryhigh then rating is high;
  case veryhigh:
    rating is loadGain;
end;
```

Based on these calculations, the different alternatives can be compared. The MoccaMuxer then will handover its connections to the device with the highest rating.

A.4   Incoming Tunnels

The basic decision process results in a rating parameter to compare alternative IP addresses. However, incoming tunnels from the communication peers (incomingTunnelRating) must also be taken into consideration, which is performed by the following decisions:

```
if (other.incomingTunnel == ipAddress) then
  rating is veryhigh;
else
  [basic decision process]
end;

rating = max(rating, incomingTunnelRating);
```

Thereby, the basic decision process determines the rating parameter as described in the previous section. A more detailed description of the fuzzy controllers can be found in [148, 149].

Appendix B

MMIP6 Registration Messages

As described in section 4.4.3, the registration is necessary before a vehicle can use an Internet Gateway to access the Internet. This appendix provides details about the messages that are exchanged for the registration. The registration procedure starts after a vehicles decided to handover its connections to a new Foreign Agent. The registration procedure in MMIP6 uses two messages: *registration request* and *registration reply*. Figure B.1 shows the message exchange between the vehicle, the Foreign Agent, and the Home Agent. If a vehicle wants to register with a new Foreign Agent, it sends a registration request message to the Foreign Agent using UDP at port 434 as specified for Mobile IPv4. The Foreign Agent processes the registration request, i.e. it updates its internal visitor list and forwards the registration request to the Home Agent of the vehicle, which is located at the MoccaProxy. The IPv6 address of the vehicle's Home Agent is specified in the registration request message. The Home Agent itself updates its internal binding with the new care-of address of the vehicle and responds with a registration reply message that is addressed to the vehicle. This registration reply is routed to the Foreign Agent, which itself processes the reply and forwards it to the vehicle. Figure B.2 shows the structure of a registration request message. The fields in this message are defined according to [145]:

▶ type: The 8 bit field type is set to 1 in order to indicate a registration request message.

▶ S: Allows simultaneous bindings.

▶ B: The vehicle requests that broadcast datagrams from the home network are transmitted to the vehicle. MMIP6 set B to 0 to avoid this.

▶ D: Decapsulation by the vehicle. D is set to 0 in MMIP6 to indicate that the vehicle does not use a co-located care-of addresses.

Vehicle
Foreign Agent
Home Agent
Registration Request
Registration Request
Registration Reply
Registration Reply
[time]

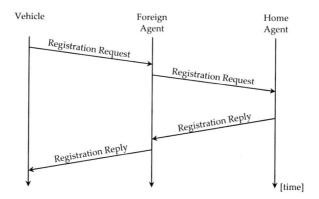

Figure B.1: Registration Procedure in MMIP6

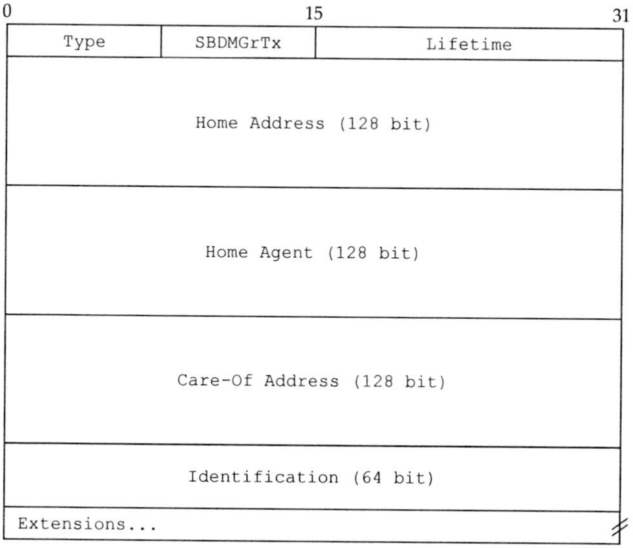

0
15
31
Type
SBDMGrTx
Lifetime
Home Address (128 bit)
Home Agent (128 bit)
Care-Of Address (128 bit)
Identification (64 bit)
Extensions...

Figure B.2: MMIP6 Registration Request Message

▶ M: Indicates that the Home Agent uses minimal encapsulation [145], which can be optionally activated in MMIP6.

▶ G: Indicates that the Home Agent uses generic routing encapsulation [145], which can be optionally activated in MMIP6.

▶ r, x: Reserved flags, are set to 0.

▶ T: Reverse tunneling requested, which is activated in MMIP6 (i.e. T = 1).

▶ Lifetime: Specifies the number of seconds remaining before the registration is considered as expired. This field has a length of 16 bit. The lifetime parameter is determined dynamically by MMIP6 using the expected time a vehicle travels in the service area of an IGW.

▶ Home Address, Home Agent, Care-Of Address: Define the respective IPv6 addresses with a length of 16 byte each.

▶ Identification: Used for matching registration request messages with registration reply messages.

▶ Extensions: Used for security considerations in Mobile IP [145].

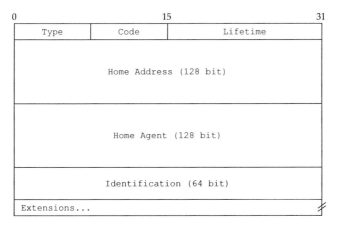

Figure B.3: MMIP6 Registration Reply Message

The registration reply message is illustrated in figure B.3. The fields in this message have the same meanings as described for the registration request message. The only differences are:

► type: The type field is set to 3 to indicate a registration reply message.

► Code: The Code field specifies the status of the registration reply, i.e. whether the registration request was granted (Code=0 or Code=1) or denied. In the latter case, the value of Code represents an error code as specified in [145].

The structure of the visitor list in the Foreign Agent and the bindings in the HA follows the specification for Mobile IPv4 [145] but uses IPv6 addresses instead of the IPv4 addresses.

Appendix C

DRIVE Implementation

In order to verify the feasibility of DRIVE, a prototype was implemented for the Linux operating system. This appendix delivers an insight into this prototype. The software is based on OpenSLP[1], a freely available implementation of the Service Location Protocol SLPv2 (see section 4.3.3). The fuzzy expert systems were realised with the help of the JFS fuzzy software toolbox[2]. The DRIVE prototype implementation consists of two main components as illustrated in figure C.1:

▶ The SLP daemon 'slpd' implements the basic Service Agent functionality.

▶ The 'libslp' library provides the basic User Agent functionality.

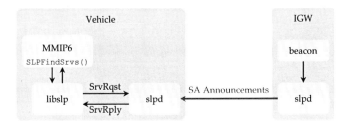

IGW: Internet Gateway ▫ MMIP6: MOCCA Mobile IPv6
SrvRply: Service Reply ▫ SrvRqst: Service Request ▫ SA: Service Agent

Figure C.1: DRIVE Implementation

---

[1]OpenSLP project page: http://www.openslp.org
[2]JFS project page: http://inet.uni2.dk/~jemor/jfs.htm

The libslp library is required in the vehicle only. It provides the application programming interface for MMIP6 to query for a more suitable IGW. This functionality is provided by a single function SLPFindSrvs(). This function sends a service request (SrvRqst) message to the in-vehicle slpd via TCP (port 427) as specified in RFC 2608 [220]. The slpd in the vehicle finds the most suitable IGW and responds with this result in a service reply (SrvRply) message. The message formats of both a SrvRqst and a SrvRply are identical with the messages specified for SLPv2 [220]. Hence, they are not discussed further on.

In order to realise the distributed Service Agent functionality in DRIVE, the SLP daemon runs in both the vehicle and the IGW. In the vehicle, it has two tasks: First, the slpd has to handle incoming SrvRqst messages from the libslp library. Second, the daemon has to process the incoming SA Announcement messages as described in section 4.4.2. At the Internet Gateways, an additional program called 'beacon' periodically generate the SA Announcements.

C.1   SA Announcements

Internet Gateways transmit SA Announcements in order to announce their presence. Figure C.2 depicts the format of a SA Announcement message. In this message, the Service Location Header specifies the message type, whereby 0xB represents an SA Announcement. <Scope List> and Authentication Blocks are used as specified in SLPv2 [220].

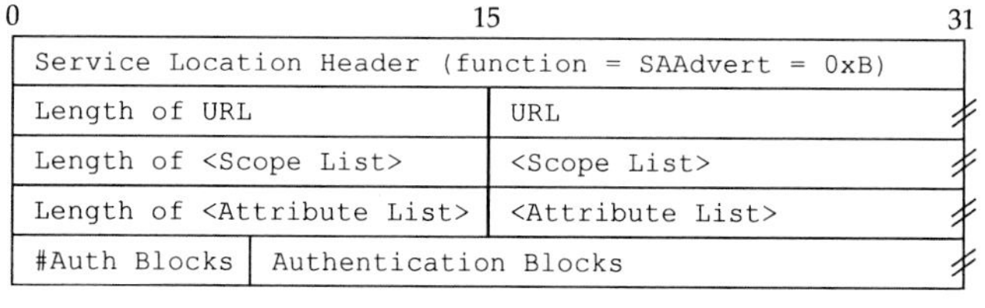

```
0                              15                           31
┌────────────────────────────────────────────────────────────┐
│ Service Location Header (function = SAAdvert = 0xB)          │
├────────────────────────────────┬───────────────────────────┤
│ Length of URL                  │ URL                       ╱│
├────────────────────────────────┼───────────────────────────┤
│ Length of <Scope List>         │ <Scope List>              ╱│
├────────────────────────────────┼───────────────────────────┤
│ Length of <Attribute List>     │ <Attribute List>          ╱│
├───────────────┬────────────────┴───────────────────────────┤
│ #Auth Blocks  │ Authentication Blocks                      ╱│
└───────────────┴────────────────────────────────────────────┘
```

Figure C.2: SA Announcement Message Format

The service URL (Uniform Resource Locator) specifies the type and location of a service according to RFC 2609 [227]. In DRIVE, the service URL has the following format:

service:service-agent://<IPv6 address of IGW>

In this URL, service-agent specifies that the provided service represents Service Agent functionality, followed by the IPv6 address of the IGW that transmitted the SA Announcement. <Attribute List> contains the status information about the IGW. The attribute names follow the defined naming conventions for non-defined attributes according to RFC 2608. The DRIVE prototype support the following three attributes:

▶ x-drive-users: Specifies the number of vehicles, which are currently registered with the Foreign Agent running on the IGW.

▶ x-drive-bandwidth: The bandwidth currently available at the IGW.

▶ x-drive-timestamp: A timestamp from the IGW, which may be derived from the GPS signal. This information is used to differentiate the SA Announcements transmitted. Moreover, this information can be useful to estimate the distance between vehicle and IGW.

These attributes are used to select the most suitable gateway, which is described in the following section.

C.2   Selection Process

The prototype uses a rectangular membership function for the fuzzyfication of the input parameters. Therefore, each input parameter is assumed to be in the range of $[0,1]$. For this range, the DRIVE prototype defines the fuzzy sets high, medium, and low. The rectangular affiliation degree for these sets are illustrated in figure C.3. In order to determine the most suitable IGW, DRIVE deploys a fuzzy expert system. This fuzzy logic system consists of three steps, as illustrated in figure C.4. In the first step, the system predicts parameters necessary for the evaluation of the different application classes. The evaluation itself and the defuzzyfication is performed in the second step. Finally, the results are averaged to determine the overall suitability of an IGW.

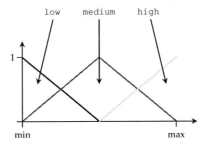

Figure C.3: Triangular Membership Function for the Fuzzy Sets low, medium, and high

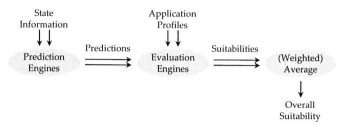

Figure C.4: Fuzzy Logic System in DRIVE

Input Parameters and Application Classes

The fuzzy system of the DRIVE prototype uses several state information parameters as input to the fuzzy system. The following state information is used in the prototype implementation of DRIVE:

- ▶ trafficDensity: The vehicle itself provides information about the density of the traffic. The density is predicted with the help of information from neighboring vehicles.

- ▶ distance: This parameter specifies the distance between the vehicle and the IGW. For example, the vehicle can calculate this distance by comparing its own position with the position of the IGW, which is contained in the SA Announcements.

- ▶ currentBw: Information about the bandwidth that is currently available on the IGW is also provided in the SA Announcements by each IGW.

- ▶ currentUsers: This parameter reflects the number of users that are currently registered with the Foreign Agent of the respective IGW. SA Announcements are used to transport this information from the gateways to the vehicles.

- ▶ delay: The packet delay has a special status in the fuzzy logic system, because it is highly correlated with the distance between vehicle and IGW. Hence, delay is assumed to be proportional to the distance parameter.

Based on this information, a set of fuzzy prediction engines calculate the suitability of an IGW for a respective application property. The implemented prototype supports the following three properties to classify applications:

1. *Interactivity:* Interactive applications are sensitive for packet delays experienced during the communication. In order to keep these delays low, the closest IGW seems to be most suitable.

2. *Streaming:* The transmission of audio and/or video streams requires relatively high data rates. Current video codecs like MPEG-2 [325] typically use an incremental compression algorithm and are, thus, highly sensitive to packet losses [326]. Streaming applications also require a continuous packet flow for a longer period of time to avoid buffer underruns.

3. *Real-Time:* Real-time applications have the hardest requirements to the communication system. They expect low and guaranteed packet delays, a very low rate of dropped packets, and a continuous packet flow.

Prediction Engines

The information described in the previous sections is processed in the prediction engines in order to determine the "most suitable" Internet Gateway. Figure C.5 depicts the dependency graph for the overall selection process, which shows the dependencies between the input information and the predicted parameters. In a first step, the DRIVE fuzzy logic system predicts the *expected* communication performance of an IGW based on the input parameters. Therefore, four prediction engines determine the following parameters:

▶ disconnects, the expected probability for disconnections,

▶ expectedUsers, the expected number of users,

▶ expectedBw, the expected bandwidth at the IGW,

▶ dropouts, the expected probability of packet losses.

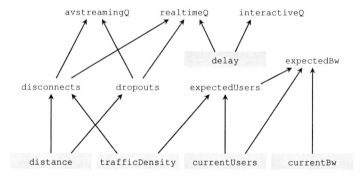

Figure C.5: Dependency Graph for the Selection Process

The following rules are used to determine the relative probability of a disconnection. Thereby, the disconnects parameter is determined by the distance between the vehicle and the IGW, and by the traffic densitiy in the vincinity of the vehicle:

```
if distance is low then disconnects is high;
if distance is medium and (trafficDensity is high or
  trafficDensity is medium) then disconnects is medium;
if (distance is medium or distance is high) and trafficDensity is low
  then disconnects is high;
if distance is high and trafficDensity is high the disconnects is low;
if distance is high and trafficDensity is medium then disconnects is low;
end;
```

The expected number of users is determined by the current number of users registered with the Foreign Agent and the current traffic densitiy in the following way:

```
if trafficDensity is high and currentUsers is low
  then expectedUsers is medium;
if currentUsers is high then expectedUsers is high;
if currentUsers is medium then expectedUsers is medium;
if currentUsers is low then expectedUsers is low;
end;
```

Similarly, the expected available bandwidth expectedBw is predicted from the current bandwidth, the current number of users using the IGW, and the expected number of users. The following rules are applied for this prediction:

```
if currentBw is high then expectedBw is high;
if currentBw is medium then expectedBw is medium;
if currentBw is low then expectedBw is low;
if expectedUsers is high and (currentUsers is low or currentUsers
  is medium) and currentBw is high then expectedBw is medium;
if expectedUsers is high and (currentUsers is low or currentUsers
  is medium) and currentBw is medium then expectedBw is low;
end;
```

The expected relative packet loss rate is basically determined by the distance between the vehicle and the IGW. As the dropouts parameter is proportional to the distance, the rules are obvious:

```
if distance is low then dropouts is low;
if distance is medium then dropouts is medium;
if distance is high then dropouts is high;
end;
```

Together with the specifications of the application properties, these expected parameters are the input for the evaluation engines.

Evaluation Engines

The evaluation module determines the suitability of an IGW for a class of applications. This way, three fuzzy engines calculate the following three parameters:

- ► `interactiveQ` for interactive applications,

- ► `avstreamingQ` for audio/video streaming applications,

- ► `realtimeQ` for real-time applications.

Interactive applications require low packet delays. Hence, `interactiveQ` is basically determined by the `delay` parameter. The following rules determine the suitability of an IGW for interactive applications:

```
if delay is high then interactiveQ is medium;
if delay is high then interactiveQ is low;
if delay is low or delay is medium then interactiveQ is high;
end;
```

Audio/Video streaming applications suffer extremely under packet losses and phases of disconnection. Hence, an IGW is only suitable for streaming applications, if both parameters `disconnects` and `dropouts` are low. The following fuzzy rules are applied for this application class:

```
if disconnects is low and dropouts is low then avstreamingQ is high;
if disconnects is medium and (dropouts is medium or dropouts is low)
  then avstreamingQ is medium;
if (disconnects is medium or disconnects is low) and dropouts is medium
  then avstreamingQ is medium;
if disconnects is high or dropouts is high then avstreamingQ is low;
end;
```

Real-time applications require short packet delays, because packets that are not delivered within the specified time become worthless. Hence, close IGWs are prefered for real-time applications. The fuzzy rules also have to consider that disconnections and packet losses may cause additional packet delays. Hence, the following rules determine the suitability of an IGW for real-time applications:

```
if delay is low and (dropouts is low or dropouts is medium) and
  (disconnects is low or disconnects is medium) then realtimeQ is high;
if dropouts is high or disconnects is high then realtimeQ is low;
if delay is medium then realtimeQ is medium;
if delay is high then realtimeQ is low;
end;
```

For these evaluations, the parameter `expectedBw` is not used in the prototype. This is due to the fact that it depends on the ability of an application to handle very low data rates. For example, an application may decide to terminate if not enough bandwidth is available, or it may decide to adapt itself to the available resources. Hence, the `expectedBw` parameter is passed immediately to the application, which is out of scope of the fuzzy system used for the decision process.

Overall Suitability

Finally, the overall suitability of an IGW has to be determined. Therefore, the results for the different application properties first need to be defuzzified. The prototype implements a centroid algorithm, which calculates the gravitiy for the fuzzy sets `high`, `medium`, and `low`. Hence, each fuzzy set is mapped onto a value in the range of $[0, 1]$, whereas 1 represents an excellent suitability for an IGW, and 0 represents complete unsuitability. In the last step, these results are averaged in order to determine the overall suitability of an IGW. Depending on the preferences of the user, application classes can be weighted optionally.

The outcome of this prototype is a list of available IGWs, which are ordered by their overall suitability. Hence, the IGW with the highes rating is the most suitable gateway and will be used for further communications.

Appendix D

Implementation of MCTP

A prototype of MCTP was implemented in order to evaluate MOCCA in general and MCTP in particular in different VANET scenarios. This prototype was developed for the Linux operating system, based on kernel version 2.6.4. This appendix gives an overview of the MCTP implementation, its integration into the TCP/IP functionality of Linux, and the basic mechanisms in the prototype to process available information.

D.1   Integration of MCTP in Linux

As illustrated in figure D.1, MCTP acts as a sublayer between TCP and IP, which examines incoming IP packets in order to control TCP appropriately (cf. section 5). The implementation of such a separated sublayer is not possible for the prototype, since the Linux operating system mixes both the TCP implementation and the IP implementation to a monolithic module [260]. Instead, the MCTP protocol state machine and its functionality are implemented in a distributed way within this monolithic module.

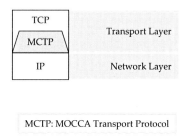

MCTP: MOCCA Transport Protocol

Figure D.1: Integration of MCTP in the TCP/IP Model

Figure D.2 depicts the integration of MCTP in the Linux operating system. The MCTP prototype implements different handler routines, which are called in different situations from within the monolithic module. In Linux, incoming IP packets as well as TCP segments are stored in *socket buffers* [260]. If an arriving socket buffer contains a TCP segment or an ICMP message of type "destination unreachable", the handler `mctp_incoming()` is called. This handler processes the incoming socket buffer in order to control the MCTP state machine appropriately. In case of a retransmission timeout, the timer function in TCP calls the `mctp_timer()` handler to perform the necessary actions. Similarly, the handler routine `mctp_output()` is called for the transmission of a socket buffer. Whereas these handlers are called implicitly from within the Linux TCP implementation, notifications about disconnections or reconnections can be set manually via the `proc` file system. This event type is handled by the routine `mctp_notification()`.

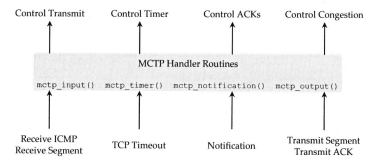

ACK: Acknowledgement ⋄ MCTP: MOCCA Transport Protocol

Figure D.2: Implementation of MCTP in Linux

The current MCTP state of each TCP connection is stored in the TCP options list, which also contains various information and states of the TCP connection itself. Depending on the current MCTP state, several mechanisms of TCP are controlled accordingly in order to perform the MCTP functionality. These are the control of socket buffer transmissions, the handling of timers/timeouts, acknowledgements, and the TCP congestion control (cf. figure D.2).

D.2   MCTP Handler Routines

Together, the four handler routines implement the MCTP protocol state machine and take appropriate actions in different situations. They handle incoming segments, timeouts, notifications, and outgoing segments. These handlers are described in the following sections.

D.2.1   Incoming Socket Buffers

Incoming socket buffers are handled by the routine `mctp_input()`, which realises the largest part of the MCTP protocol state machine. The handler is called whenever a socket buffer for an established TCP connection arrives at the end system, or in case it receives an ICMP messages. In this case, several examinations are necessary as summarised in the flow chart given in figure D.3.

Incoming socket buffers will only be handled if MCTP does not operate in DISCON-NECTED mode. In this case, `mctp_input()` first examines the transitions to and from the PARTITIONED mode. If the socket buffer contains an ICMP message of type "destination unreachable", MCTP switches into the PARTITIONED state. It then deactivates the current retransmissions and stops the transmissions by setting the congestion window to zero. This way, TCP does not transmit any data segments. Afterwards, MCTP activates the *Zero Window Probing*, which triggers TCP to transmit acknowledgement packets to the communication peer. This way, the communication peer is forced to respond to the acknowledgements if the connection is re-established after a network partitioning. Finally, the ICMP message is discarded by MCTP. Vice versa, if MCTP operated in the PARTITIONED mode and a duplicate acknowledgement arrives in the incoming socket buffer, MCTP returns to the NORMAL operation mode. In this case, MCTP sets the congestion window of TCP to two segments and immediately retransmits the queued socket buffers.

The second step deals with the transitions to the CONGESTED state. `mctp_input()` therefore checks the incoming socket buffer for an indicated congestion, i.e. by examining the ECE (ECN Echo) flag in the TCP header. If ECN indicates a pending congestion, MCTP moves into the CONGESTED state and standard TCP continues with the processing of the incoming socket buffer.

Potential segment losses are handled in the third step. If MCTP operated in the LOSS mode and receives an acknowledgement for a new TCP segment, it returns to the NORMAL state. Vice versa, if MCTP operated in the NORMAL mode and receives two consecutive duplicate acknowledgements for a TCP segment, it switches to the LOSS state and performs the following actions:

▶ MCTP forces TCP to enter the persist mode (cf. section 5.1) by setting the congestion

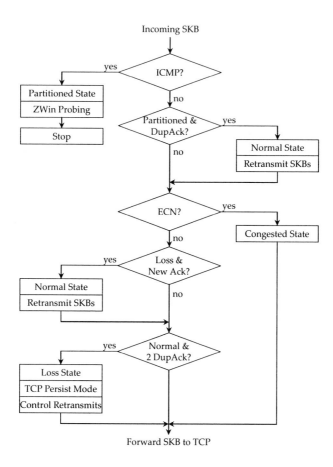

Figure D.3: Flow Chart for Handling Incoming Socket Buffers

window to zero. This way, TCP is not allowed to transmit any TCP data segments until it receives a duplicate acknowledgement from the communication peer to open its congestion window.

▶ Afterwards, MCTP retransmits the outstanding TCP segment autonomously. This way, the communication peer can receive the segment before it sends the third duplicate acknowledgement.

▶ MCTP remains in the LOSS state until it receives an acknowledgement for the retransmitted TCP segment.

After the processing of the incoming socket buffer, the buffer is forwarded to the TCP implementation in the Linux operating system.

D.2.2 Timeouts

The timeout handler routine `mctp_timer()` is called whenever a retransmission timeout occurs for a transmitted TCP segment. In this case, it first checks the state of MCTP. If MCTP operates in the CONGESTED mode, the `mctp_timer()` does nothing and leaves the handling of the timeout to the standard mechanisms implemented in TCP. Otherwise, MCTP switches into the LOSS mode in order to handle the segment loss appropriately. Thereby, MCTP performs the same actions as if MCTP receives two duplicate acknowledgements, which is described in the third step in the previous section.

D.2.3 Notifications

Notifications are handled separately since they are independent of the current MCTP state. If a notification occurs for a TCP connection, the following (pseudo) code fragment is performed:

```
begin mctp_notification()

  // Toggle State
  if (state == MCTP_DISC) then
    state = MCTP_NORMAL;
  else
    state = MCTP_DISC;
  fi

  // handle disconnection
  if (state == MCTP_DISC) then
    cwnd = 0;
    delete retransmission timers;
  fi
```

```
// handle reconnection
if (state == MCTP_NORMAL) then
  cwnd = 2;
  if (retransmit_queue not empty) then
    retransmit socket buffers from retransmit_queue;
  else
    send 2 acknowledgements;
  fi
fi
end;
```

First, the handler determines the correct state of the MCTP protocol state machine. If MCTP was in the DISCONNECTED state, MCTP switches to the NORMAL operation mode. Otherwise, MCTP enters the DISCONNECTED mode. Both situations are handled in a different way. In case of a disconnection, MCTP forces TCP to enter the persist mode by shrinking the congestion window to zero and by deactivating the retransmission timers for the TCP connection. This way, TCP does not send further TCP socket buffers. TCP remains in this state until MCTP is notified about a reconnection. In case of a re-connection, MCTP opens the congestion window by setting it to two segments and retransmits the outstanding segments immediately from the retransmission queue. If such segments are not available, MCTP sends two acknowledgements (i.e. a duplicate acknowledgement) for the last segment transmitted. This way, it notifies the communication peer about the reconnection in order to continue communications.

D.2.4 Outgoing Socket Buffers

If TCP transmits a socket buffer, it calls the mctp_outgoing() handler beforehand. Thereby, MCTP controls the outgoing segment in order to determine if it can leave the CONGESTED state: If MCTP operates in the CONGESTED state and TCP retransmits a new TCP segment, MCTP returns back to the NORMAL state and forwards the socket buffer back to TCP, which sends it out afterwards.

Acronyms

BMBF Bundesministerium für Bildung und Forschung (German Federal Ministry of Education and Research)

C

CAN Controller Area Network

CCoA Co-Located Care-of Address

CDMA Code Division Multiple Access

CE Congestion Experienced

CN Correspondent Node

CoA Care-of Address

COMCAR Communication and Mobility by Cellular Advanced Radio

CP Communication Platform

CPU Central Processing Unit

cwnd Congestion Window

CWR Congestion Window Reduced

D

DA Directory Agent

DAB Digital Audio Broadcasting

DHCP Dynamic Host Configuration Protocol

DLL Data Link Layer

DNS Domain Name System

DRIVE Discovery of Internet Gateways from Vehicles

DRiVE Dynamic Radio for IP Services in Vehicular Environments

DSR Dynamic Source Routing

DSRC   Dedicated Short Range Communication

DVB-T   Digital Video Broadcasting – Terrestrial

E

EBSN   Explicit Bad State Notification

ECE   ECN Echo

ECN   Explicit Congestion Notification

ECT   ECN-Capable Transport

ELFN   Explicit Link Failure Notification

ELN   Explicit Loss Notification

EU   European Union

F

FA   Foreign Agent

FDLC   FleetNet Data Link Control

FEC   Forward Error Correction

FNA   FleetNet Network Adaptation

FNL   FleetNet Network Layer

FORP   Flow-Oriented Routing Protocol

FPHY   FleetNet Physical

G

GPRS   General Packet Radio Service

GPS   Global Positioning System

GPSR   Greedy Perimeter Stateless Routing

GRE Generic Routing Encapsulation

GSM Global System for Mobile Communications

H

HA Home Agent

HAWAII Handoff-Aware Wireless Access Internet Infrastructure

HFA Highest Foreign Agent

HiperLAN High Performance Local Area Network

HMIPv6 Hierarchical Mobile IPv6

HSCSD High Speed Circuit Switched Data

HTTP Hypertext Transfer Protocol

I

I-TCP Indirect TCP

IANA Internet Assigned Numbers Authority

ICMP Internet Control Message Protocol

IEEE Institute of Electrical and Electronics Engineers

IETF Internet Engineering Task Force

IFA Intermediate Foreign Agent

IGW Internet Gateway

IMAP Internet Message Access Protocol

INVENT Intelligenter Verkehr und nutzergerechte Technik (Intelligent Road Traffic and User-Friendly Technologies)

IP Internet Protocol

IPsec Internet Protocol Security Architecture

IPv4 Internet Protocol Version 4

IPv6 Internet Protocol Version 6

ISO International Organization for Standardization

ISP Internet Service Provider

IST Information Society Technologies

ITS Intelligent Transportation System

L

LAN Local Area Network

LFA Lowest Foreign Agent

M

M-TCP Mobile TCP

MAC Medium Access Control

MANET Mobile Ad Hoc Network

MCTP MOCCA Transport Protocol

MMIP6 MOCCA Mobile IPv6

MMP Multicast for Mobility Protocol

MN Mobile Node

MOCCA Mobile Communication Architecture

MOST Media Oriented Systems Transport

MoTiV Mobilität und Transport im intermodalen Verkehr (Mobility and Transportation in Intermodal Road Traffic Scenarios)

MSS Maximum Segment Size

MTA Mail Transfer Agent

MTU   Maximum Transfer Unit

N

NACK   Negative Acknowledgement

NAT   Network Address Translator

NAT-PT   Network Address Translation – Protocol Translation

NEMO   Network Mobility

NOW   Network On Wheels

O

OEM   Original Equipment Manufacturer

OLSR   Optimized Link State Routing

OMA   Open Mobile Alliance

OSI   Open Systems Interconnection

OSPF   Open Shortest Path First

P

PATH   Partners for Advanced Transit and Highways

PDA   Personal Digital Assistant

PEP   Performance Enhancing Proxy

PHY   Physical

PILC   Performance Implications of Link Characteristics

POP   Post Office Protocol

Q

QoS   Quality of Service

QPSK Quaternary Phase Shift Keying

R

R/A Road Access

RED Random Early Detection

RFC Request for Comments

RIPE Réseaux IP Européens

RTO Retransmission Timeout

RTT Round Trip Time

S

S-MIP Seamless Mobile IP

SA Service Agent

SCTP Stream Control Transmission Protocol

SDP Service Discovery Protocol

SDR Service Dependent Router

SIIT Stateless IP/ICMP Translation

SIP Session Initiation Protocol

SLM Session Layer Mobility

SLP Service Location Protocol

SrvAck Service Acknowledge

SrvReg Service Register

SrvRply Service Reply

SrvRqst Service Request

SSL Secure Socket Layer

ssthresh   Slow Start Threshold

StVO   Straßenverkehrsordnung

StVZO   Straßenverkehrszulassungsordnung

T

TCP   Transmission Control Protocol

TCP BuS   TCP with Buffering Capability and Sequence Information

TCP DOOR   TCP Detection of Out-of-Order and Response

TCP FACK   TCP Forward Acknowledgement

TCP SACK   TCP Selective Acknowledgement

TCP-F   TCP Feedback

TCPW   TCP Westwood

TCPW BR   TCP Westwood Bulk Repeat

TDD   Time Division Duplex

TLS   Transport Layer Security

TRT   Transport Relay Translator

TTL   Time to Live

U

UA   User Agent

UDP   User Datagram Protocol

UMTS   Universal Mobile Telecommunications System

UPnP   Universal Plug and Play

URL   Uniform Resource Locator

UTRA   Universal Terrestrial Radio Access

V

VAE   Vehicular Alter Ego

VANET   Vehicular Ad Hoc Network

VPN   Virtual Private Network

W

W-TCP   Wireless TCP

WAP   Wireless Application Protocol

WTP   Wireless Transaction Protocol

WWW   World Wide Web

X

xDSL   Digital Subscriber Line (could be Synchronous or Asynchronous)

Bibliography

[1] A. Saad, "Das Automobil als Anwendungsgebiet der Informatik," Proceedings of the 10th GI Fachtagung Informatik und Schule, München, Germany, September 2003 [German].

[2] A. Widodo, T. Hasegawa, "Evaluations of Traffic Safety Improvement using Autonomous Traffic Flow Simulator including Inter-Vehicle Communication," Proceedings of the 1998 IEEE Global Telecommunications Conference (GLOBECOM), Sydney, Australia, November 1998.

[3] W. D. Jones, "Keeping Cars from Crashing," IEEE Spectrum, September 2001.

[4] I. Chisalita, N. Shahmehri, "Active Support for Traffic Safety Applications through Vehicular Communication," Proceedings of the 2002 International Workshop on Trends and Recent Achievements in Information Technology, Cluj-Napoca, Romania, May 2002.

[5] European Transport Safety Council (ETSC), "Intelligent Transportation Systems and Road Safety," Report, Brussels, Belgium, September 1999.

[6] A. Murphy, G. Roman, G. Varghese, "An Exercise in Formal Reasoning about Mobile Communications," Proceedings of the 9th International Workshop on Software Specifications and Design, Ise-Shima, Japan, April 1998.

[7] R. C. Heft, "The Navigation Market for Road Vehicles," Proceedings of the 1998 IEEE Position, Location and Navigation Symposium (PLANS), Rancho Mirage, California, USA, April 1998.

[8] R. Bishop, "A Survey of Intelligent Vehicle Applications Worldwide," Proceedings of the 2000 IEEE Intelligent Vehicles Symposium (IV), Dearborn, Michigan, USA, October 2000.

[9] J. Schiller, "Mobile Communications," Addison Wesley, 2003.

[10] D. Reichardt, M. Miglietta, L. Moretti, P. Morsink, W. Schulz, "CarTALK 2000 – Safe and Comfortable Driving Based Upon Inter-Vehicle-Communication," Proceedings of the 2002 IEEE Intelligent Vehicle Symposium (IV), Versailles, France, June 2002.

[11] M. Aoki, "Inter-Vehicle Communication: Technical Issues on Vehicle Control Application," IEEE Communications Magazine, October 1996.

[12] W. Enkelmann, "FleetNet – Applications for Inter-Vehicle Communications," Proceedings of the 2003 IEEE Intelligent Vehicles Symposium (IV), Columbus, Ohio, USA, June 2003.

[13] H. Rehborn, A. Haug, B. S. Kerner, M. Aleksic, U. Fastenrath, "Floating Car Data und Verfahren zur Erkennung und Verfolgung von zeitlich-räumlichen Verkehrsmustern," Straßenverkehrstechnik, Kirschbaum-Verlag, September 2003 [German].

[14] U. Fastenrath, M. Becker, "High Quality Traffic Information by Real Time Modelling," Proceedings of the 10th World Congress on Intelligent Transport Systems and Services, Madrid, Spain, November 2003.

[15] F. F. H. Fitzek, L. Badia, P. Seeling, J. G. Schulte, T. Henderson, "Mobility and Stability Evaluation in Wireless Multi-Hop Networks Using Multiplayer Games," Proceedings of the 2nd Workshop on Network and System Support for Games (NetGames), Redwood City, California, USA, May 2003.

[16] K. Mitchell, D. McCaffery, G. Metaxas, J. Finney, "Six in the City: Introducing Real Tournament: A Mobile IPv6 Based Context-Aware Multiplayer Game," Proceedings of the 2nd Workshop on Network and System Support for Games (NetGames), Redwood City, California, USA, May 2003.

[17] C. Güttler, T. D. Johansson, "Spatial Principles of Level-Design in Multi-Player First-Person Shooters," Proceedings of the 2nd Workshop on Network and System Support for Games (NetGames), Redwood City, California, USA, May 2003.

[18] S. V. Bana, P. Varaiya, "Space Division Multiple Access (SDMA) for Robust Ad-Hoc Vehicle Communication Networks," Proceedings of the 4th IEEE International Conference on Intelligent Transportation Systems (ITSC), Oakland, California, USA, August 2001.

[19] S. Corson, J. Macker, "Mobile Ad hoc Networking (MANET): Routing Protocol Performance Issues and Evaluation Considerations," RFC 2501, Internet Engineering Task Force (IETF), January 1999.

[20] C. S. Wijting, R. Prasad, "Evaluation of Mobile Ad-Hoc Network Techniques in a Cellular Network," Proceedings of the 52nd IEEE Semiannual Vehicular Technology Conference (VTC), Boston, Massachusetts, USA, September 2000.

[21] D. A. Topham, D. Ward, T. N. Arvanitis, C. C. Constantinou, "Inter-Vehicle Communications based on Mobile Ad Hoc Networks," Proceedings of the 1st International Conference on Sensors, Navigation, and Communications for Vehicles Telematics (VehCom), Birmingham, UK, June 2003.

[22] FleetNet Consortium, "FleetNet Project Homepage," http://www.fleetnet.de, 2004.

[23] W. Franz, R. Eberhardt, T. Luckenbach, "FleetNet – Internet on the Road," Proceedings of the 8th World Congress on Intelligent Transport Systems, Sydney, Australia, October 2001.

[24] NOW Consortium, "Network on Wheels Project Homepage," http://www.network-on-wheels.de, 2004.

[25] W. Franz, H. Hartenstein, B. Bochow, "Internet on the Road via Inter-Vehicle Communications," Proceedings of the Workshop on Informatics 2001: Mobile Communications over Wireless LAN: Research and Applications, Vienna, Austria, September 2001.

[26] W. Franz, C. Wagner, C. Maihöfer, H. Hartenstein, "FleetNet – Platform for Inter-Vehicle Communications," Proceedings of the 1st International Workshop on Intelligent Transportation (WIT), Hamburg, Germany, March 2004.

[27] M. Lott, R. Halfmann, E. Schulz, M. Radimirsch, "Medium Access and Radio Resource Management for Ad hoc Networks based on UTRA TDD," Proceedings of the 2nd ACM International Symposium on Mobile Ad Hoc Networking and Computing (MobiHoc), Long Beach, California, USA, October 2001.

[28] A. Ebner, H. Rohling, R. Halfmann, M. Lott, "Synchronization in Ad Hoc Networks based on UTRA TDD," Proceedings of the 13th IEEE International Symposium on Personal Indoor Mobile Radio Communications (PIMRC), Lisboa, Portugal, September 2002.

[29] A. Ebner, H. Rohling, M. Lott, R. Halfmann, "Decentralized Synchronization in Highly Dynamic Ad Hoc Networks," Proceedings of the 5th International Symposium on Wireless Personal Multimedia Communications (WPMC), Honolulu, Hawai'i, October 2002.

[30] A. El-Rabbany, "Introduction to GPS: The Global Positioning System," Artech House Publishers, 2002.

[31] M. Käsemann, H. Hartenstein, H. Füßler, M. Mauve, "Analysis of a Location Service for Position-Based Routing in Mobile Ad Hoc Networks," Proceedings of the 1st German Workshop on Mobile Ad Hoc Networks (WMAN), Ulm, Germany, March 2002.

[32] M. Mauve, J. Widmer, H. Hartenstein, "A Survey on Position-Based Routing in Mobile Ad Hoc Networks," IEEE Network, November 2001.

[33] M. Mauve, H. Hartenstein, H. Füßler, J. Widmer, W. Effelsberg, "Positionsbasiertes Routing für die Kommunikation zwischen Fahrzeugen," Informationstechnik und Technische Informatik, Universität Mannheim, 2002 [German].

[34] C. Lochert, H. Hartenstein, J. Tian, H. Füßler, D. Hermann, M. Mauve, "A Routing Strategy for Vehicular Ad Hoc Networks in City Environments," Proceedings of the 2003 IEEE Intelligent Vehicles Symposium (IV), Columbus, Ohio, USA, June 2003.

[35] H. Hartenstein, H. Füßler, M. Mauve, W. Franz, "Simulation Results and a Proof-of-Concept Implementation of the FleetNet Position-Based Router," Proceedings of the 8th IFIP International Conference on Personal Wireless Communications (PWC), Venedig, Italy, September 2003.

[36] M. Möske, H. Füßler, H. Hartenstein, W. Franz, "Performance Measurements of a Vehicular Ad Hoc Network," Proceedings of the 59th IEEE Semiannual Vehicular Technology Conference (VTC), Milan, Italy, May 2004.

[37] P. Srisuresh, K. Egevang, "Traditional IP Network Address Translator (Traditional NAT)," RFC 3022, Internet Engineering Task Force (IETF), January 2001.

[38] Dynamic DNS Homepage. http://www.dyndns.org, 2004.

[39] German Federal Office for Vehicles. http://www.kba.de, 2004.

[40] Internet Assigned Numbers Authority. http://www.iana.org, 2004.

[41] C. E. Perkins, "Mobile IP Design Principles and Practices," Addison Wesley, 1998.

[42] C. E. Perkins, "Ad Hoc Networking," Addison Wesley, 2001.

[43] D. B. Johnson, D. A. Maltz, Y.-C. Hu, "The Dynamic Source Routing Protocol for Mobile Ad Hoc Networks (DSR)," Internet Draft draft-ietf-manet-dsr-09.txt, Internet Engineering Task Force (IETF), April 2003.

[44] C. E. Perkins, E. M. Belding-Royer, S. R. Das, "Ad hoc On-Demand Distance Vector (AODV) Routing," RFC 3561, Internet Engineering Task Force (IETF), July 2003.

[45] K. C. Claffy, "Internet Measurement and Data Analysis: Topology, Workload, Performance and Routing Statistics," Proceedings of the 1999 Workshop on Numerical Analysis in Engineering (NAE), Medan, Indonesia, April 1999.

[46] R. Stevens, "UNIX Network Programming Volume 1: Networking APIs: Sockets and XTI," Prentice Hall, 1998.

[47] A. Bakre, B. Badrinath, "I-TCP: Indirect TCP for Mobile Hosts," Proceedings of the 15th International Conference on Distributed Computing Systems (ICDCS), Vancouver, Canada, June 1995.

[48] J. H. Saltzer, D. P. Reed, D. D. Clark, "End-to-End Arguments in System Design," ACM Transactions in Computer Systems, November 1984.

[49] G. Montenegro, S. Dawkins, M. Kojo, V. Magret, N. Vaidya, "Long Thin Networks," RFC 2757, Internet Engineering Task Force (IETF), January 2000.

[50] J. Border, M. Kojo, J. Griner, G. Montenegro, Z. Shelby, "Performance Enhancing Proxies Intended to Mitigate Link-Related Degradations," RFC 3135, Internet Engineering Task Force (IETF), June 2001.

[51] Defence Advanced Research Projects Agency, "Transmission Control Protocol," RFC 793, Internet Engineering Task Force (IETF), September 1981.

[52] R. Fielding, J. Gettys, J. Mogul, H. Frystyk, L. Masinter, P. Leach, T. Berners-Lee, "Hypertext Transfer Protocol – HTTP/1.1," RFC 2616, Internet Engineering Task Force (IETF), June 1999.

[53] J. Myers, M. Rose, "Post Office Protocol – Version 3," RFC 1939, Internet Engineering Task Force (IETF), May 1996.

[54] M. Crispin, "Internet Message Access Protocol – Version 4rev1," RFC 3501, Internet Engineering Task Force (IETF), March 2003.

[55] B. Carpenter, "Architectural Principles of the Internet," RFC 1958, Internet Engineering Task Force (IETF), June 1996.

[56] S. Kent, R. Atkinson, "Security Architecture for the Internet Protocol," RFC 2401, Internet Engineering Task Force (IETF), November 1998.

[57] K. Nichols, S. Blake, F. Baker, D. Black, "Definition of the Differentiated Services Field (DS Field) in the IPv4 and IPv6 Headers," RFC 2474, Internet Engineering Task Force (IETF), December 1998.

[58] R. Braden, D. Clark, S. Shenker, "Integrated Services in the Internet Architecture: an Overview," RFC 1633, Internet Engineering Task Force (IETF), June 1994.

[59] G.-S. Ahn, A. T. Campbell, A. Veres, L.-H. Sun, "Supporting Service Differentiation for Real-Time and Best Effort Traffic in Stateless Wireless Ad Hoc Networks (SWAN)," IEEE Transactions on Mobile Computing, September 2002.

[60] T.-W. Chen, "Efficient Routing and Quality of Service Support for Ad Hoc Wireless Networks," PhD Thesis, University of California Los Angeles, USA, April 1998.

[61] G. Apostolopoulos, R. Guérin, S. Kamat, S. K. Tripathi, "Quality of Service Based Routing: A Performance Perspective," Proceedings of the 1998 ACM SIGCOMM Conference, Vancouver, Canada, October 1998.

[62] S.-B. Lee, A. T. Campbell, "INSIGNIA: In-Band Signaling Support for QoS in Mobile Ad Hoc Networks," Proceedings of the 5th International Workshop on Mobile Multimedia Communication (MoMUC), Berlin, Germany, October 1998.

[63] K. Wu, J. Harms, "QoS Support in Mobile Ad Hoc Networks," Technical Report, University of Alberta, Canada, August 2000.

[64] A. Frier, P. Karlton, P. Kocher, "The SSL 3.0 Protocol," Netscape Communications Corp., November 1996.

[65] T. Dierks, C. Allen, "The TLS Protocol Version 1.0," RFC 2246, Internet Engineering Task Force (IETF), January 1999.

[66] S. Blake-Wilson, M. Nystrom, D. Hopwood, J. Mikkelsen, T. Wright, "Transport Layer Security (TLS) Extensions," RFC 3546, Internet Engineering Task Force (IETF), June 2003.

[67] C. de Laat, G. Gross, L. Gommans, J. Vollbrecht, D. Spence, "Generic AAA Architecture," RFC 2903, Internet Engineering Task Force (IETF), August 2000.

[68] D. Wisley, H. Aghvami, S. L. Gwyn, T. Zahariadis, J. Manner, V. Gazis, N. Houssos, N. Alonistioti, "Transparent IP Radio Access for Next-Generation Mobile Networks," IEEE Wireless Communications, August 2003.

[69] I. Chisalita, N. Shahmehri, "A Novel Architecture for Supporting Vehicular Communication," Proceedings of the 56th IEEE Vehicular Technology Conference (VTC), Vancouver, Canada, September 2002.

[70] N. Shahmehri, I. Chisalita, "A Peer-to-Peer Approach to Vehicular Communication for the Support of Traffic Safety Applications," Proceedings of the 5th IEEE International Conference on Intelligent Transportation Systems (ITSC), Singapore, September 2002.

[71] Chauffeur II Project Homepage. http://www.chauffeur2.net, 2004.

[72] S. Martini, V. Murdocco, "A Study on Lateral Control for Automated Driving on Heavy Truck Vehicles," Proceedings of the 2001 IEEE Intelligent Vehicle Symposium (IV), Tokyo, Japan, May 2001.

[73] CarTALK2000 Project Homepage. http://www.cartalk2000.net, 2004.

[74] F. Borgonovo, A. Capone, M. Cesana, L. Fratta, L. Coletti, L. Moretti, N. Riato, "Inter-Vehicles Communications: A New Frontier of Ad-Hoc Networking," Proceedings of the 2nd Mediterranean Workshop on Ad-Hoc Networks (MED-HOC NET), Mahdia, Tunisia, June 2003.

[75] Bundesministerium für Bildung und Forschung (BMB+F), "Mobility in Conurbations," Public Brochure, Bonn, Germany, May 2002.

[76] Bundesministerium für Bildung und Forschung (BMB+F), "Mobilität und Verkehr," Public Brochure, Bonn, Germany, July 2002 [German].

[77] INVENT Project Homepage. http://www.invent-online.de, 2004.

[78] S. Breitenberger, K. Bogenberger, M. Hauschild, K. Laffkas, "Extended Floating Car Data – An Overview," Proceedings of the 10th World Congress on Intelligent Transport Systems and Services, Madrid, Spain, November 2003.

[79] D. Manstetten, W. Krautter, A. Engeln, P. Zahn, J. Simon, F. Kuhn, P. Frank, M. Junge, "Leanability of Driver Assistance Systems," Proceedings of the 10th World Congress on Intelligent Transport Systems and Services, Madrid, Spain, November 2003.

[80] M. Michaelsen, C. Ress, "Innovative Hybrid Routing Services – INVENT Traffic Network Equaliser Approach," Proceedings of the 1st International Workshop on Intelligent Transportation (WIT), Hamburg, Germany, March 2004.

[81] PATH Project Homepage. http://www.path.berkeley.edu, 2004.

[82] L. Christodoulides, T. Sammut, R. Tönjes, "DRiVE towards Systems beyond 3G," Pro-
      ceedings of the 5th World Multi-Conference on Systemics, Cybernetics and Informatics
      (SCI), Orlando, Florida, USA, July 2001.

[83] R. Tönjes, P. Benkö, J. Ebenhard, M. Frank, T. Göransson, W. Hansman, J. Huschke,
      T. Lohmar, T. Paila, F. Sällström, W. Stahl, L. Xu, "Architecture for a Future Genera-
      tion Multi-Access Wireless System with Dynamic Spectrum Allocation," IST Mobile
      Summit 2000, Galway, Ireland, October 2000.

[84] R. Tönjes, K. Moessner, T. Lohmar, M. Wolf, "OverDRiVE – Spectrum Efficient Mul-
      ticast Services to Vehicles," IST Mobile Summit 2002, Thessaloniki, Greece, October
      2002.

[85] L. Xu, T. Paila, W. Hansmann, M. Frank, "IPv6 based Infrastructure for Wireless IP in
      Multi-Radio Environments with Quality of Service Support," Proceedings of the 26th
      IEEE Conference on Local Computer Networks (LCN), Tampa, Florida, USA, Novem-
      ber 2001.

[86] H. Soliman, C. Castelluccia, K. El-Malki, L. Bellier, "Hierarchical Mobile IPv6 mobil-
      ity management (HMIPv6)," Internet Draft draft-ietf-mipshop-hmipv6-00.txt, Internet
      Engineering Task Force (IETF), June 2003.

[87] P. R. Calhoun, J. Loughney, E. Guttman, G. Zorn, J. Arkko, "Diameter Base Protocol,"
      RFC 3588, Internet Engineering Task Force (IETF), September 2003.

[88] L. Xu, R. Tönjes, T. Paila, W. Hansmann, M. Frank, M. Albrecht, "DRiVE-ing to the
      Internet: Dynamic Radio for IP Services in Vehicular Environments," Proceedings of
      the 25th IEEE Conference on Local Computer Networks (LCN), Tampa, Florida, USA,
      November 2000.

[89] W. Hansmann, M. Frank, M. Wolf, "Performance Analysis of TCP Handover in a Wire-
      less/Mobile Multi-Radio Environment," Proceedings of the 27th IEEE Conference on
      Local Computer Networks (LCN), Tampa, Florida, USA, November 2002.

[90] COMCAR Project Homepage. http://www.comcar.de, 2004.

[91] R. Keller, T. Lohmar, R. Tönjes, J. Thielecke, "Convergence of Cellular and Broadcast
      Networks from a Multi-Radio Perspective," IEEE Personal Communications, April
      2001.

[92] R. Kroh, A. Held, M. Adlinger, R. Keller, T. Lohmar, E. Kovacs, "High-Quality Interac-
      tive and Broadband IP Services for the Vehicle on the Net – The COMCAR Approach,"

Proceedings of the 7th World Congress on Intelligent Transport Systems, Torino, Italy, November 2000.

[93] S. Blödt, "Entwicklung und Implementierung einer Dienstgüte-basierten Ressourcenverwaltung und Wegewahlstrategie in einer heterogenen Mobilfunkumgebung," Master Thesis, Technical University of Karlsruhe, Institute of Telematics, Germany, November 2001 [German].

[94] E. Kovacs, R. Keller, T. Lohmar, R. Kroh, A. Held, "Adaptive Mobile Applications over Cellular Advanced Radio," Proceedings of the 11th IEEE International Symposium on Personal Indoor Mobile Radio Communications (PIMRC), London, UK, September 2000.

[95] J. Diederich, T. Lohmar, M. Zitterbart, R. Keller, "On Integrating Differentiated Services and UMTS Networks," Proceedings of the 25th IEEE Conference on Local Computer Networks (LCN), Tampa, Florida, USA, November 2000.

[96] J. Diederich, T. Lohmar, M. Zitterbart, R. Keller, "A QoS Model for Differentiated Services in Mobile Wireless Networks," Proceedings of the 11th IEEE Workshop on Local and Metropolitan Area Networks (LANMAN), Boulder, Colorado, USA, March 2001.

[97] J. Diederich, M. Doll, M. Zitterbart, "Best-Effort Low-Delay Service," Proceedings of the 28th IEEE Conference on Local Computer Networks (LCN), Bonn, Germany, October 2003.

[98] IPonAir Project Homepage. http://www.iponair.de, 2004.

[99] M. Zitterbart, K. Weniger, O. Stanze, I. Gruber, "IPonAir – Drahtloses Internet der nächsten Generation," PIK Themenheft "Mobile Ad-Hoc-Netzwerke", December 2003 [German].

[100] H. Li, M. Lott, W. Zirwas, M. Weckler, E. Schulz, "Hierarchical Cellular Multihop Networks," Proceedings of the 5th European Personal Mobile Communications Conference (EPMCC), Glasgow, Scotland, April 2003.

[101] H. Li, D. Yu, "Performance Comparison of Ad-Hoc and Cellular Based Routing Algorithms in Multihop Cellular Networks," Proceedings of the 5th International Symposium on Wireless Personal Multimedia Communications (WPMC), Honolulu, Hawai'i, USA, October 2002.

[102] K. Weniger, M. Zitterbart, "IPv6 Autoconfiguration in Large Scale Mobile Ad-Hoc Networks," Proceedings of the 2002 European Wireless Conference, Florence, Italy, February 2002.

[103] K. Weniger, "Passive Duplicate Address Detection in Mobile Ad hoc Networks," Proceedings of the 2003 IEEE Wireless Communications and Networking Conference (WCNC), New Orleans, Louisiana, USA, March 2003.

[104] J. Wu, M. Zitterbart, "Service Awareness and its Challenges in Mobile Ad Hoc Networks," Proceedings of the Workshop of Informatics 2001: Mobile Communication over Wireless LAN: Research and Applications, September 2001.

[105] N. Frangiadakis, G. Nikolaidis, P. Schefczik, A. Wiedemann, "MxRAN Functional Architecture Performance Modeling," Proceedings of the 2002 OPNETWORK Conference, Washington, USA, August 2002.

[106] M. Gerharz, C. de Waal, M. Frank, P. Martini, "Link Stability in Mobile Wireless Ad Hoc Networks," Proceedings of the 27th IEEE Conference on Local Computer Networks (LCN), Tampa, Florida, USA, November 2002.

[107] S. Aust, D. Proetel, A. Könsgen, C. Pampu, C. Görg, "Design Issues of Mobile IP Handoffs between General Packet Radio Service (GPRS) Networks and Wireless LAN (WLAN) Systems," Proceedings of the 5th International Symposium on Wireless Personal Multimedia Communications (WPMC), Hawai'i, USA, October 2002.

[108] J. Macker, V. Park, "Anycast Routing for Mobile Networking," Proceedings of the 1999 IEEE Military Communications Conference (MILCOM), Atlantic City, New Jersey, USA, November 1999.

[109] V. Park, J. Macker, "Anycast Routing for Mobile Services," Proceedings of the 33rd Annual Conference on Information Sciences and Systems (CISS), Baltimore, Maryland, USA, March 1999.

[110] H. Sarhan, C. Yu, "Study on IP Anycast in Ad-Hoc Networks," Technical Report, Cleveland State University, Department of Electrical and Computer Engineering, Cleveland, Ohio, USA, September 2002.

[111] F. Heiler, W. Holfelder, D. Jiang, "DriveBy InfoFueling – Telematics beyond the Anytime Anywhere Paradigm," Technical Report, Mercedes-Benz USA, (Montvale, New Jersey) and DaimlerChrysler Research and Technology North America (Palo Alto, California), USA, November 2001.

[112] S. Dijkstra, W. Holfelder, M. Moody, J. de Stefano, "DaimlerChrysler IT Cruiser Telematics Concept," Technical Report, DaimlerChrysler Corporation (Auburn Hills, Michigan, USA), DaimlerChrysler Research and Technology North America (Palo Alto, California), and Sun Microsystems (Southfield, Michigan), USA, January 2001.

[113] J. Zhu, S. Roy, "MAC for Dedicated Short Range Communications in Intelligent Transport System," IEEE Communications Magazine, December 2003.

[114] K. Weniger, "Infostations System," available at http://www.tm.uni-karlsruhe.de, Institute of Telematics, Technical University of Karlsruhe, Germany, July 2001.

[115] R. Morris, J. Jannotti, F. Kaashoek, J. Li, D. Decouto, "CarNet: A Scalable Ad Hoc Wireless Network System," Proceedings of the 9th ACM SIGOPS European Workshop, Kolding, Denmark, September 2000.

[116] J. Postel, J. Reynolds, "A Standard for the Transmission of IP Datagrams over IEEE 802 Networks," RFC 1042, Internet Engineering Task Force (IETF), February 1988.

[117] D. S. J. De Couto, J. Jannotti, D. Karger, J. Li, R. Morris, "A Scalable Location Service for Geographic Ad Hoc Routing," Proceedings of the 6th ACM/IEEE International Conference on Mobile Computing and Networking (Mobicom), Boston, Massachusetts, USA, August 2000.

[118] B. Karp, H. T. Kung, "GPSR: Greedy Perimeter Stateless Routing for Wireless Networks," Proceedings of the 6th ACM/IEEE International Conference on Mobile Computing and Networking (Mobicom), Boston, Massachusetts, USA, August 2000.

[119] Y. Rekhter, T. Li, "A Border Gateway Protocol 4 (BGP-4)," RFC 1771, Internet Engineering Task Force (IETF), March 1995.

[120] J. Moy, "OSPF Version 2," RFC 2328, Internet Engineering Task Force (IETF), April 1998.

[121] J. Ioannidis, D. Duchamp, G. Maguire, "IP-based Protocols for mobile Internetworking," Proceedings of the 1991 ACM SIGCOMM Conference, Zurich, Switzerland, September 1991.

[122] F. Halsall, "Data Communications, Computer Networks and Open Systems," Addison Wesley Longman, 1996.

[123] K. Brown, S. Singh, "M-TCP: TCP for Mobile Cellular Networks," ACM SIGCOMM Computer Communication Review, October 1997.

[124] R. Gilligan, E. Nordmark, "Transition Mechanisms for IPv6 Hosts and Routers," RFC 2893, Internet Engineering Task Force (IETF), August 2000.

[125] B. Carpenter, C. Jung, "Transmission of IPv6 over IPv4 Domains without Explicit Tunnels," RFC 2529, Internet Engineering Task Force (IETF), March 1999.

[126] A. Durand, P. Fasano, I. Guardini, D. Lento, "IPv6 Tunnel Broker," RFC 3053, Internet Engineering Task Force (IETF), January 2001.

[127] B. Carpenter, K. Moore, "Connection of IPv6 Domains via IPv4 Clouds," RFC 3056, Internet Engineering Task Force (IETF), February 2001.

[128] K. Tsuchiya, H. Higuchi, Y. Atarashi, "Dual Stack Hosts using the "Bump-In-the-Stack" Technique (BIS)," RFC 2767, Internet Engineering Task Force (IETF), February 2000.

[129] P. S. G. Tsirtsis, "Network Address Translation – Protocol Translation," RFC 2766, Internet Engineering Task Force (IETF), February 2000.

[130] E. Nordmark, "Stateless IP/ICMP Translation Algorithm (SIIT)," RFC 2765, Internet Engineering Task Force (IETF), February 2000.

[131] H. Kitamura, "A SOCKS-based IPv6/IPv4 Gateway Mechanism," RFC 3089, Internet Engineering Task Force (IETF), April 2001.

[132] J. Hagino, K. Yamamoto, "An IPv6-to-IPv4 Transport Relay Translator," RFC 3142, Internet Engineering Task Force (IETF), June 2001.

[133] D. G. Waddington, F. Chang, "Realizing the Transition to IPv6," IEEE Communications Magazine, June 2002.

[134] M. Tatipamula, P. Grossetete, H. Esaki, "IPv6 Integration and Coexistence Strategies for Next-Generation Networks," IEEE Communications Magazine, January 2004.

[135] R. Hinden, S. Deering, "Internet Protocol Version 6 (IPv6) Addressing Architecture," RFC 3513, Internet Engineering Task Force (IETF), April 2003.

[136] J. Li, S. Singh, "ATCP: TCP for Mobile Ad Hoc Networks," IEEE Journal on Selected Areas in Communications, July 2001.

[137] K. Sundaresan, V. Anantharaman, H.-Y. Hsieh, R. Sivakumar, "ATP: A Reliable Transport Protocol for Ad-hoc Networks," Proceedings of the 4th ACM International Symposium on Mobile Ad Hoc Networking and Computing (MobiHoc), Annapolis, Maryland, USA, June 2003.

[138] J. Postel, "User Datagram Protocol," RFC 768, Internet Engineering Task Force (IETF), August 1980.

[139] W. Dixon, "IPsec-Network Address Translation (NAT) Compatibility Requirements," RFC 3715, Internet Engineering Task Force (IETF), March 2004.

[140] A. Huttunen, B. Swander, V. Volpe, "Negotiation of NAT-Traversal in the IKE," Internet Draft draft-ietf-ipsec-nat-t-ike-08.txt, Internet Engineering Task Force (IETF), February 2004.

[141] M. Burnside, D. Clarke, T. Mills, A. Maywah, S. Devadas, R. Rivest, "Proxy-Based Security Protocols in Networked Mobile Devices," Proceedings of the 17th ACM Symposium on Applied Computing (SAC), Madrid, Spain, March 2002.

[142] "MOST Specification, Revision 2.2," http://www.mostcooperation.com, November 2002.

[143] K. Etschberger, "Controller-Area-Network: Grundlagen, Protokolle, Bausteine, Anwendungen," Hanser Verlag, 2002 [German].

[144] R. Droms, "Dynamic Host Configuration Protocol," RFC 2131, Internet Engineering Task Force (IETF), March 1997.

[145] C. E. Perkins, "IP Mobility Support for IPv4," RFC 3344, Internet Engineering Task Force (IETF), August 2002.

[146] B. Hurler, "Implementierung eines Software-Multiplexers unter Linux," Project Thesis, Technical University of Karlsruhe, Institute of Telematics, Germany, September 2001 [German].

[147] M. Bechler, B. Hurler, V. Kahmann, L. Wolf, "A Management Entity for Improving Service Quality in Mobile Ad-Hoc Networks," Proceedings of the 1st International Conference on Wireless LANs and Home Networks (ICWLHN), Singapore, December 2001.

[148] N. Fideropoulos, "Entwurf und Implementierung eines dynamischen Handovers in IP-basierten mobilen Netzen," Master Thesis, Technical University of Braunschweig, Institute of Operating Systems and Computer Networks, Germany, December 2002 [German].

[149] M. Olbrich, "Optimization of a Dynamical Handoff in Mobile Ad Hoc Networks," Project Thesis, Technical University of Braunschweig, Institute of Operating Systems and Computer Networks, Germany, June 2003.

[150] L. Taylor, R. Titmuss, C. Lebre, "The Challenges of Seamless Handover in Future Mobile Multimedia Networks," IEEE Personal Communications, April 1999.

[151] H.-Y. Lach, C. Janneteau, A. Petrescu, "Network Mobility in Beyond-3G Systems," IEEE Communications Magazine, July 2003.

[152] R. H. Katz, E. A. Brewer, E. Amir, H. Balakrishnan, A. Fox, S. Gribble, T. Hodes, D. Jiang, G. T. Nguyen, V. N. Padmanabhan, M. Stemm, "The Bay Area Research Wireless Access Network (BARWAN)," IEEE Communications Magazine, December 2001.

[153] E. A. Brewer, R. H. Katz, Y. Chawathe, S. D. Gribble, T. Hodes, G. Nguyen, M. Stemm, T. Henderson, E. Amir, H. Balakrishnan, A. Fox, V. N. Padmanabhan, S. Seshan, "A Network Architecture for Heterogeneous Mobile Computing," IEEE Personal Communications, October 1998.

[154] S. Cheshire, M. Baker, "A Wireless Network in MosquitoNet," IEEE Micro, February 1996.

[155] K. Pahlavan, P. Krishnamurthy, A. Hatami, M. Ylianttila, J.-P. Makela, R. Pichna, J. Vallström, "Handoff in Hybrid Mobile Data Networks," IEEE Personal Communications, February 2000.

[156] L.-J. Chen, T. Sun, B. Chen, V. Rajendran, M. Gerla, "A Smart Decision Model for Vertical Handoff," Proceedings of the 4th ANWIRE International Workshop on Wireless Internet and Reconfigurability, Athens, Greece, May 2004.

[157] J. Inouye, J. Binkley, J. Walpole, "Dynamic Network Reconfiguration Support for Mobile Computers," Proceedings of the 3rd ACM International Conference on Mobile Computing and Networking (Mobicom), Budapest, Hungary, September 1997.

[158] M. Bechler, H. Ritter, "A flexible Multiplexing Mechanism for Supporting Quality of Service in Mobile Environments," Proceedings of the 34th Annual Hawai'i International Conference on System Sciences (HICSS), Maui, Hawai'i, USA, January 2001.

[159] J. Ylitalo, T. Jokikyyny, T. Kauppinen, A. J. Tuominen, J. Laine, "Dynamic Network Interface Selection in Multihomed Mobile Hosts," Proceedings of the 36th Hawai'i International Conference on System Sciences (HICSS), Big Island, Hawai'i, USA, January 2003.

[160] M. Mukaidono, H. Kikuchi, "Fuzzy Logic for Beginners," World Scientific Publishing Company, 2001.

[161] C. T. Leondes, "Fuzzy Logic and Expert Systems Applications (Neural Network Systems Techniques and Applications)," Academic Press, 1998.

[162] S. Lipperts, A. Park, "An Agent-Based Middleware: A Solution for Terminal and User Mobility," Elsevier Computer Networks, August 1999.

[163] E. Kovacs, K. Rohrle, M. Reich, "Integrating Mobile Agents into the Mobile Middleware," Proceedings of the 2nd International Workshop on Mobile Agents (MA), Stuttgart, Germany, September 1998.

[164] P. Bellavista, A. Corradi, C. Stefanelli, "Mobile Agent Middleware for Mobile Computing," IEEE Computer Magazine, March 2001.

[165] B. C. Housel, C. Samara, D. B. Lindquist, "WebExpress: A Client/Intercept based System for optimizing Web Browsing in a Wireless Environment," Journal of Special Issues on Mobility of Systems, Users, Data and Computing, Kluwer Academic Publishers, December 1998.

[166] B. D. Noble, M. Satyanarayanan, D. Narayanan, J. E. Tilton, J. Flinn, K. R. Walker, "Agile Application-Aware Adaptation for Mobility," Proceedings of the 16th ACM Symposium on Operating System Principles (SOSP), St. Malo, France, August 1997.

[167] T. Phan, G. Zorpas, R. Bagrodia, "An Extensible and Scalable Content Adaptation Pipeline Architecture to Support Heterogeneous Clients," Proceedings of the 22nd International Conference on Distributed Computing Systems (ICDCS), Vienna, Austria, July 2002.

[168] A. Fox, S. D. Gribble, Y. Chawathe, E. A. Brewer, "Adapting to Network and Client Variation Using Infrastructure Proxies: Lessons and Perspectives," IEEE Personal Communications Magazine, October 1998.

[169] G. Montenegro, "Reverse Tunneling for Mobile IP, revised," RFC 3024, Internet Engineering Task Force (IETF), January 2001.

[170] D. B. Johnson, C. E. Perkins, J. Arkko, "Mobility Support in IPv6," RFC 3775, Internet Engineering Task Force (IETF), June 2004.

[171] T. Narten, E. Nordmark, W. Simpson, "Neighbor Discovery for IP Version 6 (IPv6)," RFC 2461, Internet Engineering Task Force (IETF), December 1998.

[172] S. Deering, R. Hinden, "Internet Protocol, Version 6 (IPv6) Specification," RFC 2460, Internet Engineering Task Force (IETF), December 1998.

[173] S. Thomson, T. Narten, "IPv6 Stateless Address Autoconfiguration," RFC 2462, Internet Engineering Task Force (IETF), December 1998.

[174] R. Droms, J. Bound, B. Volz, T. Lemon, C. Perkins, M. Carney, "Dynamic Host Configuration Protocol for IPv6 (DHCPv6)," RFC 3315, Internet Engineering Task Force (IETF), July 2003.

[175] A. Conta, S. Deering, "Generic Packet Tunneling in IPv6 Specification," RFC 2473, Internet Engineering Task Force (IETF), December 1998.

[176] R. Koodli, "Fast Handovers for Mobile IPv6," Internet Draft draft-ietf-mipshop-fast-mipv6-00.txt, Internet Engineering Task Force (IETF), October 2003.

[177] S. Pack, Y. Choi, "Performance Analysis of Fast Handover in Mobile IPv6 Networks," Proceedings of the 8th IFIP International Conference on Personal Wireless Communications (PWC), Venice, Italy, September 2003.

[178] R. Hsieh, Z. G. Zhou, A. Seneviratne, "S-MIP: A Seamless Handoff Architecture for Mobile IP," Proceedings of the 22nd IEEE Conference on Computer Communications (Infocom), San Francisco, California, USA, April 2003.

[179] A. T. Campbell, J. Gomez, S. Kim, A. G. Valkó, C.-Y. Wan, Z. R. Turányi, "Design, Implementation and Evaluation of Cellular IP," IEEE Personal Communications, June 2000.

[180] Z. D. Shelby, D. Gatzounas, A. Campbell, C.-Y. Wan, "Cellular IPv6," Internet Draft draft-huitema-multi-homed-01.txt, Internet Engineering Task Force (IETF), November 2000.

[181] A. Campbell, J. Gomez, C.-Y. Wan, S. Kim, Z. Turanyi, A. Valko, "Cellular IP," Internet Draft draft-ietf-mobileip-cellularip-00.txt, Internet Engineering Task Force (IETF), June 2000.

[182] R. Ramjee, T. F. L. Porta, L. Salgarelli, S. Thuel, K. Varadhan, L. Li, "IP-Based Access Network Infrastructure for Next Generation Wireless Data Networks," IEEE Personal Communications, August 2000.

[183] R. Ramjee, T. L. Porta, S. Thuel, K. Varadhan, S.-Y. Wang, "HAWAII: A Domain Based Approach for Supporting Mobility in Widearea Wireless Networks," Proceedings of the 7th International Conference on Network Protocols (ICNP), Toronto, Canada, November 1999.

[184] R. Ramjee, T. L. Porta, S. Thuel, K. Varadhan, L. Salgarelli, "IP micro-mobility support using HAWAII," Internet Draft draft-ietf-mobileip-hawaii-00.txt, Internet Engineering Task Force (IETF), June 1999.

[185] A. T. Campbell, J. Gomez, S. Kim, C.-Y. Wan, Z. R. Turányi, A. G. Valkó, "Comparison of IP Micromobility Protocols," IEEE Wireless Communications, February 2002.

[186] T. Ernst, "Network Mobility Support Goals and Requirements," Internet Draft draft-ietf-nemo-requirements-02.txt, Internet Engineering Task Force (IETF), February 2004.

[187] V. Devarapalli, R. Wakikawa, A. Petrescu, "Network Mobility (NEMO) Basic Support Protocol," Internet Draft draft-ietf-nemo-basic-support-03.txt, Internet Engineering Task Force (IETF), June 2004.

[188] H. Zhou, M. W. Mutka, L. M. Ni, "IP Address Handoff in the MANET," Proceedings of the 23nd IEEE Conference on Computer Communications (Infocom), Hong Kong, China, March 2004.

[189] W. Adjie-Winoto, E. Schwartz, H. Balakrishnan, J. Lilley, "The Design and Implementation of an Intentional Naming System," Proceedings of the 17th ACM Symposium on Operating System Principles (SOSP), Kiawah Island, South Carolina, USA, December 1999.

[190] A. C. Snoeren, H. Balakrishnan, M. F. Kaashoek, "Reconsidering Internet Mobility," Proceedings of the 8th Workshop on Hot Topics in Operating Systems (HotOS), Elmau, Germany, May 2001.

[191] B. Landfeldt, T. Larsson, Y. Ismailov, A. Seneviratne, "SLM, a Framework for Session Layer Mobility Management," Proceedings of the 1999 IEEE International Conference on Computer Communications and Networks (ICCCN), Boston, Massachusetts, USA, October 1999.

[192] D. A. Maltz, P. Bhagwat, "MSOCKS: An Architecture for Transport Layer Mobility," Proceedings of the 17th IEEE Conference on Computer Communications (Infocom), San Francisco, California, USA, April 1998.

[193] A. C. Snoeren, H. Balakrishnan, "An End-to-End Approach to Host Mobility," Proceedings of the 6th ACM/IEEE International Conference on Mobile Computing and Networking (Mobicom), Boston, Massachusetts, USA, August 2000.

[194] L. Ong, J. Yoakum, "An Introduction to the Stream Control Transmission Protocol (SCTP)," RFC 3286, Internet Engineering Task Force (IETF), May 2002.

[195] S. J. Koh, M. J. Chang, M. Lee, "mSCTP for Soft Handover in Transport Layer," IEEE Communications Letters, March 2004.

[196] C. Huitema, "Multi-homed TCP," Internet Draft draft-huitema-multi-homed-01.txt, Internet Engineering Task Force (IETF), November 1995.

[197] M. Py, "Multi Homing Translation Protocol (MHTP)," Internet Draft draft-py-multi6-mhtp-01.txt, Internet Engineering Task Force (IETF), November 2001.

[198] J. Broch, D. A. Maltz, D. B. Johnsson, "Supporting Hierarchy and heterogeneous Interfaces in Multi-hop Wireless Ad Hoc Networks," Proceedings of the 4th International Symposium on Parallel Architectures, Algorithms and Networks (ISPAN), Fremantle, Australia, June 1999.

[199] T. Randhawa, L. Lamont, S. Hardy, "Integrating WLANs and MANETs to the IPv6 based Internet," Proceedings of the 2003 IEEE International Conference on Communications (ICC), Anchorage, Alaska, USA, May 2003.

[200] T. Clausen, P. Jacquet, "Optimized Link State Routing Protocol (OLSR)," RFC 3626, Internet Engineering Task Force (IETF), October 2003.

[201] H. Lei, C. Perkins, "Ad Hoc Networking with Mobile IP," Proceedings of the 2nd European Personal Mobile Communication Conference (EPMCC), Bonn, Germany, September 1997.

[202] U. Jörnsson, F. Alriksson, T. Larsson, P. Johansson, G. Q. Maguire Jr., "MIPMANET – Mobile IP for Mobile Ad Hoc Networks," Proceedings of the 1st ACM International Symposium on Mobile Ad Hoc Networking and Computing (MobiHOC), Boston, Massachusetts, USA, August 2000.

[203] W. Su, M. Gerla, "IPv6 Flow Handoff in Ad Hoc Wireless Networks Using Mobility Prediction," Proceedings of the 1999 IEEE Global Telecommunications Conference (GLOBECOM), Rio de Janeiro, Brazil, December 1999.

[204] S. Deering, "Host Extensions for IP Multicasting," RFC 1112, Internet Engineering Task Force (IETF), August 1989.

[205] B. Cain, S. Deering, I. Kouvelas, B. Fenner, A. Thyagarajan, "Internet Group Management Protocol, Version 3," RFC 3376, Internet Engineering Task Force (IETF), October 2002.

[206] S. Deering, B. Haberman, T. Jinmei, E. Nordmark, B. Zill, "IPv6 Scoped Address Architecture," Internet Draft draft-ietf-ipv6-scoping-arch-01.txt, Internet Engineering Task Force (IETF), February 2004.

[207] J. Mysore, V. Bharghavan, "A New Multicasting-Based Architecture for Internet Host Mobility," Proceedings of the 3rd ACM International Conference on Mobile Computing and Networking (Mobicom), Budapest, Hungary, September 1997.

[208] A. Helmy, "A Multicast-based Protocol for IP Mobility Support," Proceedings of the 2nd International Workshop on Networked Group Communication (NGC), Palo Alto, California, USA, November 2000.

[209] J. Wu, G. Maguire, "Agent based seamless IP Multicast Receiver Handover," Proceedings of the 5th IFIP International Conference on Personal Wireless Communications (PWC), Gdansk, Poland, September 2000.

[210] R. Wakikawa, J. T. Malinen, C. E. Perkins, A. Nilsson, A. J. Tuominen, "Global Connectivity for IPv6 Mobile Ad Hoc Networks," Internet Draft draft-wakikawa-manet-globalv6-02.txt, Internet Engineering Task Force (IETF), November 2002.

[211] A. Mihailovic, M. Shabeer, A. H. Aghvami, "Multicast for Mobility Protocol (MMP) for Emerging Internet Networks," Proceedings of the 11th IEEE International Symposium on Personal, Indoor and Mobile Radio Communications (PIMRC), London, UK, September 2000.

[212] Y.-C. Tseng, C.-C. Shen, W.-T. Chen, "Integrating Mobile IP with Ad Hoc Networks," IEEE Computer, May 2003.

[213] S.-Y. Ni, Y.-C. Tseng, Y.-S. Chen, J.-P. Sheu, "The Broadcast Storm Problem in a Mobile Ad Hoc Network," Proceedings of the 5th ACM/IEEE International Conference on Mobile Computing and Networking (Mobicom), Seattle, Washington, USA, August 1999.

[214] A. Nilsson, C. E. Perkins, A. J. Tuominen, R. Wakikawa, J. T. Malinen, "AODV and IPv6 Internet Access for Ad hoc Networks," ACM SIGMOBILE Mobile Computing and Communications Review, July 2002.

[215] A. Striegel, R. Ramanujan, J. Bonney, "A Protocol Independent Internet Gateway for Ad-Hoc Wireless Networks," Proceedings of the 26th IEEE Conference on Local Computer Networks (LCN), Tampa, Florida, USA, November 2001.

[216] A. Misra, S. Das, A. McAuley, S. K. Das, "Autoconfiguration, Registration, and Mobility Management for Pervasive Computing," IEEE Personal Communications, August 2001.

[217] B. A. Miller, T. Nixon, C. Tai, M. D. Wood, "Home Networking with Universal Plug and Play," IEEE Communications Magazine, December 2001.

[218] P. Dobrev, D. Famolari, C. Kurzke, B. A. Miller, "Device and Service Discovery in Home Networks with OSGi," IEEE Communications Magazine, August 2002.

[219] G. G. Richard III., "Service Advertisement and Discovery: Enabling Universal Device Cooperation," IEEE Internet Computing Magazine, September/October 2000.

[220] E. Guttman, C. Perkins, J. Veizades, M. Day, "Service Location Protocol, Version 2," RFC 2608, Internet Engineering Task Force (IETF), June 1999.

[221] E. Guttman, "Service Location Protocol Modifications for IPv6," RFC 3111, Internet Engineering Task Force (IETF), May 2001.

[222] UPnP Forum, "Device Definition Version 1.0 for UPnP Version 1.0," available at http://www.upnp.org, December 2002.

[223] Jini Architecture Specification. Available at http://www.jini.org, August 2003.

[224] Bluetooth Consortium, "Specification of the Bluetooth System – Core System Package age [Host Volume] Version 1.2, Part B: Service Discovery Protocol," available at http://www.bluetooth.org, November 2003.

[225] Salutation Consortium, "Salutation Architecture Specification Version 2.0c (Part 1–3)," available at http://www.salutation.org, June 1999.

[226] C. Lee, S. Helal, "Protocols for Service Discovery in Dynamic and Mobile Networks," International Journal of Computer Research, Special Issue on Wireless Systems and Mobile Computing, September 2002.

[227] E. Guttman, C. E. Perkins, J. Kempf, "Service Templates and Services Schemes," RFC 2609, Internet Engineering Task Force (IETF), June 1999.

[228] C. Maihöfer, "A Survey of Geocast Routing Protocols," IEEE Communication Surveys, June 2004.

[229] O. Storz, "Entwurf und Implementierung eines optimierten Service-Discovery-Proto-kolls für fahrzeugbasierte Netze," Master Thesis, Technical University of Karlsruhe, Institute of Telematics, Germany, September 2002 [German].

[230] O. Storz, "DRIVE – Ein effizientes Service Discovery Protokoll für fahrzeugbasierte Netze," Proceedings of the 13th Fachtagung Kommunikation in Verteilten Systemen (KiVS), Leipzig, Germany, April 2003 [German].

[231] M. Bechler, O. Storz, W. Franz, L. Wolf, "Efficient Discovery of Internet Gateways in Future Vehicular Communication Systems," Proceedings of the 57th IEEE Vehicular Technology Conference (VTC), Jeju, Korea, April 2003.

[232] E. Gustafsson, A. Jonsson, C. E. Perkins, "Mobile IPv4 Regional Registration," Internet Draft draft-ietf-mobileip-reg-tunnel-07.txt, Internet Engineering Task Force (IETF), October 2002.

[233] M. Zouari, "Optimierung von Mobile IP für Szenarien der Verkehrstelematik," Master Thesis, Technical University of Braunschweig, Institute of Operating Systems and Computer Networks, Germany, August 2003 [German].

[234] S. S. Wang, M. Green, M. Malkawi, "Adaptive Handoff Method Using Mobile Location Information," Proceedings of the 2001 IEEE Emerging Technologies Symposium on Broadband Communications for the Internet Era Symposium, IEEE Press, 2001.

[235] W. Teerapabkajorndet, P. Krishnamurthy, "Comparison of Performance of Location-Aware and Traditional Handoff-Decision Algorithms in CDPD Networks," Proceedings of the 54th IEEE Vehicular Technology Conference (VTC), Atlantic City, New Jersey, USA, October 2001.

[236] S. Kyriazakos, D. Drakoulis, G. Karetsos, "Optimization of the Handover Algorithm based on the Position of the Mobile Terminals," Proceedings of the 2000 Communications Symposium on Vehicular Technology and Communications (CSVT), Leuven, Belgium, October 2000.

[237] Y. Ko, N. Vaidya, "Geocasting in Mobile Ad Hoc Networks: Location-Based Multicast Algorithms," Proceedings of the 2nd IEEE Workshop on Mobile Computing Systems and Applications (WMCSA), New Orleans, Louisiana, USA, February 1999.

[238] J. Xie, I. E. Akyildiz, "A Distributed Dynamic Regional Location Management Scheme for Mobile IP," Proceedings of the 21st IEEE Conference on Computer Communications (Infocom), New York, USA, June 2002.

[239] H.-C. Chao, Y.-M. Chu, M.-T. Lin, "The Implication of the Next-Generation Wireless Network Design: Cellular Mobile IPv6," IEEE Transactions on Consumer Electronics, August 2000.

[240] A. Stephane, A. H. Aghvami, "Fast Handover Schemes for Future Wireless IP Networks: A Proposal and Analysis," Proceedings of the 53rd IEEE Vehicular Technology Conference (VTC), Vienna, Austria, May 2001.

[241] H.-C. Chao, C.-Y. Huan, "Micro-Mobility Mechanism for Smooth Handoffs in an Integrated Ad-Hoc and Cellular IPv6 Network Under High-Speed Movement," IEEE Transactions on Vehicular Technology, November 2003.

[242] Information Science Institute, "Transmission Control Protocol," RFC 793, Internet Engineering Task Force (IETF), September 1981.

[243] W. Stevens, "TCP/IP Illustrated, Volume 1: The Protocols," Addison Wesley, 1994.

[244] R. Caceres, L. Iftode, "The Effects of Mobility on Reliable Transport Protocols," Proceedings of the 14th International Conference on Distributed Computing Systems (ICDCS), Poznan, Poland, June 1994.

[245] G. Holland, N. Vaidya, "Analysis of TCP Performance over Mobile Ad Hoc Networks," Proceedings of the 5th ACM/IEEE International Conference on Mobile Computing and Networking (MOBICOM), Seattle, Washington, USA, August 1999.

[246] S. Bae, K. Xu, S. Lee, M. Gerla, "TCP Behavior across Multihop Wireless and Wired Networks," Proceedings of the 2002 IEEE Global Telecommunications Conference (GLOBECOM), Taipei, Taiwan, November 2002.

[247] H. Lim, K. Xu, M. Gerla, "TCP Performance over Multipath Routing in Mobile Ad Hoc Networks," Proceedings of the 2003 IEEE International Conference on Communications (ICC), Anchorage, Alaska, USA, May 2003.

[248] W. Stevens, "TCP Slow Start, Congestion Avoidance, Fast Retransmit, and Fast Recovery Algorithms," RFC 2001, Internet Engineering Task Force (IETF), January 1997.

[249] V. Paxson, M. Allman, "Computing TCP's Retransmission Timer," RFC 2988, Internet Engineering Task Force (IETF), November 2000.

[250] D.-M. Chiu, R. Jain, "Analysis of the Increase and Decrease Algorithms for Congestion Avoidance in Computer Networks," Computer Networks and ISDN Systems, June 1989.

[251] M. Allman, V. Paxson, W. Stevens, "TCP Congestion Control," RFC 2581, Internet Engineering Task Force (IETF), April 1999.

[252] T. D. Dyer, R. V. Boppana, "ATP: A Reliable Transport Protocol for Ad-hoc Networks," Proceedings of the 2th ACM International Symposium on Mobile Ad Hoc Networking and Computing (MobiHoc), Long Beach, California, USA, October 2001.

[253] Z. Fu, P. Zerfos, S. Lu, L. Zhang, M. Gerla, "The Impact of Multihop Wireless Channel on TCP Throughput and Loss," Proceedings of the 22nd IEEE Conference on Computer Communications (Infocom), San Francisco, California, USA, April 2003.

[254] J. Ott, D. Kutscher, "Drive-Thru Internet: IEEE 802.11b for Automobile Users," Proceedings of the 23rd IEEE Conference on Computer Communications (Infocom), Hong Kong, China, March 2004.

[255] M. Lott, "Performance of a Medium Access Scheme for Inter-Vehicle Communication," Proceedings of the 2002 International Symposium on Performance Evaluation of Computer and Telecommunication Systems (SPECTS), San Diego, California, USA, July 2002.

[256] R. Caceres, L. Iftode, "Improving the Performance of Reliable Transport Protocols in Mobile Computing Environments," IEEE Journal on Selected Areas in Communications, June 1995.

[257] S. Floyd, T. Henderson, "The NewReno Modification to TCP's Fast Recovery Algorithm," RFC 2582, Internet Engineering Task Force (IETF), April 1999.

[258] M. Mathis, J. Mahdavi, S. Floyd, A. Romanow, "TCP Selective Acknowledgment Options," RFC 2018, Internet Engineering Task Force (IETF), October 1996.

[259] M. Mathis, J. Mahdavi, "Forward Acknowledgement: Refining TCP Congestion Control," Proceedings of the 1996 ACM SIGCOMM Conference, Stanford, California, USA, August 1996.

[260] K. Wehrle, F. Pählke, H. Ritter, D. Müller, M. Bechler, "The Linux Networking Architecture," Pearson Education, 2004.

[261] P. Sarolahti, A. Kuznetsov, "Congestion Control in Linux TCP," Proceedings of the 2002 USENIX Technical Conference, Monterey, California, USA, October 2002.

[262] A. Eitner, "Entwicklung eines Transportprotokolls zur effizienten Kommunikation in der Verkehrstelematik," Master Thesis, Technical University of Braunschweig, Institute of Operating Systems and Computer Networks, Germany, January 2003 [German].

[263] H. Balakrishnan, V. N. Padmanabhan, S. Seshan, R. H. Katz, "A Comparison of Mechanisms for Improving TCP Performance over Wireless Links," Proceedings of the 1996 ACM SIGCOMM Conference, Stanford, California, USA, August 1996.

[264] R. G. Mukhtar, S. V. Hanly, L. L. H. Andrew, "Efficient Internet Traffic Delivery over Wireless Networks," IEEE Communications Magazine, December 2003.

[265] M. Gerla, M. Y. Sanadidi, R. Wang, A. Zanella, C. Casetti, S. Mascolo, "TCP West-wood: Congestion Window Control Using Bandwidth Estimation," Proceedings of the 2001 IEEE Global Telecommunications Conference (GLOBECOM), San Antonio, Texas, USA, November 2001.

[266] G. Yang, R. Wang, M. Y. Sanadidi, M. Gerla, "Performance of TCPW BR in Next Generation Wireless and Satellite Networks," Proceedings of the 2003 IEEE International Conference on Communications (ICC), Anchorage, Alaska, USA, May 2003.

[267] C.-J. Kao, W. Liao, C.-H. Chien, J.-C. Liu, "Improving TCP Performance in Heterogeneous Mobile Networks," Proceedings of the 57th IEEE Vehicular Technology Conference 2003 (Spring), Jeju, South Korea, May 2003.

[268] K. Tsukamoto, Y. Fukuda, Y. Hori, Y. Oie, "New Flow Control Schemes of TCP for Multimodal Mobile Hosts," Proceedings of the 57th IEEE Vehicular Technology Conference 2003 (Spring), Jeju, South Korea, May 2003.

[269] F. Wang, Y. Zhang, "Improving TCP Performance over Mobile Ad-Hoc Networks with Out-of-Order Detection and Response," Proceedings of the 3rd ACM International Symposium on Mobile Ad Hoc Networking and Computing (MobiHoc), Lausanne, Switzerland, June 2002.

[270] C. Parsa, J. J. Garcia-Luna-Aceves, "Improving TCP Congestion Control over Internets with Heterogeneous Transmission Media," Proceedings of the 5th International Conference on Network Protocols (ICNP), Toronto, Canada, October 1999.

[271] V. Tsaoussidis, H. Badr, "TCP Probing: Towards an Error Control Schema with Energy and Throughput Performance Gains," Proceedings of the 6th International Conference on Network Protocols (ICNP), Osaka, Japan, November 2000.

[272] P. Sinha, N. Venkitaraman, R. Sivakumar, V. Bharghavan, "WTCP: A Reliable Transport Protocol for Wireless Wide-Area Networks," Proceedings of the 5th ACM/IEEE International Conference on Mobile Computing and Networking (MOBICOM), Seattle, Washington, USA, August 1999.

[273] Z. Fu, B. Greenstein, X. Meng, S. Lu, "Design and Implementation of a TCP-Friendly Transport Protocol for Ad Hoc Wireless Networks," Proceedings of the 10th International Conference on Network Protocols (ICNP), Paris, France, November 2002.

[274] T. Goff, J. Moronski, D. S. Phatak, V. Gupta, "Freeze-TCP: A true End-to-End TCP Enhancement Mechanism for Mobile Environments," Proceedings of the 19th IEEE Conference on Computer Communications (Infocom), Tel Aviv, Isra, March 2000.

[275] L. S. Brakmo, S. W. O'Malley, L. L. Peterson, "TCP Vegas: New Techniques for Conges-
       tion Detection and Avoidance," Proceedings of the 1994 ACM SIGCOMM Conference,
       London, UK, September 1994.

[276] L. S. Brakmo, L. L. Peterson, "TCP Vegas: End to End Congestion Avoidance on a
       Global Internet," IEEE Journal on Selected Areas in Communications, October 1995.

[277] C.-P. Fu, "TCP Veno: End-to-End Congestion Control over Heterogeneous Networks,"
       PhD Thesis, Chinese University of Hong Kong, China, June 2001.

[278] S. Stotz, "Performance-Analyse von Transportprotokollen in mobilen Kommunika-
       tionssystemen," Project Thesis, Technical University of Braunschweig, Institute of Op-
       erating Systems and Computer Networks, Germany, January 2003 [German].

[279] J. P. Monks, P. Sinha, V. Bharghavan, "Limitations of TCP-ELFN for Ad hoc Net-
       works," Proceedings of the 2000 Workshop on Mobile and Multimedia Communi-
       cation, Marina del Rey, California, USA, October 2000.

[280] H. Balakrishnan, R. H. Katz, "Explicit Loss Notification and Wireless Web Per-
       formance," Proceedings of the 1998 IEEE Global Telecommunications Conference
       (GLOBECOM), Sydney, Australia, November 1998.

[281] W. Ding, A. Jamalipour, "Delay Performance of the New Explicit Loss Notification
       TCP Technique for Wireless Networks," Proceedings of the 2001 IEEE Global Telecom-
       munications Conference (GLOBECOM), San Antonio, Texas, USA, November 2001.

[282] B. S. Bakshi, P. Krishna, N. H. Vaidya, D. K. Pradhan, "Improving Performance of
       TCP over Wireless Networks," Proceedings of the 17th International Conference on
       Distributed Computing Systems (ICDCS), Baltimore, Maryland, USA, May 1997.

[283] K. Ramakrishnan, S. Floyd, D. Black, "The Addition of Explicit Congestion Notifica-
       tion (ECN) to IP," RFC 3168, Internet Engineering Task Force (IETF), September 2001.

[284] K. Chandran, S. Raghunathan, S. Venkatesan, R. Prakash, "A Feedback Based Scheme
       For Improving TCP Performance in Ad-Hoc Wireless Networks," Proceedings of the
       18th International Conference on Distributed Computing Systems (ICDCS), Amster-
       dam, The Netherlands, May 1998.

[285] D. Kim, C.-K. Toh, Y. Choi, "TCP BuS: Improving TCP Performance in Wireless Ad
       Hoc Networks," Proceedings of the 2000 IEEE International Conference on Commu-
       nications (ICC), New Orleans, Louisiana, USA, June 2000.

[286] D. Kim, C.-K. Toh, Y. Choi, "TCP BuS: Improving TCP Performance in Wireless Ad Hoc Networks," IEEE Journal on Communications and Networks, June 2001.

[287] B. Braden, D. Clark, J. Crowcroft, B. Davie, S. Deering, D. Estrin, S. Floyd, V. Jacobson, G. Minshall, C. Partridge, L. Peterson, K. Ramakrishnan, S. Shenker, J. Wroclawski, L. Zhang, "Recommendations on Queue Management and Congestion Avoidance in the Internet," RFC 2309, Internet Engineering Task Force (IETF), April 1998.

[288] J. H. Salim, U. Ahmed, "Performance Evaluation of Explicit Congestion Notification (ECN) in IP Networks," RFC 2884, Internet Engineering Task Force (IETF), July 2000.

[289] Wireless Application Protocol (WAP) Forum, "Wireless Profiled TCP," WAP-225-TCP-20010331-a, Part of the WAP 2.0 Specification, March 2001.

[290] Open Mobile Alliance (OMA) Homepage. http://www.openmobilealliance.org, 2004.

[291] NTT DoCoMo Inc., "i-mode Protocol Stack for new FOMA Handsets," available at http://www.nttdocomo.co.jp, 2004.

[292] V. Jacobson, R. Braden, D. Borman, "TCP Extensions for High Performance," RFC 1323, Internet Engineering Task Force (IETF), May 1992.

[293] M. Allman, S. Floyd, C. Partridge, "Increasing TCP's Initial Window," RFC 2414, Internet Engineering Task Force (IETF), September 1998.

[294] J. Mogul, S. Deering, "Path MTU Discovery," RFC 1191, Internet Engineering Task Force (IETF), November 1990.

[295] J. McCann, S. Deering, J. Mogul, "Path MTU Discovery for IP version 6," RFC 1981, Internet Engineering Task Force (IETF), August 1996.

[296] B. McLarnon, "Information Technology Trends," Defence R&D Canada, Communications Research Centre, available at http://www.ndu.edu, September 2001.

[297] R. R. Stewart, Q. Xie, K. Morneault, C. Sharp, H. J. Schwarzbauer, T. Taylor, I. Rytina, M. Kalla, L. Uhang, V. Paxson, "Stream Control Transmission Protocol," RFC 2960, Internet Engineering Task Force (IETF), October 2000.

[298] V. Harms, "Evaluierung des Stream Control Transmission Protocol in der Verkehrstelematik," Project Thesis, Technical University of Braunschweig, Institute of Operating Systems and Computer Networks, Germany, January 2003 [German].

[299] S. M. Huq, "The Evaluation of Congestion Control in the Stream Control Transmission Protocol (SCTP)," Project Thesis, Technical University of Braunschweig, Institute of Operating Systems and Computer Networks, Germany, June 2003.

[300] A. Gonçalvès, "Evaluierung und Optimierung des Transportprotokolls Wireless Profiled TCP in der Verkehrstelematik," Master Thesis, Technical University of Braunschweig, Institute of Operating Systems and Computer Networks, Germany, September 2003 [German].

[301] J. Noonan, P. Perry, J. Murphy, "A Study of SCTP Services in a Mobile-IP Network," Proceedings of the 2002 Information Technology and Telecommunications Conference (IT&T), Waterford, Ireland, October 2002.

[302] H. Ritter, "Bedarfsorientierte Dienstgüteunterstützung durch adaptive Endsysteme," VDI Verlag, 2001 [German].

[303] A. S. Tanenbaum, "Computer Networks," Prentice Hall, 2003.

[304] H. Balakrishnan, S. Seshan, R. H. Katz, "Improving Reliable Transport and Handoff Performance in Cellular Wireless Networks," ACM Wireless Networks, Kluwer Academic Publishers, February 1995.

[305] S. Vangala, M. A. Labrador, "Performance of TCP over Wireless Networks with the Snoop Protocol," Proceedings of the 27th IEEE Conference on Local Computer Networks (LCN), Tampa, Florida, USA, November 2002.

[306] A. Moustafa, "TCP over Mobile Ad-Hoc Access Networks," Master Thesis, Ottawa-Carleton Institute for Computer Science, Carleton University, Ottawa, Canada, December 2002.

[307] J. Kienzle, "Analyse von Einzelfahrzeugdaten – Verkehr verstehen," Master Thesis, University of Stuttgart, Institut für Straßen- und Verkehrswesen, Germany, August 2001 [German].

[308] L. Breslau, D. Estrin, K. Fall, S. Floyd, J. Heidemann, A. Helmy, P. Huang, S. McCanne, K. Varadhan, Y. Xu, H. Yu, "Advances in Network Simulation," IEEE Computer, May 2000.

[309] D. McDysan, D. Spohn, "ATM – Theory and Application," McGraw Hill, 1995.

[310] O. Kyas, G. Crawford, "ATM Networks," Prentice Hall, 2002.

[311] A. Ebner, H. Rohling, L. Wischhof, R. Halfmann, M. Lott, "Performance of UTRA TDD Ad Hoc and IEEE 802.11b in Vehicular Environments," Proceedings of the 57th IEEE Semiannual Vehicular Technology Conference (VTC), Jeju, Korea, April 2003.

[312] G. Hoffmann, S.-M. Nielsen, "Beschreibung von Verkehrsabläufen an signalisierten Knotenpunkten," Forschung Straßenbau und Straßenverkehrstechnik, Heft 693, Bundesministerium für Verkehr, Abteilung Straßenbau, 1994 [German].

[313] S. Jaap, "Design and Implementation of Typical Road Traffic Scenarios," Project Thesis, Technical University of Braunschweig, Institute of Operating Systems and Computer Networks, Germany, January 2004.

[314] M. Rudack, M. Meineke, M. Lott, "On the Dynamics of Ad Hoc Networks for Inter Vehicle Communication (IVC)," Proceedings of the 2002 International Conference on Wireless Networks (ICWN), Las Vegas, Nevada, USA, June 2002.

[315] D. Forsberg, J. T. Malinen, J. K. Malinen, T. Weckström, M. Tiusanan, "Distributing Mobility Agents Hierarchically Under Frequent Location Updates," Proceedings of the 6th International Workshop on Mobile Multimedia Communications (MoMuC), San Diego, California, USA, November 1999.

[316] "Straßenverkehrszulassungsordnung (StVZO)," Bundesrepublik Deutschland, Justizministerium, Bonn, Germany, March 2004 (last change) [German].

[317] "Straßenverkehrsordnung (StVO)," Bundesrepublik Deutschland, Justizministerium, Bonn, Germany, January 2004 (last change) [German].

[318] H. Füßler, J. Widmer, M. Käsemann, M. Mauve, H. Hartenstein, "Beaconless Position-Based Routing for Mobile Ad-Hoc Networks," Technical Report, TR-03-001, Universität Mannheim, Germany, 2004.

[319] NISTNet Project Page. http://www.snad.ncsl.nist.gov/itg/nistnet, 2004.

[320] J.-C. Bolot, "End-to-End Packet Delay and Loss Behavior in the Internet," Proceedings of the 1993 ACM SIGCOMM Conference, San Francisco, California, USA, September 1993.

[321] K. Mochalski, J. Micheel, S. Donnelly, "Packet Delay and Loss at the Auckland Internet Access Path," Proceedings of the 3rd Workshop on Passive and Active Measurement Workshop (PAM), Fort Collins, Colorado, USA, March 2002.

[322] RIPE Network Coordination Center. http://www.ripe.net, 2004.

[323] M. Bechler, W. J. Franz, L. Wolf, "Mobile Internet Access in FleetNet," Proceedings of the 13th Fachtagung Kommunikation in Verteilten Systemen (KiVS), Leipzig, Germany, February 2003.

[324] G. Fodor, A. Eriksson, A. Tuoriniemi, "Providing Quality of Service in Always Best Connected Networks," IEEE Communications Magazine, July 2003.

[325] R. Steinmetz, K. Nahrstedt, "Multimedia Fundamentals," Prentice Hall, 2002.

[326] J. M. Boyce, R. D. Gaglianello, "Packet Loss Effects on MPEG Video Sent Over the Public Internet," Proceedings of the 6th ACM International Conference on Multimedia, Bristol, UK, September 1998.

Epilogue

Many people wondered about the admittedly "untypical" representation of the Internet throughout my thesis – and smiled about my explanations for this abstract representation. IMHO, this effigy looks like an (abstract) cloud as well as a traverse section of a human brain as well as a sponge, which is all correct:

▶ *The Internet is like a Cloud:* This is naturally evident, because a cloud is the mostly used representation for the Internet in current literature.

▶ *The Internet is a Brain:* This should be also evident, because "If it's not in your head, you will find it in the Internet."

▶ *The Internet is like a Sponge:* This is my private and favourite paraphrase for the Internet, because the Internet is able to soak up all the information that is available elsewhere on the world. Of course, you can wring out this sponge – but if you do it not carefully enough, you will get a flood of (information) drops back. Moreover, you can wring it out several times, and you will always get different drops of information to the same topic. (Notice that this is in contrast to a cloud, which dissapears after a heavy rain!)

For those who are interested in the origins of my private Internet representation: Indeed, it is a sponge.